DENIED

Denied

Women, Sports, and the Contradictions of Identity

Michelle J. Manno

NEW YORK UNIVERSITY PRESS

New York

NEW YORK UNIVERSITY PRESS
New York
www.nyupress.org

© 2023 by New York University
All rights reserved

Library of Congress Cataloging-in-Publication Data
Names: Manno, Michelle J., author.
Title: Denied : women, sports, and the contradictions of identity /
Michelle J. Manno.
Description: New York : New York University Press, [2023] |
Includes bibliographical references and index.
Identifiers: LCCN 2022059257 | ISBN 9781479882229 (hardback) |
ISBN 9781479885381 (paperback) | ISBN 9781479891849 (ebook other) |
ISBN 9781479885718 (ebook)
Subjects: LCSH: Women athletes—Social conditions. | Sports—Social aspects. |
Sex discrimination in sports. | Racism in sports. | Sexual minorities and sports.
Classification: LCC GV709 .M36 2023 | DDC 796.082—dc23/eng/20221216
LC record available at https://lccn.loc.gov/2022059257

This book is printed on acid-free paper, and its binding materials are chosen for strength and durability. We strive to use environmentally responsible suppliers and materials to the greatest extent possible in publishing our books.

Manufactured in the United States of America

10 9 8 7 6 5 4 3 2 1

Also available as an ebook

For Leah

And for all of us who have ever felt too much or not enough

CONTENTS

AUTHOR'S NOTE

As I revised this book in the summer of 2022, the sociopolitical topography of the United States was shifting in real time. The Supreme Court had overturned *Roe v. Wade*, effectively making abortion illegal in almost half of the country. Four states banned transgender minors from receiving gender-affirming medical treatments like hormones and surgeries. Florida enacted a law—what many are calling "don't say gay"—that banned all discussion of gender identity and sexual orientation from classrooms, and a number of states are attempting to do the same. The sports world was not immune to this changing landscape, and transgender athletes have become a particular target for conservative vitriol. As of this writing, eighteen states have banned transgender athletes from playing on school sports teams that align with their gender identities.

Additionally, in the winter of 2022, after being charged and convicted of drug possession and smuggling (for carrying two vape cartridges with less than one gram of hash oil) in Russia, Women's National Basketball Association (WNBA) star Brittney Griner was freed from a Russian penal colony following a prisoner exchange with convicted Russian arms dealer Viktor Bout. Bout, nicknamed the Merchant of Death, was serving a twenty-five-year sentence in the United States. The United States maintained that Griner was wrongfully detained and used as a political bargaining chip in the increasingly tense relationship between the United States and Russia. Many have argued that Griner's Blackness and queerness complicated her case—Russia is notoriously anti-LGBTQ—and contributed to the US government's initial silence around her arrest and subsequent lack of urgency to secure her release. Griner's race, gender, and sexuality (as well as her liberal political views) are further complicating the conversation around her release, as US Marine Paul Whelan—a White man, originally considered to be part of the prisoner exchange—was ultimately left behind. In response, Donald Trump Jr.

tweeted that the Biden administration "was apparently worried that their DEI score would go down if they freed an American Marine."[1]

Throughout this book, I draw throughlines between the experiences of the women athletes I feature and the broader US society in which their experiences are situated. I try to connect their micro-level experiences to the macro-level social structures that are continuously operating to shape their everyday. What these recent sociopolitical events in the United States demonstrate is the ongoing way that social structures impact individuals' everyday lives, particularly those who hold marginalized identities like many of the athletes in this book. I also argue throughout the book that sport as an institution cannot be divorced from the larger context in which it exists. It is therefore unsurprising that sport is one of the primary sites in which the political backlash of the day is playing out in ways that ultimately cost us all, but specifically at the expense of transgender athletes and other marginalized athletes.

Denied is a book about a group of athletes in a particular time and place navigating the unsettled terrain of identity in an institution that was not constructed with them in mind. And while their experiences may be unique, the lessons we can learn from them are generalizable, especially right now.

A NOTE ON LANGUAGE

When writing a book involving complex identity categories like race, gender, and sexuality, it's important to be intentional about language. Language is powerful, and the words we choose to use can promote inclusion or perpetuate inequity. Language can also serve as a form of erasure. What terminology is included (or excluded) extends to *who* is included (or excluded). And those decisions matter beyond theory or method because behind the terminology are real people who are being made either visible or invisible by such decisions.

Language is complex, and it is also evolving and political. The terminology used to refer to the identity categories I include in this book is fluid. Terms change over time and will likely continue to do so, in formal ways (e.g., official classifications) and in popular culture and imagination. Racial categories in the US Census, for example, have changed from decade to decade, reflecting the evolving politics and science of a given era. Categories are always inherently incomplete and unable to capture the complexity of human existence.[1] Even when terminology is durable, remaining or reemerging in common usage over time, *meaning* often changes. The word "queer," for example, a former slur, has been reclaimed by many LGBTQ+ people as an affirming and empowering identity, especially for younger generations.

When it comes to gender, terminology is equally complex. The phrase "female athlete," for instance, is sociologically incorrect as the word "female" refers to those assigned female at birth, a biological sex category. The phrase "woman athlete" refers to someone who identifies as a woman, a socially constructed gender category. Using "women" or "woman" instead of "female" is more trans inclusive in that not all women are female. I have been intentional in this book to try to keep sex and gender as the distinct categories that they are, and I chose to use the phrases "woman athlete" and "women athletes" for this reason. And, yet, commonsense understanding and popular usage consistently conflates sex and gender, as does scholarly literature. Ultimately, the phrase "female athletes" still comes up often in this book in direct quotes from individuals and scholarly sources.

Additionally, much of the analysis in this book is grounded in problematizing the gender binary, the idea that there are two distinct and complementary genders—men and women (assigned male and female at birth, respectively)—and that those men and women will identify with their sex assigned at birth (cisgender) and express masculinity and femininity in normative ways. The risk in relying so heavily on the gender binary as a foundational concept is that it inherently excludes intersex people and trans people—those who do not fit neatly into binary sex and gender categories—and centers the identities and experiences of cisgender people as normative. Despite this, the gender binary is an important concept in this book because I argue that it is the lens through which women athletes are policed. Their ability to embody and express normative femininity matters for how they are perceived and treated. As an idea, the gender binary is used to erase intersex and trans existence. And as a tool for policing gender and sexuality, the gender binary is used to punish intersex and trans people along with cisgender people who cannot adequately conform. When binary ideas about gender are talked about in this book, it is done so always with the deep understanding that they are, by nature, exclusionary.

The words I use to identify the women athletes involved in this book include both the words they used to describe themselves at the time and my own interpretations and analysis. Many of the athletes, for example, referred to themselves as "gay" or "bisexual" while others called themselves "lesbians." When directly quoting the athletes, those are the words you will see. In my analysis, however, I often use the broader term "queer" to describe many of the athletes' sexual identities and the ways they challenge the gender binary through their gender expressions. None of the athletes identified as trans, genderqueer, or nonbinary at the time of this study. Nonetheless, many of them were queering gender in complex ways through their expressions and embodiments of masculinity. My decision to use the word "queer" is an attempt to acknowledge the breadth of identities that exist within the category, as well as to give meaning to the athletes' experiences, which are shaped by both their gender and sexual identities.

Lastly, I chose to capitalize the "B" in Black and the "W" in White when referring to racial identity categories, including in words like "Blackness" and "Whiteness," with the exception of direct quotes. In response to George Floyd's murder in 2020, many in the news media changed their style guidelines and began capitalizing "Black" when referring to people, in part to recognize that "Black" represents a group of people with a shared history and culture. Reactions to this change were, perhaps predictably, mixed as were reactions to whether "White" would be similarly capitalized. The *Chronicle of Higher Education* as well as the *New York Times* continue to use a lowercase "w" in "white" because it is believed that White people don't possess shared history and culture and, importantly, because White supremacist hate groups often capitalize "White." Setting aside the latter, what is missing from this discussion is that even though White people often fail to see themselves as part of a racial group, they do have race. Failing to recognize this makes Whiteness the default, marking it invisible and thereby marking only non-Whites with race and racial identities. As Amanda Lewis writes, "Whether all whites have self-conscious racial identities may or may not matter as much for their life chances as external readings of them as white."[2] She goes on to add that

> because of their social location (as dominants) whites historically have had the luxury of racializing others without necessarily, except strategically, developing or invoking a strong racial consciousness. Yet they remain an important racial collectivity despite their lack of felt groupness. They are a passive social collectivity that can become, at strategic moments, a self-conscious group (e.g., race riots, choosing a school for children, hiring a new employee). In highlighting that whites are a social collective, this does not negate their heterogeneity. There are multiple ways of expressing or doing whiteness. However, there is at any particular time a dominant form that shapes the lives of all those living within that particular racial formation.[3]

In explaining why she capitalizes White, Eve Ewing says, "When we ignore the specificity and significance of Whiteness—the things that it is, the things that it does—we contribute to its seeming neutrality and thereby grant it power to maintain its invisibility."[4] She continues her explanation as follows:

As is the case with all power structures, its invisibility does crucial work to maintain its power. In maintaining the pretense of its invisibility, Whiteness maintains the pretense of its inevitability, and its innocence. As long as White people do not ever have to interrogate what Whiteness is, where it comes from, how it operates, or what it does, they can maintain the fiction that race is other people's problem, that they are mere observers in a centuries-long stage play in which they have, in fact, been the producers, directors, and central actors.[5]

The choices we make as writers around when to capitalize the "B" in Black and the "W" in White (or the "B" in Brown) matter. In this book, I intentionally center the experiences of queer, Black women in elite-level sports, which is why I capitalize Black. These athletes' Blackness shapes their experience in profound ways, particularly when cast against the seemingly invisible backdrop of Whiteness—to which they are always compared and will always fall short—which is why I also capitalize White. Words can obscure and reveal, and I believe that real change happens through revelation.

Undoubtedly, the decisions I made around language in this book will not be perfect and will not satisfy every reader. I chose the terminology in this book with genuine intentions of inclusivity, and at the time of this writing, I used the words that were contemporarily available and analytically meaningful. Where the terminology falls short, as it is bound to do, I encourage readers to focus on the words of the athletes themselves. They were and always will be the best narrators of their own stories.

GLOSSARY

CISGENDER: Individuals whose gender identities align with their sex assigned at birth.

CISNORMATIVE: The privileging of cisgender identity as the norm or assumed gender identity.

GENDER BINARY: The belief that there are only two distinct and complementary genders—men and women. The gender binary is based off of the belief that there are only two distinct sexes—male and female.

GENDER EXPRESSION: The way an individual expresses gender externally, often through behavior, clothing, or bodily characteristics. Gender expression may or may not align with an individual's gender identity.

GENDER NONCONFORMITY: Gender identity, expression, or behavior that does not conform to the expectations of an individual's assigned gender.

HETERONORMATIVE: The privileging of heterosexuality as the norm or assumed sexual orientation.

HETEROPATRIARCHY: A societal structure that privileges heterosexuality and patriarchy.

MISOGYNOIR: A term coined by Moya Bailey to describe the specific anti-Black racist misogyny experienced by Black women.

NONBINARY: A gender identity in which an individual does not identify as one of the binary gender categories of man or woman. Some nonbinary people identify as both, in between, or completely outside of binary gender categories.

QUEER: An umbrella term to include nonheterosexual sexualities and nonbinary gender identities and expressions.

TRANSGENDER, OR TRANS: Individuals whose gender identities do not align with their sex assigned at birth.

TRANSMISOGYNOIR: A term coined by the writer Trudy to describe the anti-Black racist transphobia experienced by Black trans women.

Introduction

In March 2018, Nike put out a commercial titled "Until We All Win" featuring Serena Williams that commemorated International Women's Day. Although Williams is arguably the greatest tennis player of all time, she has had to endure racist and sexist discourse that has questioned her place in women's tennis—indeed, in the game of tennis at all—as well as her womanhood. This history of doubting and denying Williams is the foundation for the commercial and what makes it so compelling. In the ad, against the backdrop of scenes of Williams as a young person and an adult, hitting serves, doing the splits as she fires back a volley, and celebrating wins, she can be heard saying, "I've never been the right kind of woman. Oversized and overconfident. Too mean if I don't smile. Too Black for my tennis whites. Too motivated for motherhood." And as she bows in the final scene, Williams says, "But I am proving, time and time again, there's no wrong way to be a woman."

The day after the commercial aired, news outlets ranging from the *Washington Post, Fortune,* and *Elle* to *SBNation,* CBS Sports, and *USA Today* published articles touting the powerful message of Nike's ad, highlighting its relevance both to Williams's life and career and to all women living in a society that tells them repeatedly that they're not good enough. The commercial aired during the ninetieth Academy Awards, during which many award commentators referenced the important role of #MeToo and #TimesUp as those movements had shined a spotlight on widespread sexual assault and harassment against women in the film, radio, business, and sports industries. To be sure, Williams's message is about her struggles in the tennis world as a woman who has never conformed to hegemonic notions of femininity. Williams does not fit the prototypical tall, slim, ponytail-wearing image of a woman tennis player. "I've never been the right kind of woman. Oversized and overconfident" makes that clear. Importantly, her message is also about her struggles in the tennis world as a Black woman who could never conform to hegemonic notions of Whiteness. "Too Black for my tennis whites" makes this stark. Taken together, however, those four short sentences—"I've never been the right kind of woman. Oversized and overconfident. Too mean if I don't smile. Too Black for my tennis whites."—invoke gender *and* race in explicit and important ways. Thus, while unacknowledged by media outlets in their praise of the ad, #BlackLivesMatter is just as crucial to the discussion as are #MeToo and #TimesUp, perhaps more so.

We cannot understand the experiences of Serena Williams or the importance of this advertisement without reckoning with how her Blackness informs and is informed by her expressions of gender. Throughout their careers, Serena Williams and her sister, Venus, have been the subjects of tremendous racialized and gendered ridicule. At a tournament in Indian Wells, California, in 2001, fans booed Serena for most of her semifinal match and allegedly shouted racial epithets and threats at her father, Richard, as he walked through the stands. As Venus dropped out of the semifinal match minutes before she was set to compete against Serena, many alleged that their matches were fixed by their father. As Serena wrote for *Time*, "The false allegations that our matches were fixed hurt, cut and ripped into us deeply. The undercurrent of racism was painful, confusing and unfair. In a game I loved with all my heart, at one of my most cherished tournaments, I suddenly felt unwelcome, alone and afraid."[1] This incident kept Serena Williams from competing at Indian Wells for fourteen years. She didn't compete against Venus there for another seventeen years, meeting for the next time in March 2018.

During an exhibition match in Brazil in 2012, Caroline Wozniacki impersonated Serena Williams by stuffing towels in her skirt and shirt to imitate Williams's breasts and buttocks. She then picked up her tennis racket and waited for her opponent, Maria Sharapova, to serve, exaggeratingly adjusting her breasts. Wozniacki played through a point before removing the towels. While Wozniacki received backlash from many commentators, Serena Williams said she was not personally offended by the impersonation, stating, "I don't think she meant anything racist by it."[2] In 2014, the Russian Tennis Federation president, Shamil Tarpischev, appeared on a late-night Russian talk show and referred to Serena and Venus Williams as the "Williams brothers," saying further, "It's frightening when you look at them."[3] Tarpischev was forced to pay a $25,000 fine for his comments and was banned for one year by the Women's Tennis Association. During the 2017 Australian Open, tennis commentator Doug Adler described Venus Williams as charging with a "gorilla effect,"[4] noting that her style of play was becoming more aggressive after her opponent's missed serves. Adler contends that he was referring to Venus's tactics as "guerrilla," not comparing her to a gorilla. EPSN fired Adler over his remarks, and he has since filed a lawsuit alleging emotional distress and lost TV opportunities. At a press conference in 2017, tennis legend Ilie Nastase commented on Serena Williams's pregnancy, saying, "Let's see what colour it has. Chocolate with milk?"[5] Nastase was referring to Williams's interracial relationship with her now-husband, Alexis Ohanian, who is White. The International Tennis Federation banned Nastase from acting in any official capacity until 2020 and fined him $10,000 for this comment, as well as for several other sexist remarks made to women competitors and journalists during the event.

Although these examples are some of the most recent and most visible—they involve prominent tennis and media personalities and often occurred on an international stage—they are by no means the only or the most egregious examples of the racist and misogynistic vitriol applied to Venus and Serena Williams over the course of their careers.[6] In 2001, sportscaster Sid Rosenberg called Venus Williams an "animal" and said that it was more likely that the Williams sisters would be featured in *National Geographic* magazine than in *Playboy*.[7] Compounding his impact, Rosenberg defended his remarks, saying they were "zoological," not racist.[8] In a *Rolling Stone* article in 2013, Stephen Rodrick described Serena Williams's body as "black, beautiful and built like one of those monster trucks that crushes Volkswagens at sports arenas."[9] Moreover, Twitter remains a mainstay for racist and misogynistic commentary from anonymous individuals about the Williams sisters. Serena, in particular, is regularly referred to as animal-like (gorilla being the most frequent likening), frightening, unattractive, and manly. Through such relentless and countless criticisms, the Williams sisters have been reminded that they don't belong, inside tennis or out. In this way, "too Black for my tennis whites" is but a thinly veiled metaphor for race in the contemporary United States. As Claudia Rankin wrote in *Citizen*,

Serena and her big sister Venus Williams brought to mind Zora Neale Hurston's "I feel most colored when I am thrown against a sharp white background." . . . Hurston's statement has been played out on the big screen by Serena and Venus: they win sometimes, they lose sometimes, they've been injured, they've been happy, they've been sad, ignored, booed mightily . . . they've been cheered, and through it all and evident to all were those people who are enraged they are there at all—graphite against a sharp white background.[10]

The Nike ad is both captivating and timely. Witnessing this commercial live for the first time was exhilarating. In those thirty seconds, legacies of White supremacy and sexism were unraveled by the very woman who has endured perhaps the most volatile forms of them on the national sporting stage. By the end of the commercial, as Williams is heard saying, "But I am proving, time and time again, there's no wrong way to be a woman," I had tears in my eyes. And then I thought, "But is she?" Serena Williams undoubtedly holds a mirror to society's racism and sexism every time she steps on the tennis court. Or dances in a Beyoncé video. Or marries a wealthy White man and has a biracial child. And while she can serve as an example of how far we've come—as is evident in the very creation and airing of the Nike ad—Serena Williams's experiences also make clear how much farther we have to go. Because, as I will argue throughout this book, there does still seem to be a right and a wrong way to be a woman in this world. That rightness and wrongness are tied to long histories of White and male domination that continue to manifest themselves, albeit in continually modified forms, today. And there is perhaps no better social institution in which to witness the dogged persistence of these histories than sport.

The particular experience of Serena Williams mirrors those of many other notable Black women athletes like Brittney Griner, Gabby Douglas, Simone Biles, CeCe Telfer, and Caster Semenya, who have all endured varied, yet similar, judgments for their (in)ability or (un)willingness to embody hegemonic White heterofemininity. Their collective experiences highlight a unique form of criticism faced by Black women, what Moya Bailey has termed "misogynoir." Misogynoir describes the "uniquely co-constituted racialized and sexualized violence that befalls Black women as a result of their simultaneous and interlocking oppression at the intersection of racial and gender marginalization."[11] As Bailey argues, "What happens to Black women in public space isn't about them being *any* woman of color. It is particular and has to do with the ways that anti-Blackness and misogyny combine to malign Black women in our world."[12] The existence of misogynoir is why, for example, it's not enough to connect Serena Williams's Nike ad to #MeToo without also tying it tightly to #BlackLivesMatter.

Fully appreciating the experience of Serena Williams in and outside of tennis or Brittney Griner in and outside of basketball necessitates an analysis that seriously examines the intersection of anti-Blackness and misogyny. It also requires, however, contending with how gender and race inform and are informed by sexuality. Embedded within gendered notions of "the right kind of woman" are assumptions about sexuality, centered on Whiteness, which have shadowed women athletes, and especially women athletes of color, for decades. Despite her profound success in college and the Women's National Basketball Association (WNBA), Griner has faced unending critique of her gender presentation and sexuality—she expresses gender nonnormatively and came out as queer publicly in 2013. When she was awarded "best female athlete" at the ESPYS in 2012, Twitter users unleashed an onslaught of racist and heterosexist commentary questioning Griner's sex (many insisted her award should have been for "best male athlete"), mocking her sexuality, and labeling her "frightening."[13] Such commentary of Griner became so commonplace that Brian Floyd published an article titled "Every Time Brittney Griner Is on TV, This Happens." The substance of the article is simply screenshots of tired tweets questioning whether Griner "pees standing up" followed by a plea from Floyd: "Can we please move past this? Thanks!"[14]

The questioning of Griner's sex and the policing of her gender—and the persistent lesbian stereotyping of women athletes in general—make it abundantly clear that being the right kind of woman is one who is not "oversized and overconfident" and, as a result, is attractive to men and subject to the male gaze. It is also, importantly, about how ideologies about gender and sexuality are racialized. Griner's treatment within social media is particularly unforgiving not just because she challenges dominant notions of what it means to be a woman or because she is openly queer but because she is doing so as a Black woman. As David Leonard argues,

Griner's inability to cross over, to secure mass appeal, wasn't purely about gender and sexuality or the predominant expectations of female athletes; it was also about the ways in which her blackness profiled her in profound ways. Described as tough, masculine, and physical, much of which comes from a 2010 incident in which she hit an opponent, Griner has faced the burden of race, gender, and sexuality. Able to dunk and brawl, rocking braids and tattoos, Griner exists in greater proximity to the black male athlete than to her white female counterparts. Her point of entry is through her physicality, athleticism, and "freakish" body as opposed to her breasts, butt, and beauty.[15]

Many media analysts predicted that Griner's androgynous gender displays coupled with her unparalleled athletic ability (defined most often by her ability to dunk) would revolutionize women's sports.[16] Every time she dunks, wears a bowtie, or gets another tattoo, Griner is pushing the boundaries of race, gender, and sexuality in important ways. Yet, as she does, she simultaneously brings about intense backlash, proving there is much more work to be done before we might see Griner featured in a Nike ad saying, "But I am proving, time and time again, there's no wrong way to be a woman."

Black Feminist Thought and Intersectionality

For more than fifty years, Black feminist scholars, activists, and organizers have argued against the inadequacy of analyzing Black women's experiences solely through the lens of race or gender, ignoring the important ways identities and systems of oppression intersect. The idea of intersectionality, first articulated by the founders of the Combahee River Collective in their 1977 statement and conceptually coined by legal scholar Kimberlé Crenshaw in the 1980s, is at its core about recognizing how racism and sexism interlock to frame Black women's lives.[17] When Brittney Cooper, a cofounder of the Crunk Feminist Collective, was asked whether her Blackness or womanhood mattered more, her response encapsulates the essence of intersectionality: "Find me the moment in which I'm not one of those at exactly the same moment that I am the other and I will answer your question."[18]

Intersectionality is important not just as a way to understand how individuals' identities overlap and intertwine (*what* might matter to a given person) but also as a way to more fully understand the impact of interlocking systems of oppression on an individual's experience (*how* things matter differently for people based on their social locations within the geography of social categories).

> Sexism, for example, is experienced differently by Black women than white women in part because it is not the only source of oppression that Black women face; it is complicated by institutional racism and the particular way that white patriarchy imparts racial hierarchy on Black bodies. . . . A similar argument has been made about how an overly simplistic view of racialized oppression of Black people often fails to consider the particular ways that gender roles and relationships are invoked as part of the system of white racism in the United States imaginary.[19]

Prevailing analyses within sport literature have examined sport through a variety of critical lenses, demonstrating the many ways the institution of sport perpetuates inequality. These analyses, however, have tended to focus singularly on gender, race, class, or sexuality, without adequately addressing how multiple aspects of identity and oppression create interlocking structures that variously impact athletes' everyday lived experiences.[20] Feminist sport scholars, for instance, have meticulously demonstrated how sport is a primary site through which gender is constructed (particularly masculinity) and power relations between men and women are played out. Many of these analyses have failed to account for the importance of race, thereby centering Whiteness and foregrounding the experiences of White athletes. Similarly, scholars examining the experiences of gay and lesbian athletes within sports have, for the most part, done so in isolation from considerations of race, resulting in a significant lack of understanding of the experiences of queer athletes of color. Race scholars studying sport have elucidated how sporting bodies are racialized and how the institution perpetuates racism, leading to differential experiences for Black and White athletes in particular. Much of this work has focused primarily on Black men athletes, however, making invisible the experiences of Black women athletes and other athletes of color.[21]

Following the work of Black feminist scholars like Beth Richie, I argue that we need to queer critical sport scholarship, weaving together disparate theories of gender, race, and sexuality in order to make sense of the unique experiences of Black women athletes and, specifically, queer, Black, and gender-nonconforming athletes within the institution of sport.[22] A Black feminist queer theory of sport decenters the dominant narratives of White women athletes, White gay men athletes, and Black men athletes by bringing analyses of gender, sexuality, and race into conversation with each other. It requires moving beyond categorical differences between athletes toward an understanding of how gender, race, and sexuality recursively structure the experiences of athletes within the institution of sport. Queering critical sport scholarship opens up a space for analyses of gender, race, and sexuality to sit side by side and, in that space, to more fully illustrate the interstice where Black women athletes are situated within the institution of sport. It is at this juncture that *Denied* begins.

This book tells a story about the everyday experiences of elite-level women athletes, particularly Black women basketball players. It is about how meanings associated with gender, sexuality, and race are made and remade daily within the context of sports, how those meanings intersect and are variously applied to individual athletes, and how those meanings are resisted, renegotiated, and redefined by individual athletes. This is an analysis about whether and how individuals within a given institutional context are allowed the agency to reach their full human capacities or whether they are confined to narrow definitions of what they should do and who they should become. It is about the power of social structures at the macro level shaping the lives of individuals at the micro level and how individuals, in various and uneven ways, push back against those structures.

The primary argument I make in this book is that women athletes are strictly policed based on gender and sexuality in complex and contradictory ways. This policing occurs at both the individual (player to player, coach to player) and institutional levels, and it is informed by the ideologies that support the larger structures of gender and sexuality operating within society. Most importantly, the policing of women athletes is racialized, meaning that racial meanings are embedded within ideologies of gender and sexuality, leading to inequitable experiences for athletes based on race. As a result, Black, queer women athletes—particularly those who are masculine-presenting in their gender expressions—experience the most severe forms of policing. Using ethnographic and interview data, I demonstrate how ideologies of gender, sexuality, and race differentially converge to shape the everyday lived experiences of elite women athletes.

The Context of Midwest State University

This book is informed by the nine months I spent with the Midwest State University (MWSU) women's basketball team as well as additional interviews with current and former elite-level women athletes.[23] My first day at MWSU, I was met at the entrance to the gymnasium by Johnny Jacobs, one of the assistant coaches.[24] Jacobs, wearing a bright yellow t-shirt and baggy blue shorts and dripping in sweat, said to me, "I'd give you a hug but I'm all sweaty." We shook hands instead. As I walked in, I could hear the familiar sounds of bouncing basketballs against glass and metal, squeaking tennis shoes on freshly cleaned hardwood, and high-pitched whistles echoing against a backdrop of thumping hip-hop music. Despite the air conditioning, the late August air was thick and sweet, the mustiness of sweat and rubber mingling with the cloying scent of sugary sports drink. Many of the players were there, finishing a three-on-three pick-up game they had been playing with some of the staff. Johnny introduced me as one of the new team managers.[25]

I chose MWSU and the women's basketball team for several important reasons. First, I wanted to explore the everyday lived experiences of collegiate women athletes because, quite simply, there is hardly anything written about this unique group. Although much sociological research on sport has focused on middle school and high school girls, much less has examined collegiate women athletes and none (as of this writing) has focused on that group of athletes from an ethnographic perspective.[26] Second, I chose basketball as opposed to other sports for several key reasons. Black women participate in collegiate basketball more than any other National Collegiate Athletic Association (NCAA) sport; they make up 31 percent of all basketball players across levels and 46 percent of Division I basketball players.[27] I was intent on decentering the experiences of White women athletes, so it was important to examine a sporting context in which Black women are overrepresented. Additionally, gender and sport scholars have long argued that contact and team sports such as basketball are stigmatized as "lesbian sports" more than individual sports such as track or tennis.[28] And, as a former collegiate basketball player myself, studying the sport was methodologically strategic, the details of which are articulated in the appendix.

Third, I chose the MWSU women's basketball team because they compete at the Division I level and, during the season I spent with the team, were ranked among the top twenty-five teams in the United States. As a result, the team received significantly more fanfare and media coverage, both locally and nationally, than the average women's basketball team. Many of the MWSU players went on to compete internationally and in the WNBA. Put simply, they represent the best of the best. Studying the most elite athletes was important to me because I wanted to explore how race, gender, and sexuality were playing out within a context where the stakes were highest. MWSU is such a context and, as I will argue throughout the book, what's at stake is much more than merely winning and losing games.

Ultimately, this is a book about a very specific group of athletes in a very particular time and place. It is a snapshot rather than a panorama. And although snapshots can reveal quite a lot when it comes to a particular moment, they are also limited. As such, there are a number of things this book does not cover. First, this book is focused on women athletes within the context of the United States and is largely concerned with the experiences of Black women athletes and the experiential differences between Black and White women athletes. This is not because it is unimportant to understand the experiences of other athletes of color, but the MWSU athletes as well as the athletes interviewed were either Black, White, or biracial (Black/White). Additionally, Black/White inequities remain the starkest within the United States broadly and within institutions such as sports.[29] A main argument of this book is that Blackness, particularly when intersected with gender nonconformity and queerness, is specifically targeted for containment and control. While all people of color are affected by White supremacy, there is something distinctive about the way anti-Blackness is perpetuated that deserves specific attention.

Second, this book is concerned with what happens in the lives of elite-level women athletes at the intersection of race, gender, and sexuality, although it is true that other important structures are operating simultaneously to impact their experiences. Class, for example, has been central to how the institution of sport has been constructed. Changes in the economic, social, and political landscape over the late nineteenth and early twentieth centuries, most notably through shifts in the kinds of work available to men as well as increasing momentum of the women's movement, began to erode the foundation of men's interpersonal, institutional, and societal dominance over women.[30] As Tony Collins has argued, modern sport is "a production of capitalism, shaped and moulded by class society and its consequent oppression of women and non-white peoples."[31] Class also impacts the kinds of sports that athletes participate in, particularly when considering the relationship between race and class. Sports like hockey and lacrosse, for instance, require substantial resources that continue to shape who has access to participation. Indeed, many of the MWSU athletes told me that had it not been for their athletic scholarships they would not have attended college at all, let alone MWSU. Class is undeniably integral to the institution of sport, and it impacts individual athletes in numerous ways. However, it is beyond the scope of this book to offer a full analysis of these processes.

What's to Come

In what follows, I tell the story of the MWSU women's basketball team and a select group of former elite women athletes as it relates to their experiences within the "contested terrain" of sport.[32] It is an attempt to shine a light on how larger structures of gender, sexuality, and race interweave and are imposed upon individuals as well as how those individuals resist, redefine, and relocate themselves within those structures in sometimes explicit but often subtle ways. It is a multilayered story about women in sports, and it is also much more than that.

Chapter 1 lays the foundation for the overall narrative by exploring the complex web of gender, sexuality, and race that envelops women athletes, along with the stickiness that comes with navigating the competing and often contradictory demands placed on these athletes. Using a particularly explosive locker-room vignette as a backdrop, I argue that the MWSU athletes, and women athletes broadly, are constrained by institutional and societal demands around their gender expressions that are complex and often in conflict with one another. This is particularly the case when examining how gender and sexuality are racialized. Thus, this chapter also offers a more detailed exploration of the importance of intersectionality in understanding women athletes' everyday lived experiences.

In chapter 2, I use an especially significant "crisis moment" for the MWSU women's basketball team—the filming of a rap video reenactment—as a means to demonstrate how ideologies of race, gender, and sexuality collide. I utilize Mark Anthony Neal's concept of legible and illegible Black masculinities in order to make sense of the behavior of the MWSU coaching staff in response to this crisis moment.[33] Ultimately, I argue that the MWSU coaching staff policed their players' expressions of gender and sexuality—policing that was problematized by race—in an attempt to promote an image of the team as heterosexual in order to secure highly sought-after recruits. I also compare the experiences of the MWSU team with those of well-known Black women athletes who are variously, albeit differently, policed for their legible and illegible expressions of race, gender, and sexuality.

Chapter 3 explores the lesbian stereotyping of women athletes. I document the pervasiveness of the stereotype as well as how it is variously applied and experienced by the athletes at MWSU. Drawing on the work of C. J. Pascoe, I introduce the term "dyke discourse" as a tool to constrain women athletes.[34] I demonstrate how the dyke discourse—commentary aimed at women athletes regarding the presence of lesbians in sport and an imagined contagion of lesbianism—is leveraged by athletes' families and friends as a way to enforce boundaries around their gender and sexuality. The dyke discourse is also utilized by opposing teams in an attempt to dissuade recruits (and their families) from attending particular programs, like MWSU. Building on previous chapters, I illustrate how such practices are differently applied to athletes based on race, gender expression, and sexuality.

In chapter 4, I outline how sport, as a masculine institution created by and for men, sets the stage for the cultural contradiction experienced by many women athletes, specifically those involved in contact and team sports like basketball. Drawing from interviews with the MWSU athletes as well as examples from popular culture, I discuss how ideologies of race, gender, and sexuality impact whether and how women athletes experience contradictions of identity. Relatedly, I utilize Arlie Hochs-child's concept of "gender strategies" in chapter 5 as a way to under-stand and interpret how women athletes, including the MWSU athletes, sometimes overemphasize femininity during sport participation. Such strategies, both implicit and explicit, range from the rather benign (e.g., wearing makeup and bows, shaving their legs) to the more extreme (e.g., altering training regimens to exclude weightlifting). Importantly, I situ-ate these findings within a structural framework that recognizes how an athlete's decision to engage in gender strategies can be viewed as much about individual preference as it is about resistance, however subtle, against structures designed to curtail their individual agency.

In the final chapter, I contend that we must continue to see how struc-tures of oppression adapt to changing times and how new forms of in-equality emerge to maintain the status quo. Ultimately, by shedding light on how structures of gender, sexuality, and race get reproduced within the institution of sport, we will be able to more fully understand the everyday lived experiences of women athletes and to discover new ways of encouraging resistance and enacting meaningful change within sport and in society more broadly.

1

"We Should Get You Skirts"

The Complex Web of Gender, Sexuality, and Race

With time quickly winding down and just seconds left in the first half, Rowan Dawson dribbled up the court, weaving through defenders, keeping an eye ahead for open teammates.[1] Dawson spotted teammate Kameron James unguarded near the basket and lobbed her the ball over the outstretched arms of their opponents. James caught the pass and finished the play with an easy layup as time expired. The buzzer sounded, and Midwest State University (MWSU) went into halftime with a twelve-point lead over their opponent.

As the voice of the announcer echoed through the rafters, the MWSU players slowly jogged down the long stadium tunnel to their locker room. One by one, the players filed in and sat down, their warm-up jerseys draped over the backs of their chairs and paper cups of water and Gatorade waiting on the tables in front of them. Despite being in the lead by a dozen points, the players wore dejected expressions: some hung their heads, others slouched, many with their eyes unmoving from the tiny cups in front of them.

Several silent minutes passed before Eve Callaway, MWSU team captain, turned her head and shouted, "Man, we're a bunch of bitch asses!" Others followed, emphatically stating, "We gotta pick it up!" and "Come on, y'all!" Seemingly buoyed by the collective rousing, the players slipped on their warm-up shirts and replenished themselves with the drinks in front of them, some taking slow sips and others guzzling the liquid in two or three quick gulps and then crushing the thin paper cups between their sweat-glistened fists. The room fell silent again. They waited.

Meanwhile, the MWSU coaching staff—head coach Jessica King and her five assistants, Missy Harwood, Grant Williams, Johnny Jacobs, Louis Jackson, and Vanessa Robinson—huddled together in the locker-room lobby, poring over pages of first-half statistics. Coach King's screams could be heard clearly over the muffled voices of the other coaches as they discussed offensive rebounding differentials, assist-to-turnover ratios, and fast-break points. Listening from inside the locker room, none of the players said a word. No one even moved.

The door flung open, and Coach King stormed in, brow furrowed and red-faced. The rest of the MWSU coaching staff slid in hesitantly behind her, staying close to the door. A blanket of silence washed over the room, and it felt as if everyone was holding their breath. Coach King slammed her clipboard down hard onto the table in front of her and shouted, "You're just a bunch of WUSS ASSES! I've never had a team with no toughness and no heart! I'm trying to find some toughness, but I got a bunch of PANSIES out here! You guys just sit there and take it up the ass. You don't even try to be tough. This is sissy league shit. We should get you skirts instead of shorts!" Furious, she stomped over to the trashcan and kicked it hard with the tip of her snakeskin stiletto. She swung back around, her piercing eyes scanning the players in front of her. "I don't have a bitch. I don't have a bitch. I got a bunch of nice girls. And you can't win games like that!"

Coach King then zeroed in on Jizeal Lane, a lean 6'3" post player who struggled with rebounding in the first half despite being up against much smaller opponents. Pointing directly at Jizeal, Coach King yelled, "*Everything* is more important to you than this, than your basketball career. You're too worried about getting your hair done and going to do this and that. You're not a competitor, a baller." Jizeal argued back, "I am!," but Coach King continued, unfazed.

"You're not committed," she said accusatorily. "You're laughing on the plane, not watching film, eating the wrong things." Jizeal tried to respond but Coach King interrupted. "I need you to be nasty. Be a *bitch*, a baller. You're nice and sweet and kind but be that off the court!" Jizeal, clearly defeated, did not respond.

Coach King then directed her anger at Tiffany Davidson, a 6'5" post player with a wide frame. "And YOU!" she shouted. "You can't even catch the ball! All you do is fumble the ball." She walked to the back row of seats where Tiffany was sitting, leaned directly in front of her, and mimicked fumbling a basketball with her hands while she pursed her lips and squealed "Ooh, ooh, meh, meh!" in a high-pitched tone. She paused for a moment and then, continuing to mock Tiffany through exaggerated hand gestures and awkward fumbling motions, she purposefully knocked over the cups of water and Gatorade on the table, spilling the contents everywhere. Tiffany and her teammates sat stunned, unmoving as liquid spread across the table, into their laps, and onto the floor. Coach King continued to scream at Tiffany to which her only response was "Yes, ma'am." Unsatisfied, King scoffed and as she turned around to walk back toward the front of the room, mocked Tiffany again. "Yes ma'am," she sarcastically mimicked in a babylike tone.

With each passing second, Coach King became more enraged. She told Jizeal she should stay upstairs in the locker room for the second half and put her feet up in the massage chair. She looked directly at Sara Parker, another 6'5" post player, and told her that the team's poor performance "starts with your fucking ass." She then went around the room pointing at individual players and repeating, "and your fucking ass . . . and her fucking ass!" Coach King grabbed the stat sheet from assistant coach Grant Williams and sat down hard in a chair at the front of the room. Clenching the sheet tightly in her fist, she listed off players' stats—"Jizeal, two rebounds!"—and lamented their poor performance— "They're almost out-rebounding us!" She stood up, crumpled the paper in her hand, and began shouting again. Her voice got louder and higher with each exasperated scream, at times cracking and hoarse. Her face was flushed and her eyes glowing as she glared at the players, often squinting in disgust. The room was so silent that you couldn't hear anything but the heaviness of Coach King's breathing, her chest visibly moving up and down with each exaggerated inhale and exhale. She continued to pace around the room, occasionally sitting down in her chair and then popping up again quickly, agitated. Everyone just watched. No one said a word.

With just more than three minutes left before the start of the second half, the team was released and headed back to the court. Some of the players attempted to reenergize the team with encouraging, yet hesitant, shouts of "Let's go!" and "We got this!" As Jizeal ran past the coaches, Coach King turned to her assistants and asked, "What's wrong with her? Is she having a boyfriend problem or something?" Johnny Jacobs replied, "I don't know," while the others, emotionless, just shook their heads.[2]

* * *

The above locker-room vignette depicts one moment amid countless others that collectively make up a season for the MWSU women's basketball team. The details of this vignette are not particularly unique. During my nine months spent with the MWSU women's basketball team—a highly competitive, National Collegiate Athletic Association (NCAA) Division I program—expletive-laden diatribes, thrown clipboards, kicked basketballs, and denigrating threats were quotidian, as is unfortunately the case in many sporting environments.[3] On the surface, then, Coach King's locker-room rant merely mirrors what we often witness on television or in scenes from any number of popular sports movies—red-faced coaches standing nose-to-nose with and screaming at rigid, deferent players, eyes averted or cast downward in shame. Such tactics are often justified as attempts to motivate players when they are perceived as not performing up to their coaches' expectations. It is certainly true that this was partly what was happening in the MWSU locker room that afternoon. Despite having a double-digit lead over their opponent at halftime, both the MWSU players and coaches were largely dissatisfied with their performance. While their opponent was undersized, less experienced, and its players generally less skilled than the elite MWSU athletes, they were executing well and keeping the game competitive. MWSU should have had a significant lead at the half, but their underperformance resulted in their holding on to only a slight advantage. Some of Coach King's comments alluded to this. When she shouted, "They're almost out-rebounding us!" or bemoaned having a team with "no toughness and no heart," King was referencing the players' athletic performance. They were not giving as much effort as they should have, and it showed in the game's statistics. I highlight this particular locker-room event, however, because it is an important illustration of the larger context in which the MWSU athletes are operating, a context that is rife with ideological contradictions and complexities about gender, sexuality, and race. Taken apart phrase by phrase, we can identify how the MWSU players are beholden not merely to expectations of superior athletic performance but also to conflicting and contrasting expectations around gender, sexuality, and race.

The Atmosphere of Sport

The experiences of the MWSU athletes, within the locker room and otherwise, cannot be fully understood outside of the specific context of sport and the ideological web woven around them. To say that the locker-room vignette is as much about race, gender, and sexuality as it is about athletic performance is to acknowledge how any one individual instance is connected to a larger structure from which it receives its meaning. Everyday acts, as Thomas Holt says, are links in a larger historical chain.[4] To know what is gendered or racialized about what happened in the MWSU locker room that afternoon necessitates knowing what historical structures created such conditions in the first place and continually shape their manifestations. It is, as Amanda Lewis and John Diamond articulate, the difficulty in keeping larger histories in mind amid everyday realities and "the challenge of paying attention simultaneously to the very bigness and the very smallness of its effects and to the connections between the two."[5] Moreover, understanding the gendered and raced nature of the locker-room scene requires understanding how sport is a gender- and race-making institution. Rather than merely processing some sort of natural way gender and race exist, the institution of sport produces a set of rules around gender and race—it teaches gendered and racial lessons—and, in doing so, actively genders and racializes its participants.[6] How gender and race operate within sport is particular to the context of sport and would not occur independently from the institution.[7] As Carmen Maria Machado writes, there is, always, the atmosphere to consider.[8]

Deeply defined by characteristics synonymous with hegemonic masculinity, and informed by sociohistorical structures, sport fundamentally shapes and creates our expectations around gender, race, and sexuality. As Shari Dworkin and Michael Messner contend,

> Sport has proven to be one of the key institutional sites for the study of the social construction of gender. Organized sport, as we now know it, was created in the late nineteenth and early twentieth centuries by and for White middle-class men to bolster a sagging ideology of "natural superiority" over women and over race- and class-subordinated groups of men. Thus, although sport was seemingly based in natural physical endow-

ments, it was socially constructed out of the gender, race, and class-based stratification systems of Europe and the United States.[9]

Gender and race are "present in the processes, practices, images and ideologies, and distributions of power" within sport.[10] As an institution, it is defined by "vastly unequal distributions of power, authority, prestige, and resources between women and men (and, indeed, between different social classes and racial groupings of men)."[11] The dearth of media coverage of women's sports and the persistent perception that girls and women play modified versions of the "real thing" are just two examples of such inequitable distributions of power.[12] Douglas Hartmann writes that sport represents a "contested terrain" in which "racial images, ideologies and inequalities are constantly and very prominently constructed, transformed, and struggled over."[13] As a result of operating within a society that is deeply structured by race, gender, and sexuality and as an institution that was fundamentally designed to maintain divisions along these lines, sport actively constructs what gender, race, and sexuality mean and, in doing so, (re)produces inequities and (re)creates inequities.

How this happens is a result of the everydayness of gender, race, and sexuality. Daily interactions that occur within sport—between coaches and players or between players, for example—serve to draw boundaries around what is expected and accepted in terms of normative understandings of race, gender, and sexuality. What happened in the locker room between Coach King and the MWSU players that gameday afternoon was the everyday making of these macro-level structures coming to life in micro-level ways.[14] It was the real-time creation of explicit and implicit rules and regulations—"*be a bitch, a baller*"—around gender, race, and sexuality. These interactions, as explosive as Coach King's fury that day, and in many much more subtle ways that will be outlined in this book, collectively comprise the everydayness of gender, race, and sexuality within sport. On their own, such interactions may seem insignificant. Taken together, however, they create an intersecting, complicated, and often-conflicting web that constricts the everyday lived experiences of the MWSU athletes in deeply consequential ways.

Expectations of Gender

In early 2019, actor Natasha Lyonne was featured on a panel hosted by *The Cut* in which she remarked: "The female experience for me has always been: Am I enough, and am I too much?"[15] Lyonne's comment encapsulates much of what occurred during those fifteen minutes in the MWSU locker room. Coach King's tirade illuminates how gender operates within larger society and, at the same time, derives complex meaning within the institutional confines of sport as a social institution. On the one hand, pejoratives like "wuss" and "sissy" are used to signal to players that they're not being tough enough, that they're not competing hard enough. These words become stand-ins for the deeper meanings embedded within them and thus simultaneously send another set of messages. For instance, when King calls her players "wuss asses" and "pansies" and compares their performance to "sissy league shit," she is invoking slurs typically used to disparage men who do not conform to hegemonic definitions of masculinity (e.g., White, heterosexual, middle-class), men who are weak and effeminate (i.e., not athletic), men who are, in short, perceived to be more like women.[16] Indeed, the meanings behind words like "wuss," "pansy," and "sissy" closely align with character traits rooted in definitions of hegemonic femininity, including passivity and deference.[17] Similarly, in telling her players they should get skirts instead of shorts, King is explicitly linking feminine-gendered signifiers such as clothing to traits such as weakness, inferiority, and incompetence, thereby reinforcing deeply rooted beliefs in the inferiority of women and femininity.

In part, this type of speech is characteristic of her coaching style. Coach King is fierce, flashy, and, from what I perceived, enjoys being feared. Coaches like her often utilize humiliating comments to motivate their players.[18] It is illuminating that in the locker room that day (and many other days after that), in the midst of being engulfed in anger, the words that King chose to use were dripping with disparagement of characteristics commonly associated with traditional femininity. She wants "bitches" and "ballers," players who will get "nasty" on the court. She doesn't want "a bunch of nice girls," like Jizeal, who King presumes care about getting their hair done as much or more than they care about their athletic performance. By denigrating her players' expressions of femininity, King explicitly marks feminine character traits and behaviors as not aligning with athleticism. The inherent assumption is that the MWSU players were performing poorly because they were performing traits characteristic of femininity. Within the context of elite-level sports, there is nothing worse than "acting like a girl."

Faced with King's criticisms, the obvious solution is for the MWSU athletes to more readily embrace and embody masculinity—to be "ballers," to give her the toughness and heart she was begging them for, at least on the court. Although doing so might appease King, such a strategy comes with its own set of costs, at least off the court. According to Cecelia Ridgeway, gender acts as a powerful cultural frame that organizes social relations between individuals.[19] The use of the word "frame" here is illustrative, as gender operates both as a rigid structure—confining individuals to culturally based, commonsense understandings of what they should look, act, and feel like—as well as a basic structure on which our most fundamental ways of being among and interacting with each other rests. Ridgeway argues that "sex/gender works as a coordinating device for social relations through the construction of shared cultural beliefs about presumed differences in character and behavior that are associated with sex category. By this common knowledge, someone classified as female can be expected to behave in a specific way that is different from someone classified as male, and this provides an initial, orienting frame for coordinating behavior with them."[20]

For decades, social psychologists exploring the content of and mechanisms behind gender stereotypes have argued that these forms of common knowledge—alternatively called gender proscriptions and prescriptions—serve as regulatory tools for maintaining gender inequity. Gender stereotypes consist of rules about how we *should* behave (prescriptions) and how we *should not* behave (proscriptions) based on our sex assigned at birth (and the assumed alignment between sex category, gender identity, and gender expression).[21] For example, agentic attributes such as assertiveness and competitiveness are prescriptive for men, and communal attributes like kindness and supportiveness are prescriptive for women. Proscriptive characteristics for men include weakness and passivity and, for women, characteristics like arrogance and dominance. Societal gender rules are made up of these prescriptions and proscriptions, guiding our own behaviors as well as our expectations of others. Importantly, gender pre/proscriptions are connected to status beliefs that serve to assign the highest value to traits most closely aligned with men and masculinity.[22]

Gender prescriptions and proscriptions are meaningful not just because they dictate our everyday, routine behaviors and interactions with others but also because they reinforce the gender binary and gender hierarchies through mechanisms of policing and punishment. Violation of gender proscriptions can result in a "backlash effect." First articulated by Laurie Rudman, the backlash effect "emerges when agentic women are judged as similarly competent but less likeable and hirable, compared with identically behaving men."[23]

> For example, women encounter backlash when they violate gender stereotypes by seeking political office, expressing anger, or vying for a managerial role. Although the majority of existing work has focused on backlash against stereotype-violating women, recent evidence suggests that stereotype-violating men encounter backlash as well. For example, men encounter backlash when they violate gender stereotypes by working in early elementary education, requesting a family leave from work, and behaving modestly on a job interview. Indeed, stereotype-violating men may actually be more susceptible to backlash than women. Specifically, while women typically experience backlash only when displaying female-proscriptive traits (but not when they fail to display female-prescriptive traits), men experience backlash when they display male-proscriptive traits and when they fail to display male-prescriptive traits.[24]

Gender prescriptions and proscriptions also impact trans people's experiences in nuanced ways. Trans women, for example, encounter both sexism and cissexism and must contend with the gender pre/proscriptions for cisgender women and those for transgender women. Trans women have, as Jill Yavorsky argues, "dualistic behavioral constraints" in which they are limited in their ability to enact authority so as not to be labeled a "bitch" (sexism) *and* so as not to have their gender identities questioned (cissexism): "Whereas cis women are able to maintain a feminine identity because slurs such as 'bitch' feminize and stigmatize them (rather than masculinize and stigmatize them), trans women's masculine practices carried the additional penalty of undermining gender authenticity."[25] Other scholars have similarly demonstrated how trans women experience greater levels of discrimination in the workplace than trans men.[26]

Status incongruity is a key component of backlash. Put another way, the presence of women in leadership positions, for example, is not enough on its own to elicit backlash. Rather, women leaders' expressions of agency result in backlash because agency is tied to high status and women are proscribed against having high status. This dominance penalty for women who enact agency is thus motivated by a desire to reinforce the gender hierarchy and is justified by perceived status violations of agentic women (i.e., the status incongruity between women's ascribed and achieved status).[27]

While the research on the backlash effect has primarily focused on professional women in organizational leadership roles, examples abound that demonstrate the same effect for women in sports, particularly for women who enter into previously male-dominated positions such as referees or sportscasters. For instance, when Beth Mowins called her first game on *Monday Night Football*, she was subject to intense criticism of her voice. Mowins's voice was labeled "annoying" and "shrill" and likened to the sound of being scolded by an ex-girlfriend or a mother.[28] Chicago sports radio host Julie Dicaro is often told that her voice is "too high, too low, too young-sounding, too Chicago-sounding, too harsh, too soft, and 'just generally obnoxious.'"[29] In response to Jessica Mendoza's calling of a Major League Baseball playoff game, exasperated baseball watchers tweeted things like "We watch sports to get away from women" and "SOS there's a woman talking during my baseball watching."[30] After National Basketball Association referee Lauren Holtkamp called a controversial technical foul against Chris Paul during a game, he told reporters afterward, "This might not be for her."[31] When Paul was criticized for what many considered to be a sexist comment, his fans flocked to Twitter to defend him with comments like "get back in the kitchen" and "if women are going to ref they should not be handled with kid gloves."[32]

Backlash as a mechanism of gender policing is a "preemptive strike that stops women long before they reach the finish line."[33] Backlash maintains gender hierarchies and forces women into delicate balancing acts "akin to driving over rough terrain while keeping one hand on the wheel and the other reassuringly on passengers' backs."[34] In later chapters, I will outline the specific ways the MWSU athletes experienced various forms of backlash as a result of their enactment and embodiment of masculinity, although I preface it here to highlight how the institutional context of sport sets the stage for the experience of gender-specific backlash. Being the "bitches" and "ballers" that Coach King desires means engaging in gender proscriptive behavior that will likely serve the MWSU players well on the court while punishing them off the court.

Expectations of Sexuality

Fully understanding the ideological work being done around gender within King's locker-room rant requires acknowledging how gender and heterosexuality are intricately interconnected or "inextricably bound up."[35] While gender and sexuality are distinct, they are mutually reinforcing and lead to a commonsense understanding of gender as a cultural signifier of sexuality. In other words, gender is often used as a stand-in for sexuality wherein normative gender presentations imply heterosexuality and nonnormative gender presentations imply nonheterosexuality. As a result, gender transgressions are always also, at least in part, perceived to be threats to heterosexuality. Inherent in gender prescriptions directing women to be "nice" or "helpful" and gender proscriptions warning women not to be "demanding" or "competitive" are also messages about sexuality. It is not surprising then that when women engage in gender proscriptions (i.e., "acting like men") they are judged more harshly than when they simply fail to follow gender prescriptions by, for example, not being "nice." Gender policing is fundamentally about policing (hetero)sexuality.

When Coach King asks for "bitches" and "ballers," she is asking her players to engage in masculinized, gender proscriptive behaviors that bring with them assumptions about sexuality. Players who are tough and nasty on the court are perceived to be acting like men and, as a result, are often presumed to be lesbians. Sport scholars have thoroughly demonstrated how the lesbian stigma associated with women's sports, especially contact and team sports like basketball, has led to perceptions of women athletes as lesbians. Historically, fears of women athletes' "mannishness" were linked to sexual deviance, and it was assumed that, by taking on masculine characteristics through sport participation, women athletes would also develop masculine "sexual characteristics and interests."[36] Indeed, the image of the "lesbian boogeywoman" is pervasive in women's sports, despite increasing acceptance of nonnormative sexualities within society and within sports.[37] As I will explore further in chapter 3, lesbian stereotyping is an essential component of the experiences of all of the athletes at MWSU, as well as others interviewed for this book.

Which Women? Racialized Expectations of Gender and Sexuality

Analyzing the locker-room vignette exposes the complicated and often contradictory expectations around gender and sexuality that women athletes face within the institution of sport. Although it is much less obvious, Coach King's rant in the locker room also reveals important messages about race and, in particular, illuminates how expectations around gender and sexuality are deeply racialized. Despite the tendency to think of them as discrete or parallel entities, gender, sexuality, and race are co-constructed, relational categories, given meaning through the ways they continuously overlap and inform one another.[38] Attempting to articulate the unique experiences of Black women who experience race and gender marginalization, Black feminist scholars have argued for increased attention to the processes whereby race and gender, among other categories of difference, compose interlocking systems of oppression.[39] Feminist legal scholar Kimberlé Crenshaw coined the phrase "intersectionality" to locate Black women's particular experiences with employment discrimination. As she argued, "The intersection of racism and sexism factors into Black women's lives in ways that cannot be captured wholly by looking at the race or gender dimensions of those experiences separately."[40]

Understanding the experiences of women athletes, like those at MWSU and beyond, within the institution of sport requires reckoning with the intersecting processes of meaning-making that occur along the lines of race, gender, and sexuality, particularly as this intersectional process relates to our understandings of femininity and womanhood. Cultural understandings of what it means to be a woman, centered largely on idealized standards of beauty, have always been racialized. Historical racial tropes of Black people as animalistic and "closer to nature" collide with controlling images of hypersexuality to create a unique frame within which Black women, including Black trans women, have always been typecast.[41] Women of color have always been situated outside of the boundaries of "true womanhood," firmly grounded in Whiteness, heterosexuality, and emphasized forms of femininity— Whiteheterofemininity. As Susan Cahn writes, "Racialized notions of sexual virtue and feminine beauty were underpinned by another concept, that of the virile or mannish black female. African American women's work history as slaves, tenant farmers, domestics, and wageworkers disqualified them from standards of femininity defined around the frail or inactive female body."[42]

Standards of femininity centered on the frailness of womanhood applied only to White women. Participating in sport, therefore, was masculinizing only for White women, since Black women were already defined as "mannish" by intersecting racial and gender tropes. Considering the experiences of contemporary athletes like Brittney Griner through an intersectional lens is also instructive. As a queer, Black woman who embodies Black masculinity, Griner is subjected to a particular kind of racialized and gendered scrutiny that "isn't purely about gender and sexuality, about dominant expectations of female athletes, but also the ways that her Blackness restricts and confines her."[43]

Importantly, Black femininity has always been constructed as inferior and inherently incongruent with idealized White womanhood; as such, Black women's deviation from Whiteheterofemininity has been historically guaranteed. As Crenshaw explains,

> certain gender expectations for women intersect with certain sexualized notions of race, notions that are deeply entrenched in American culture. Sexualized images of African Americans go all the way back to Europeans' first engagement with Africans. Blacks have long been portrayed as more sexual, more earthly, more gratification-oriented. These sexualized images of race intersect with norms of women's sexuality, norms that are used to distinguish good women from bad, the madonnas from the whores. Thus Black women are essentially prepackaged as bad women within cultural narratives about good women.[44]

The construction of "good" and "bad" categories of women has served many purposes, one of which is to shore up structures of White supremacy and heteropatriarchy. As Patricia Hill Collins writes, "Many of the attributes extant in Black female stereotypes are actually distorted renderings of those aspects of Black female behavior seen as most threatening to white patriarchy. For example, aggressive Afro-American women are threatening because they challenge white patriarchal definitions of femininity."[45] Gender and sexuality are inextricably connected to race and, as a result, gender policing is as much about controlling the boundaries of femininity and heterosexuality as it is about maintaining ideologies of White supremacy. Patricia Hill Collins further contends that "ideas about sexuality are so integral to understandings of Black gender ideology as well as broader gender ideology in the United States, neither Black masculinity nor Black femininity can be adequately understood let alone transformed without attending to the politics of sexuality."[46]

Scholars across disciplines have articulated how racialized notions of gender have created vastly inequitable everyday lived experiences for Black girls and women. In her book *Invisible No More*, Andrea Ritchie meticulously outlines how gender-specific forms (e.g., sexual harassment, assault, rape) and gender-specific contexts (e.g., sex work) of policing disproportionately make women of color into targets of police violence. Such policing depends on long-standing controlling images—the "monstrous and licentious 'Jezebel'"—which denigrate Black femininity and situate Black women's bodies as deserving of control by state-sanctioned police violence.[47]

The media that circulate misogynoir help maintain White supremacy by offering tacit approval of the disparate treatment that Black women negotiate in society. Whether the Jezebel, mammy, Sapphire, and later the "welfare queen" or even the "strong Black woman" archetype, misogynoiristic portrayals of Black women shape their livelihoods and health. As media studies scholars attest, negative images and narratives do more than affect the self-esteem of the populations depicted. Misogynoiristic caricatures materially impact the lives of Black women by justifying poor treatment throughout all areas of society and throughout US history.[48]

Education scholars have similarly argued that Black girls are disciplined differently and, in many cases, more harshly in schools than Black boys and White and Latina girls due to failing to comply with normative gender expectations.[49] According to Connie Wun, Black girls are often punished in schools for nonviolent infractions such as being "disrespect-ful" or "talking back"—coded language for "failing to meet dominant cis-gendered expectations of femininity."[50] The labeling of Black girls as "defiant" or "disobedient" and "the subsequent disciplinary actions are characterized by underlying racial stereotypes and assumptions about appropriate behaviors, which often indicate that girls are expected to be obedient and docile."[51] Given the tendency to criminalize normal everyday behaviors of Black girls, Wun argues that we must "examine the racial/gendered phobic impulse to characterize her as a problem."[52] Monique Morris likewise contends that Black girls are placed into polar-izing categories:

> They are either "good" girls or "ghetto" girls who behave in ways that ex-acerbate stereotypes about Black femininity, particularly those that relate to socioeconomic status, crime, and punishment. When Black girls do engage in acts that are deemed "ghetto"—often a euphemism for actions that deviate from social norms tied to a narrow, White middle-class defi-nition of femininity—they are frequently labeled as nonconforming and thereby subjected to criminalizing responses.[53]

Black girls are especially susceptible to punishment in schools (and beyond) because of commonsense understandings of Black femininity as inferior, buoyed by long-standing controlling images of Black girls and women as "hypersexual, conniving, loud, and sassy."[54]

Returning to the locker-room scene that opens this chapter, when Coach King tells Jizeal, "I need you to be *nasty*. Be a *bitch*, a *baller*. You're nice and sweet and kind but be that off the court," she is invoking ra-cialized and gendered ideologies of women in ways that create an im-possible paradox of expectations for Jizeal and for all the players. King wants her almost all-Black team to be "bitches" in a society that already perceives Black women as such. She wants her players to be "ballers"—to embrace and embody masculinity—in a society that already perceives women athletes, and Black women athletes in particular, as mannish and lesbians.[55] King wants her team to be nice off the court, in a society where women's "niceness" is prescribed and can lead to sexual victimization, and where Black women are continually resisting societal perceptions of being unjustifiably angry.[56] And she threatens to replace her players' basketball shorts with skirts because they aren't performing athletically to their potential, and, in doing so, she denigrates femininity and reinforces the notion that women athletes are only ever playing modified versions of the "real thing"—the men's game. For the MWSU players to be all of these things at once is an impossible fiction, not just because such expectations are fundamentally unattainable but because they are inherently contradictory and, most importantly, accessible only to women who possess and conform to Whiteheterofemininity (and maybe not even to them).[57]

Indeed, "the controlling image of the 'bitch' constitutes one representation that depicts Black women as aggressive, loud, rude, and pushy."[58] Gymnast Gabby Douglas faced criticism during the 2016 Olympic Games in Rio for not smiling after her teammate Simone Biles won a gold medal, inciting the creation of the Twitter hashtag #CrabbyGabby. In response to a series of questionable calls against her during the 2018 US Open final—including a penalty for breaking her racket after losing a serve and accusations of receiving improper coaching—Serena Williams called umpire Carlos Ramos a liar and a thief. She was fined $17,000 and received both intense media backlash and support. Echoing what was obvious to many commentators who have followed Williams's career, Rebecca Traister writes,

> I don't care much about the rules of tennis that Serena Williams was accused of violating at Saturday night's U.S. Open final. Those rules were written for a game and for players who were not supposed to look or express themselves or play the game as beautifully and passionately as either Serena Williams or the young woman who eventually beat her, 20-year-old Naomi Osaka, do. They are rules written for a sport that, until Williams and her sister came along, was dominated by white players, a sport in which white men have violated those rules in frequently spectacular fashion and rarely faced the kind of repercussions that Williams—and Osaka—did on Saturday night.[59]

Williams was penalized, therefore, not merely for allegedly violating the rules of tennis but, more importantly, for violating the racialized and gendered rules of society. Expressions of anger and rage, however justified, fall squarely outside of the boundaries of womanhood, and Black womanhood especially. In her memoir *Becoming*, Michelle Obama writes, "Since stepping into public life, I've been held up as the most powerful woman in the world and taken down as an 'angry black woman.'"[60] Kimberley Wilson, a contestant on the widely popular reality show *The Great British Bake Off*, experienced online vitriol by viewers who accused her of being arrogant, too self-satisfied, too confident, and not showing enough vulnerability, deference, and graciousness. Other commenters went so far as to suggest that she "know her place." Such examples illuminate the continued perception of Black women, inside and out of the sporting context, as uncivil.[61] More importantly, they underscore the everyday reality that Black women, regardless of context and achievement, must navigate a minefield of expectations rooted in White supremacy and patriarchy that require them to be everything all the time in exactly the right proportions.

Cathy Park Hong's concept of minor feelings is illustrative here. Minor feelings are "the racialized range of emotions that are negative, dysphoric, and therefore untelegenic, built from the sediments of everyday racial experience and the irritant of having one's perception of reality constantly questioned or dismissed."[62] Minor feelings occur when people accuse Gabby Douglas of being unsupportive of her teammate for not smiling, when Serena Williams is penalized repeatedly for rules infractions that others routinely get away with, and when Kimberley Wilson is labeled too self-satisfied for baking a good cake. Minor feelings are also, as Hong says,

> the emotions we are accused of having when we decide to *be* difficult—in other words, when we decide to be honest. When minor feelings are finally externalized, they are interpreted as hostile, ungrateful, jealous, depressing, and belligerent, affects ascribed to racialized behavior that whites consider *out of line*. Our feelings are overreactions because our lived experiences of structural inequality are not commensurate with their deluded reality.[63]

When Serena Williams fought back against Ramos's allegation of cheating, she was giving voice to her continuous experiences of sexism and racism in a sport where she continually dominates yet has never been fully accepted. Her externalization of these minor feelings—dubbed "verbal abuse" by the US Open referee office—resulted in a substantial fine and news headlines about her "furious rant." As Traister adds, "One thing black women are never allowed to be without consequence is livid."[64]

* * *

The MWSU athletes are actively navigating a sporting landscape rife with complex and contradictory rules around gender, sexuality, and race. They are, in dramatic moments and in hundreds more ordinary, always managing the impossible task that is living at the nexus of intersecting societal structures of oppression while simultaneously trying to compete in elite-level athletics. From the outside, the MWSU team is highly competitive and at the peak of its programmatic success. From the inside, it is a group of mostly Black, some queer, and a few gender-nonconforming women contending with the everyday machinations of race, gender, and sexuality in an institution that was not designed for them. Too often, rather than being celebrated for their successes as athletes, they are accused of being failures as women—at once too much and never enough.

2

"Don't Be So Blunt with It"

The Racialized Policing of Gender and Sexuality

It was mid-December, and the usually bustling Midwest State University (MWSU) campus was quiet. Classes were suspended until the new year, and most students were away spending the holidays with family and friends. Because winter break falls in midseason, the MWSU basketball players were required to stay on campus. Much of their time was filled with practices, traveling, and playing games, but the players did have some occasional free time as they were not attending classes and completing homework. After practice one day, some of the players gathered in one of their dorm rooms to hang out and listen to music. It had recently snowed, and they were bored, stuck inside without much to do until the next practice, weight training, or film session. Trying to pass the time and have a little fun, the players playfully danced and sang along to their favorite hip-hop songs. Inspired, they decided to film a reenactment of a popular hip-hop music video at the time.

In that video, a group of rappers—all Black and mostly men—are singing, dancing, and interacting with a group of partially clothed women, most of whom are women of color. One rapper, shirtless and in boxer shorts, is shown getting out of a bed full of women wearing only underwear. He and the women are draped across one another. The camera then pans to another room where more women, wearing not much more clothing, are watching television, shooting pool, and dancing. Two other rappers are shown playing cards and throwing money into the air while women in cut-off jean shorts and see-through midriff shirts dance behind them. Another rapper is depicted lying in bed and singing while taking photos of a woman who is straddled on top of him, slowly undressing to the beat of the music. In a scene that cuts in and out throughout the video, the group of rappers are standing in front of a swimming pool, wearing sunglasses, leather jackets, and gold jewelry, and dancing and singing to the music. At the same time, women in bikinis are getting sprayed with water guns while others are playfully pushed into the pool. Another woman is sitting in the lap of one of the rappers as they float on a large, colorful pool float. She is smiling and kissing his cheek with her arms wrapped tightly around his neck.

In imitating these scenes, the MWSU players took on the various roles of the people in the video. Some of them—Eve Callaway, Kyle Kingsley, Nikki Randall, and Nicole "Prince" Davis—portrayed the rappers, dressing in fitted backward baseball caps, men's tank tops, and baggy jeans or boxer shorts. Other players—Jizeal Lane, Karolina Markovich, Naomi Pierce, and Tiffany Davidson—acted as the women in the video, wearing elaborate makeup, short shorts, and revealing tops or perhaps just bras. Isis Smith shot the film while Lauryn Brown stood off to the side, laughing at her teammates. Using one of their dorm suites as the set, the players reenacted parts of the video described above while the song played in the background. They sang and danced with each other in the living room and lounged on the beds together as close as they could get to how it was performed in the music video.

Thinking it was creative and funny, one of the players posted the video to Facebook to share with their friends. The MWSU coaching staff, however, saw the video as anything but funny. Alerted to its existence by an unknown source, the coaches demanded the immediate removal of the video and called an emergency team meeting. During the meeting, the players were forced to watch their parody on a large projector screen—typically reserved for watching game film—in front of the coaches and, as one player put it, "explain themselves."

Girl-on-Girl Action

The MWSU coaches, and Coach King in particular, were incensed over the video, and their reactions represent an important crisis moment in which the boundaries around race, gender, and sexuality are pushed and promptly reinforced. The scenes in the video are clearly sexualized, as the men are often shirtless and the women are all in either revealing clothing or no clothing at all, just underwear. Almost all the interactions between the men and women in the video involve sexualized touching or sexual innuendos. Moreover, the song itself is about sex. The players were reprimanded for making the video and posting it on the internet, not because it involved a series of sexually explicit interactions between men and women but because those interactions were taking place *between women*. Some of the players appeared to be "acting like boys" and all of them appeared to be queer. Considering the long history of women's sports—particularly team contact sports like basketball—being typecast as lesbian, the coaches' anger over the portrayal of "girl-on-girl action" in the video is in large part about battling this ever-present stereotypical image.[1]

To understand how such a seemingly benign event could cause a reaction of this magnitude, I asked several of the MWSU players about the video and the coaching staff's reaction.[2] Freshman guard Kyle Kingsley described the situation as a harmless attempt at having fun during some downtime. "It was over winter break," Kyle tells me. "When it snowed really bad here and we were stuck in the room. We had nothing to do, and man, we made a video because we were just so close. We put it on the internet. It wasn't meant to be anything like that. It was just to be fun. So, we put it on the internet and I guess it got back to our coach. And it didn't seem that bad to us. But they called us in here to watch it in front of them."

"They called the whole team in?" I asked.

Kyle replied, "They called the whole team in to watch."

"To watch the video in front of the coaches?" I repeated.

Kyle continued:

In front of them. And then we watching it. It wasn't that bad. It was just like, you know, it feels weird watching it in front of them. I don't know. I mean we were just laughing. We would just like turn our head and would laugh. We knew it wasn't meant to be anything like that. I mean it would be the same thing if they was a boy in the video.

"Right," I responded. "So, what was the big deal about the video?"

"It might have been a big deal, I guess, because we're all girls," Kyle adds. "But at the same time, we're all teammates. It's not like we had random girls in the video that nobody's ever seen."

"So, they were upset that you guys made the video because . . . ," I ask, trailing off at the end.

Kyle tells me, "It's probably mostly that we put it on the internet for people to see." Once uploaded to Facebook, the video went from an innocuous attempt at having fun during a snowstorm to a crisis akin to an actual snowstorm. The broad visibility of the video was problematic for MWSU not because it could be seen but because of what exactly could be seen within it. Senior and team captain Eve Callaway explained it to me this way:

> So, we made a video. And like all of us are like, really close, you know. So, like, we have straight teammates who doesn't mind like, dancing on us or dancing with us or just having fun with us. So, we did the video and she [Coach King] was like, "This doesn't look good for the program. You guys look like a bunch of lesbians!" And we just like, "Who cares?"

Reflecting on Coach King's reaction, Jizeal Lane told me similarly,

> When we did that or whatever and she [Coach King] was just like, "That's not okay because that just gives, that just shows that, oh, it's girl-on-girl action." Me and Prince on the couch, she whispering in my ear. You know, we was just acting but I mean she was whispering in my ear. Naomi and Karolina in the bed with Eve, you know, half dressed. It was a nice video but like I understood where she was coming from. It did make it seem like our whole team was gay because only two people wasn't in the video.

The girl-on-girl action portrayed in the video made it appear as though the entire MWSU team was queer, which presented an image problem for the coaches. Moreover, several of the players were specifically playing the role of the Black male rappers in the video. Therefore, the video sent another set of messages that is more complicated than simple perceptions of lesbianism. The stereotype of women athletes as lesbians is as old as women's sports themselves. Girl-on-girl action, while troublesome for a program, can be handled. The real problem here was the racialized portrayal of girl-on-girl action with a handful of Black women acting like Black men. The MWSU coaches' response to the video is about the specific intersections of race, gender, and sexuality literally playing out within and between the players' bodies. The demand for the removal of the video is an indictment of lesbianism and, in particular, an explicit and exacting regulation of queer, Black women's bodies performing masculinity.

Body Legibility

Bodies are key sites of social construction—how we physically construct ourselves—and power relations—how others attach meaning and value to our bodies and how we express resistance to those meanings.[3] Cultural narratives about the inherent value of certain kinds of bodies and their uses have long histories tied to White supremacy, patriarchy, heterosexism, and other structures of oppression. Colonialist ideologies about race used to construct racial hierarchies and cement White supremacy are centered on notions of Black bodies as subhuman, sexually and criminally deviant, immoral, and uncontrollable.[4] These racial scripts have been and continue to be intricately tied to ideologies of gender and sexuality. As Patricia Hill Collins notes, "For both women and men, Western social thought associates Blackness with an imagined uncivilized, wild sexuality and uses this association as one lynchpin of racial difference. Whether depicted as 'freaks' of nature or as being the essence of nature itself, savage, untamed sexuality characterizes Western representations of women and men of African descent."[5] The legacy of American colonial history lives on in modern racial tropes that both celebrate and loathe, commodify and criminalize the Black body.[6] As Ben Carrington writes, "Within the post/colonial present, the binary structure of contemporary stereotypes means that the black body becomes either *sub*-human or *super*-human—never just common, never ordinary, never defined by its unspectacular *humanity*."[7] As kihana miraya ross argues, "The *thingification* of black people is a fundamental component of this nation."[8]

Contemporary racial imagination thus oscillates between idealization and condemnation of the Black body, rendering it, in many ways, ambivalent. Such ambivalence serves White supremacy as it "allows constructions of the Other to remain both 'fixed' and to adapt (and sometimes to even reverse its connotations) in different historical contexts in order for it to make sense to its particular location and to 'work.'"[9] This kind of racialized ambivalence—the both/and inherent in modern racial discourse—is ultimately what allows us to relentlessly criminalize Black men on the whole *and* elect Barack Obama as president of the United States twice. It is a context in which we can demonize Black women through the lenses of any number of controlling images like the "Jezebel" and "Welfare Queen" and exalt Beyoncé as our "Queen Bey."[10]

Another way to understand the simultaneous celebration and denigration of Black bodies is through Mark Anthony Neal's concept of legible and illegible Black masculinities. As Neal asserts, "That the most 'legible' black male body is often thought to be a criminal body and/or a body in need of policing and containment—incarceration—is just a reminder that the black male body that so seduces America is just as often the boogeyman that keeps America awake at night."[11] Constructions of Black masculinity that are not clear enough to be read through the lens of our collective racial imagination, those that exist outside of the frame of the "criminalblackman,"[12] are illegible. Importantly, the legible Black body is "continually recycled to serve the historical fictions of American culture" that prescribe and perpetuate anti-Blackness.[13] This continued recycling of the legible Black body breathes new life into deep-rooted racial narratives, leaving them modified yet intact in "postracial" America. The (il)legibility of Black bodies is thus what allows us to put the Dallas Cowboys' Ezekiel Elliot's wet, naked body on the cover of *ESPN* magazine's 2017 "body issue" for mass consumption *and* turn a blind eye toward—if not outright support—the inexorable mass incarceration of Black men, and increasingly Black women, in our country.[14]

If the most legible Black man's body is a criminal body in need of containment, the most legible Black woman's body is a hypersexual body in need of regulation. Black feminist scholars such as Angela Davis, Kimberlé Crenshaw, Dorothy Roberts, Beth Richie, and Patricia Hill Collins have detailed how myths about Black women's sexuality have been used to perpetuate controlling images of Black women as deviant and immoral. These images have been repeatedly repurposed to fit the popular racial imaginations of the current moment. The uncontrollable, overly sexual "Jezebel," for instance, has existed since slavery and continues on in modern popular culture as a way to perpetually exclude Black women from notions of "ideal femininity" or "true womanhood."[15] As Dorothy Roberts contends,

> From the moment they set foot in this country, Black women have fallen outside the American ideal of true womanhood. This contradiction became especially pronounced during the Victorian era. The nineteenth-century image of the True Woman was delicate, refined, and chaste. Although she was considered physically and intellectually inferior to men, she was morally superior to them. She was perfectly suited to the home, where she served as mother and wife. All of her attributes were precisely the opposite of those that characterized Black women.[16]

Depicted as "purely lascivious" and morally inferior to White women, the most legible Black woman's body during slavery was embodied by the "Jezebel."[17] Modern iterations of the "Jezebel" saturate popular culture, most notably within hip-hop songs and music videos.[18] Racialized sexual scripts that play out in hip-hop culture and media, such as the "Diva," "Gold Digger," and "Freak," all contain remnants of "Jezebel" imagery. These modernized controlling images buoy the popular notion that Black women's bodies are most legible as sexually deviant bodies, existing well beyond the boundaries of traditional White womanhood. As Resmaa Menakem claims, "The White body sees . . . Black bodies as dangerous and needing to be controlled, yet also as potential sources of service and comfort."[19]

Ultimately, White supremacy is maintained through the construction of legible Black bodies, the relative ease with which they can be read in ways that match popular perceptions of what those bodies should look like and should be doing. Legibility is important not just because of the apparent neatness with which it organizes our collective racial imagination, but because it has material consequences attached to it. Legible Black bodies are readable precisely because they are perceived as in need of unerring control. The legible "criminalblackman" necessitates policing and incarceration—the literal containment of the body. The legible "Jezebel" or "Freak" compels social and state-sponsored demonization—the literal regulation of what the body can and cannot do.[20]

Layers of Legibility

It is within this context of legibility that we can best understand the MWSU coaches' reactions to their players' music video parody. The

MWSU players were critiqued for their legibility *and* illegibility. The players, in their various roles, embodied both legible Black femininities and masculinities; some of them took on the role of "Jezebel," while others portrayed the "criminalblackman" or "thug," as embodied by the image of the Black rapper.[21] These representations, while fictional, presented problems for the MWSU coaches because, at their most basic level, they put on display racialized stereotypes that are often accompanied by social derision and inherently require social control. The "Jezebel" and "thug" are in direct contrast to the role-model "girl next door" image that puts parents and their young children in the MWSU stands during game time.

The harshness of the coaches' critique is, of course, amplified by the fact that both masculine and feminine portrayals of Black legibility were enacted by women. The players who took on the "Jezebel" roles were perpetuating a legible narrative consistent with controlling images of Black women that have long permeated our collective imaginations. Such portrayals in and of themselves are problematic for MWSU. As Prince tells me,

> You know, why throw a whole bunch of guys in the video? Now we're hos. I mean, either way it go, you know what I'm saying? You put guys in the video, you're a ho. You put girls in the video, you're gay. So, I mean either way, you're gonna get criticized. Do you think it would've looked better if we put a whole bunch of football players in there and we're all dancing on them half-ass naked? What that look like? "Oh, at Midwest State, they're fucking hos and they're all over the guys," kinda thing. You know? It's always something, right?

In her response, Prince illustrates how all women face a cultural double standard around sexuality in which men are congratulated for their sexual prowess and women are called "hos." More than that, however, the type of racialized, hypersexualized femininity embodied in the video was consistent with commonsense tropes like the "Jezebel." The coaches perceived such portrayals as problematic, to be sure. The players who took on the roles of the rappers, however, were presenting an altogether different type of problem. As Black women enacting Black masculinity through nonnormative gender expressions and explicit forms of queerness—butch/femme "girl-on-girl action"—these players were simultaneously legible and illegible. The script of Black man/rapper as deviant and hypersexual was clearly legible. The bodies through which such imagery was performed were not. The incongruity of the players "acting like boys" and the obvious lesbianism on display in the video left the coaches in complete panic, and with only one conceivable response—erasure.

Taken within a larger societal context that continues to struggle with women's expressions of masculinity, especially for queer women, the MWSU coaches' concerns are not entirely unfounded. The experiences of Women's National Basketball Association (WNBA) star Brittney Griner serves as one telling example. Griner, who set National Collegiate Athletic Association (NCAA) women's basketball records for most career blocks and dunks, has consistently been met with criticism regarding her sex, gender, and sexuality. Griner's Blackness, coupled with her masculine gender presentation and unapologetic queerness, makes her (il)legible: she cannot be easily read through any standard gendered or racial lens. In some ways, she fits popular narratives of Black men athletes as menacing and criminal. David Leonard has written at length about how Black men athletes, particularly professional athletes in the National Basketball Association (NBA), cannot escape the legibility of the criminal Black body. As he argues, "Black bodies, even those living the 'American Dream,' functioning as million-dollar commodities, are contained and imagined as dangerous, menacing, abject, and criminal—as inherently threatening."[22] At 6'8" and over 200 pounds, Griner fits the script of the menacing Black man athlete—enhanced no doubt by a 2010 incident in which she punched an opposing player in the face after a hard foul—with a legible Black body in need of social control. Griner is not, however, a Black man and, in this way, has an (il)legible body, perhaps in need of even more control.

Griner's (il)legibility is relentlessly policed, particularly on social media sites. In June 2016, internet trolls inundated Griner with "Happy Father's Day" messages on Instagram and Twitter.[23] While such messages are in part a result of a court settlement in which Griner agreed to pay child support for the daughters of her former wife, Glory Johnson, they are, at the same time, indictments of her masculinity, her Blackness, and her queerness. Similar to the kinds of vitriol projected at Serena Williams throughout her career, Griner has long been exposed to harassment about her sex and gender. As Laura Abraham wrote in a 2013 profile on Griner, "Brittney Griner is now the first man to play in the WNBA. . . . Brittney Griner threw down two dunks last night. One for each of her testicles. . . . Brittney Griner suspended for first three games next season after testing positive for a penis. This is a tiny sample of the ugly invective regularly hurled at Griner on Twitter and other social-media forums."[24] Griner's (il)legibility as a queer, Black masculine woman requires social control, just as the MWSU players' queer, Black masculinity performed in the video necessitated regulation. Caught in a web of (il)legibility, the MWSU athletes' bodies were subject to policing and control. Although all of the players involved in the video were reprimanded, those who most embodied legible Black masculinity were most heavily critiqued. Similar to the "hegemonic practice of policing young Black males who defy dominant expectations with baggy shorts, trash talking, 'bling-bling,' and hypermasculinity," the MWSU coaches sought to regulate the embodiment and enactment of legible Black masculinity by queer, Black women.[25] Demanding the removal of the video was a conscious effort to make supposed deviant Black bodies invisible—a racist, heterosexist, and transmisogynistic practice. Heteropatriarchy and anti-Blackness worked in tandem to construct a context in which a harmless attempt at having fun with teammates led to an institutional crisis requiring swift sanctions. The MWSU players took down the video. Unfortunately for the coaches, somebody had already seen it and, as will be explained next, tried to use it against MWSU.

The Power of Recruiting

This crisis moment is one of many examples of how the MWSU women's basketball players' identities and expressions of those identities were policed during the course of a season. Aside from the numerous formal rules that govern collegiate sports through entities such as the NCAA, each team has its own set of policies covering everything from how many hours of studying they must complete each week to what they can and cannot eat to whether they can have social media accounts and so on. Witnessed less are the informal rules, those that, although not written down in any handbook, are embedded in the team's culture and govern the players' decisions at every turn. These disciplinary moments "communicate key messages . . . about who is and is not a full citizen" within a given context.[26] My time spent with the MWSU program revealed a context riddled with disciplinary moments that sent clear messages to the players about who is and is not a full citizen at MWSU—who is and is not free to be themselves, to express those selves openly, and to be proudly included as a member of the team above and beyond their athletic contributions. Disciplinary moments were routine at MWSU. They occurred at both the individual and institutional levels. The most egregious ones, however, occurred in relation to one of the most important aspects of collegiate athletics: recruiting. In what follows, I outline how many of the players' (il)legibility represented a problem for MWSU not just because of how it perpetuated easily read racialized tropes about gender and sexuality but because those tropes could serve as a disadvantage to MWSU in its efforts to secure highly sought-after recruits.

Recruiting is one of the most important aspects of college sports. Colleges and universities go to great lengths to secure the most talented, highly sought-after recruits because, simply, talent wins games. Recruiting is also one of the most expensive aspects of college sports—for the schools and the players attempting to get recruited. "The recruiting process is a lengthy and expensive endeavour; players are tracked from their middle school days through high school, are courted by coaching staffs through various communication media and through various 'handlers,' are visited at their games and during in-home meetings, are brought to campus and are ultimately awarded a full scholarship."[27] The number of spots available on any given college athletic team is small, as are the odds that an athlete will receive a scholarship. For example, only about 6 percent of all women who play high school basketball will go on to play in college at any level, and just over 1 percent of those athletes will play at the Division I level.[28] The high-stakes nature of athletic recruiting has led to the formation of recruiting firms and athletic "showcases," providing coaches and athletes greater exposure to one another, often at significant cost ($1,000 per showcase entry in some cases).[29] For many athletes and their families, spending thousands of dollars on travel leagues and recruiting consultants seems worth it in order to achieve a coveted athletic scholarship. And for college programs the cost can be seen as an investment; spending money on acquiring the most talented athletes, in theory, leads to winning more games, which in turn leads to greater revenue.[30]

Competition between programs for the best athletes can lead to instances of unethical recruiting practices and, in some cases, illegal behavior. Men's college programs have long been plagued by recruiting scandals involving inappropriate use of funds and, in the worst cases, allegations of sexual assault. A network of corruption involving a "thriving black market for teenage athletes" recently uncovered by the FBI implicated over a dozen people, including a number of men's NCAA assistant basketball coaches and an Adidas executive.

> Across three complaints, two broad schemes were alleged. One involved bribing four assistant coaches—at Arizona, Auburn, Oklahoma State and Southern California, all programs in the so-called Power 5 conferences of college sports—to persuade players to send business to certain financial advisers once they turned professional. The other involved efforts to secretly funnel money from Adidas to three players and their families in exchange for the players' commitments to play at two Adidas-sponsored college programs and to later sign sponsorship deals with the company once they turned pro.[31]

The University of Louisville, one of the universities implicated in the scandal, had recently received a number of sanctions as a result of a two-year investigation into recruiting violations involving the use of strippers and escorts to entice young prospects. According to reports, former assistant Andre McGee "arranged and paid for adult entertainment and sex acts at . . . a campus dormitory that houses athletes."[32] Similarly, Baylor University is facing a federal lawsuit alleging that dozens of football players at the university committed a range of sexual assault crimes, many of them occurring within the context of recruiting. According to the lawsuit, elite recruits were promised sex by "hostesses" of the Baylor Bruins—women tasked with socializing with recruits and families during campus visits—creating a culture of sexual violence in which several women were assaulted.[33]

Negative Recruiting

Recruiting scandals such as these are almost unheard of within women's collegiate athletics. When official recruiting violations do occur, they usually involve transgressions such as impermissible communication between coaches and recruits (e.g., during "quiet" or "dead" periods when contact is not allowed) or academic-related infractions rather than illegal or violent behavior.[34] Women's collegiate sports have, however, long been beset by an egregious, if unofficial, form of recruiting infraction: antilesbian recruiting tactics. Since the early 1990s, scholars have identified how negative recruiting tactics couched in homophobia and antilesbian rhetoric have permeated women's sports, particularly team and contact sports like basketball.[35]

> Though negative recruiting is prohibited by the NCAA, it is often used to attack lesbians in sports. Several lesbian coaches I talked with knew that negative recruiting was used against them by other coaches in their conference. This information is passed along through informal networks of athletes and coaches. . . . By playing on the fears of young women and their parents, coaches hope to gain an advantage in recruiting new talent.[36]

Questions about the presence of lesbian players on a team are common during the recruiting process, as are insinuations about lesbians on other teams.[37] As Luke Cyphers and Kate Fagan found in their article on antilesbian recruiting, "Pitches emphasizing a program's family environment and implicit heterosexuality are often part of a consciously negative campaign targeted at another program's perceived sexual slant. In a survey of more than 50 current and former college players, as part of The Magazine's seven-month look at women's basketball recruiting, 55 percent answered 'true' when asked if sexual orientation is an underlying topic of conversation with college recruiters."[38]

When I asked the MWSU players whether they thought other schools used the fact that there were queer players on the team against them, almost all of them emphatically agreed. Sara, for instance, said it happens "all the time" and when I asked her what she meant, she replied, "If one university wanted to break down another one, they'll tell the parent the whole team's gay. 'Your daughter goes there, she's gonna be gay, too.'" Kyle similarly told me, "Yeah, we've probably been—not probably—I know we've been stereotyped as 'Don't want to go there, the whole team is gay, the coach is gay,' you know."

Referencing the fact that MWSU and its rival university, Prairie View State, often compete against each other for recruits, Jizeal revealed that "Joel McQue from Prairie View, he be telling the recruits, 'Oh, the coach is gay and she turns everybody else gay on the team.'" Confirming her teammates' perceptions, Isis told me, "Certain people use like gay and lesbianism against others. It's becoming like a recruiting defense, I guess. Which is sad but it's true." The MWSU players weren't the only ones acutely aware of how antilesbian recruiting strategies were used within collegiate women's basketball broadly and against the MWSU program specifically. MWSU assistant coach Dee Dee Johnson told me how she's heard that other programs have used antilesbian rhetoric against MWSU: "People go 'Oh, don't go there. You're gonna wind up gay' or 'They're going to turn you into a dyke.'"

While antilesbian recruiting strategies can be cultivated through coded language like "wholesome" and "family-friendly," the players and coaches at MWSU tell stories of blatant antigay recruiting tactics used by other programs against them. There are no data on the impact of anti-lesbian recruiting tactics—how many players were dissuaded from join-ing a program because they were told that the team is not "wholesome" or that "they'll turn you into a dyke"—but there are myriad anecdotal examples.[39] The MWSU players felt as though the presence of lesbian players and coaches on a team is an important issue to some players and, perhaps even more so, to some parents.[40] When team captain Rowan Dawson was deciding which program to sign with, she was at first reluc-tant to commit to MWSU because she found out that two or three of the players on the team were queer. She was worried she would be hit on. Rowan told head coach Jessica King about her concern, and this is how she describes the exchange:

And I was like, "Coach King, no, I'm not fittin' to be around them." It was just bad. I had it bad. And so, I was like, "No." She was like, "No, you don't have to be around it. Don't even pay attention to it. I don't want you mess-ing up your college career over such and such and all this type stuff." I was like, "I'm just saying, like I don't want to be around it." And she was like, "They're not gonna bother you, you know. As long as you respect them, they're going to respect you. Like they're not going to throw it in your face." I'm like, "Okay, whatever." So, I took a second chance and came here. I don't know, that kind of had me in a way. It was just like "Eww, I don't want to be around that."

While Rowan was ultimately convinced by Coach King to attend MWSU despite her fears of being turned by the few queer players on the team, there are probably some recruits who were not. In talking about her own experience being recruited by MWSU and rival program Charleston State, Tiffany Davidson told me she decided against Charleston State because there weren't any "girly girls," which she used as code for straight. As she told me, "I was recruited heavily by Charleston State, and one of the reasons why we didn't go there is because [my mom] didn't feel like I would fit in on that team. You see what I'm saying? Like, that's the kind of effect that it has."

"Did you feel that way?" I asked.

"Um, yeah," Tiffany replied. "There's just like not—when I was getting recruited there, there weren't any girly girls there, you know what I mean? Or just somebody I could go shopping with, you know? There was nobody there."

"There weren't any gay people that wanted to go shopping with you?" I replied, half-jokingly.

Smiling, Tiffany added, "Well, anybody who'd look like I'd shop—maybe I'm being a stereotype—there wasn't anybody who I know I'd be like, 'Hey, you want to go to Banana Republic?' You know?" Tiffany ultimately chose MWSU over Charleston State because there were more women like her—heterosexual and feminine-presenting—on the MWSU team at the time.

It's impossible to predict how losing Tiffany as a recruit impacted Charleston State. It's equally impossible to predict how the success of the MWSU program might have changed if Rowan had decided not to attend because of her desire to not be around queer players. But, having spent an entire season with MWSU, it would not be an understatement to say that things would have been different, as Rowan undoubtedly impacted the outcome of several games throughout the season and her career at MWSU. A commanding presence on the court at 6'1" and 185 pounds, Rowan Dawson could oscillate between positions with ease, playing point guard for some plays and posting up on the block during others. She could just as easily sink three-pointers as she could slice through multiple defenders on her drives to the basket. She could block, jump, and steal. She was, in no uncertain terms, the go-to player. She became a part of just a handful of players in MWSU women's basketball history to score at least 1,000 points during her career. Rowan was selected in the first round of the WNBA draft and as of this writing, has played several seasons in the league and internationally.

While there is no way to definitively say that MWSU would not have been as successful without Rowan Dawson, her career statistics support speculating as much. Recruiting Rowan was crucial for the MWSU program and Coach King played a key role in ensuring that Rowan felt comfortable attending MWSU despite the presence of queer players. Telling Rowan "they're not going to bother you" and "they're not going to throw it in your face" was something Coach King could be sure about in some ways as her players' expressions of gender and sexuality were strictly policed.

Within the context of antilesbian recruiting, coaches are left navigating an intricate maze of fear, silence, denial, and hypervigilance, and many go to extremes in order to combat lesbian images of their teams.[41] MWSU coaches denounced the players' video because of its explicit, racialized girl-on-girl action. This denunciation was directly connected to recruiting and an overarching attempt by the MWSU coaching staff to make the team appear, at the very least, not *all* queer. Rowan, who was not part of the video, explained why. "Oh yeah, that was awful," she tells me. "Like I just looked at them like, 'You guys are fucking stupid.'"

"So, talk to me about that, [Coach King] doesn't want recruits to think . . . ?" I started.

"That we're all just dykin," Rowan interjected.

"Why?" I added.

Rowan responded plainly:

Because that puts our program at risk. Like, "Oh well, I don't want my daughter around that foolishness." You know, and we could possibly lose a recruit from that just because we're acting like boys and kissin' on another girl. And some little girls now, they're like really uncomfortable with that. Like, "I'm not, I don't want to go to that college because they're all gay." Like, ew. And you know, that could mess up our program, our reputation. So, I see where she's coming from in so many ways and it's just like, I don't know, respect yourself. Like, it's cool to do it behind closed doors, but like, when you're representing an institution like, just chill.

The possibility of MWSU being seen as a team that's "all just dykin," was perceived as tremendously damaging, particularly in efforts to secure recruits. Removing the video, however, was not enough. More needed to be done. During my time spent with the program and through my interviews with the MWSU players, I discovered a sporting context in which coaches promoted a culture of "don't ask, don't tell" and players were encouraged to "tone down" or otherwise hide their sexuality in an effort to present the program as heterosexual—or at least not "too gay"—and, as a result, land the nation's top recruits.

Toning It Down

The responsibility for successful recruiting is not something that falls solely on the shoulders of the coaching staff. The players are equally important to the equation and can often play a significant role in a recruit's decision about whether to attend their university. When recruits come on an official visit, the players are responsible for hosting the recruit in their dorm room or apartment, taking them to classes, and otherwise showing them the ropes on campus. More than that, players are often encouraged to sell their school by highlighting extracurricular activities such as going to parties or nightclubs. As MWSU captain Eve Calloway told me, "As players you're supposed to do whatever it takes to get the kids there." For many women's basketball programs, including MWSU, doing whatever it takes is often less about persuading recruits about the wonders of their school's dining options or the campus arcade and more about convincing them and their parents that their team is (at least mostly) heterosexual.

Given that half of the MWSU women's basketball team (at the time) self-identified as gay or bisexual, and given that many of those players constructed masculine gender presentations, crafting an image of the team as heterosexual was highly unlikely.[42] Instead, the MWSU coaching staff attempted to present an image of the team as not *all* gay or not *overtly* gay by creating explicit boundaries around what the players could and could not do and actively policing those boundaries. Carefully constructing this team image was an attempt both to counter or dilute antilesbian recruiting that was being used against MWSU and, at the same time, appeal to top recruits that were considering attending MWSU. The coaches did this by creating a somewhat passive "don't ask, don't tell" environment in which it was acceptable for players to be queer as long as they "toned it down," especially when in the company of highly sought-after recruits. "When you say it was like 'don't ask, don't tell,'" I ask Prince, "where was that coming from?" Prince replied:

> I feel like it was more of like Coach would be more like, "Okay, if you're gay, you're gay, but don't be so blunt with it." Like, you know what I'm saying? Like, one time I got in trouble for allegedly using the boy's bathroom. But I really didn't use it, I just walked around the corner, but I didn't go in there. I was just joking around. I just had opened the door and I closed it, but I didn't go inside. And when me and her had a talk it was more like, "You know, everybody knows you're gay, but you don't have to be so, you know, blunt with it." You know, like trying to kinda, just, I guess be like, "Hey, I'm gay, I can use the boy's bathroom because I look like a boy" kinda thing. But I wasn't really thinking like that. I wasn't really trying to do that. I was just joking, you know what I'm saying? But I guess that's what she was saying like, okay, 'cause I look like a boy that don't mean you have to sag your pants so that the whole world knows you're gay or wear a big rainbow watch and you know all this extra stuff to bring attention to yourself.

"Does that ever bother you that you . . . ," I wondered.

"It did bother me at first," Prince responded. "I felt like she was just saying that I wanted the gay attention, which I really don't. Like, I mean, I feel like everybody already know, so I don't have to be overly about it." Pausing, Prince added, "But at the same time, I understood what she was saying. I understood, like, you know, I don't have to go over and beyond just to say 'Hey, I'm gay,' even though I wasn't trying to do that. But it just made me realize more when I got older that I don't have to go all out, you know, to make it known. It's already there kinda thing."

The policing of the players' expressions of their sexuality was intimately tied to policing their gender expressions in such a way that gender and sexuality were often conflated and used interchangeably. Prince, whose gender expression most closely aligns with legible Black masculinity, was "too blunt" not just because she identifies as gay but because she presents a very particular kind of racialized, legible masculinity that the coaches perceived as being "extra" and done solely to bring undue attention to herself. In such a context, there can be no such thing as pretending to use the men's restroom. Simple acts of whimsy take on much deeper, more consequential meanings when they are done under the microscope of coaches in constant fear of what others will think. In Prince's retelling of this event, it's clear that she's actively working through how to balance genuine self-expression and the coaches' expectations and perceptions. Telling Prince—the most masculine-presenting of all of the MWSU players—"if you're gay, you're gay" while simultaneously telling her that the way she expresses her sexuality through her gender presentation is "too much," conveys a conditional acceptance that is confusing and harmful. Moreover, the accusation that Prince's performativity of queerness was intentionally extra, despite her repeated attempts to explain that she wasn't trying to bring attention to herself, is an explicit act of erasure and manipulation. What's more, Prince is left engaging in a significant amount of "emotion work" to appease Coach King and ease the gender panic surrounding her presumed use of the men's bathroom and the perceived flaunting of her queerness.[43] As Lain Mathers argues, this type of emotion work is often expected of trans and genderqueer people "to appease cisgender people's discomfort with gender transgressions."[44]

No Men's Clothes

The MWSU players spoke at length about how they were expected to modify their behavior in front of recruits. Time and again, the players talked about coaches instructing them to portray an image, however false, of the team as heterosexual. Almost all of the players stated that the primary expectation from the coaching staff was to "tone it down." As Sara, an MWSU senior, told me: "We do have some gay females on our team, obviously. And our coaches told us, 'Look, the parents are very anti-gay. You have to watch what you do. You have to watch what you say." You know, in a sense of tone down being yourself. Tone down what you wear. Dress unknown so it's not bluntly out there that you're gay." Isis, MWSU's senior point guard, told me similarly, "The only strategy is tone it down." When I asked Isis what it meant to tone it down, she replied, "They don't even give us examples. They just say 'tone it down' and basically you know where to go from there." Other players, however, believed that it was very clear what was meant by "tone it down." In fact, when asked, most of the players referenced avoiding wearing masculine-gendered clothing, talking about girlfriends, and talking about or doing "gay things." Sara elaborates that "[it's okay to wear] tomboyish stuff. Stuff that you really would, like a tight shirt, and if you want baggy jeans. Baggy jeans would be fine with some Converse. But not like baggy shirt, baggy jeans, drawers showing. You know? Not stuff you would, not men's clothes. Don't come out with men's clothes on."

Rowan, seemingly agreeing with the coaches' requests, tells me, "[Players should] dress appropriate. Don't be having your boxers all out and saggin' and all that. Keep it up, keep it together." Reflecting on her own experience with toning it down, a former MWSU player and assistant coach, Sophie, told me, laughing, "This was the funny thing. 'Cause we had one of the top recruits come, you know, had a visit. And it was like for some reason known that we couldn't take her to anything gay. We had to act straight. I remember this night, we had to act . . . I have pictures of me in a little skirt, like, you know? It's just stupid."

No Girls Around

In addition to making sure they wore "appropriate" (read: feminine or androgynous) clothing during recruiting visits, players also discussed how they were encouraged not to talk about their girlfriends in front of recruits or their parents. As Jizeal recalls, "They was just like 'Y'all don't be bringing no girls around that y'all talk to because her mom just, she's not with that gay stuff.'" Tiffany elaborated on similar restrictions:

> You'll get a parent who comes on a recruiting visit with their child, and they kind of imply that they've heard that your school is—your team is full of lesbians. So, if as a coach you know that they're coming on a visit, you don't ask your players to change their identity or become something

they're not. But as a coach, you're like, "Let's not do anything crazy." You know what I mean? You know? Like, "Don't have your girlfriend around and we have a recruit here," you know?

Sara went even further to suggest that "if you're gay and you have a friend there, don't introduce her as your girlfriend. Just be like, 'This is my friend.'" MWSU players also spoke of how recruits were often placed with straight hosts so, as Kameron describes it, they would remain open to coming to MWSU:

> Obviously, we will get information from them. You know, they [coaches] are doing most of the recruiting. They will let us know, like maybe such-and-such's mom isn't okay with lesbians or maybe this player is a little bit more uncomfortable with lesbians. So, in order to accommodate her and to maintain her interest, we're gonna put her with the girls who are not lesbians and who are more feminine. Or we're gonna let the whole team know, "Hey, this mom isn't okay with lesbians, so kind of moderate your behavior a little bit more." You know? So yeah, absolutely. It's sad, but it happens.

Supporting Kameron's account, Nikki tells me that a "certain selection of people"—straight players—are chosen to show recruits around.

No Gay Places or Activities

Sophie, reflecting on how the coaches often told hosts to take recruits somewhere "nice," a code for straight, tells me, "So they tell the host, 'Okay, make sure you take her to, like, a nice place. Don't get out of control,' stuff like that. And then, you know, I guess they told 'em, 'Make sure you don't take them anywhere that's gay.'" While not explicitly stated, the players seemed to understand that "gay places" included obvious spaces such as gay and lesbian bars and clubs, public places frequented predominantly by LGBTQ people (e.g., restaurants in certain neighborhoods), as well as apartments of gay friends. Nikki similarly describes how players are told not to say or do "gay things" (activities) they might normally do and how they "try to lean it towards what we think they are or what they tell us they are." For instance, Tiffany told me of a time when the players and coaches were discussing where to take a certain recruit who was presumed to be straight on a Sunday afternoon. Apparently, one of the coaches suggested a popular park that is near the MWSU campus. Laughing, Tiffany tells of the players' responses. "And we were like, 'Mmm, no. Like, no. No!' Especially, you know what I mean? Like, no. No! You wouldn't do that on a Sunday." In suggesting a visit to this park, the coaches didn't understand that on a Sunday afternoon the park would be populated with a lot of queer people due to its close proximity to a well-known LGBTQ neighborhood. The players therefore pushed back on that recommendation.

In addition to avoiding queer spaces, the players also knew that they should avoid talking about anything gay. When I inquired about this, the players often used the terms "gay" and "inappropriate" or "crazy" interchangeably. In talking to me about how she should answer a recruit's potential questions about the presence of queer players on the team, Isis tells me, "I mean if she has questions, answer them. Be truthful. Just don't say anything like completely inappropriate. Like that's the only thing." I asked Isis to explain since it seemed to me that talking about your girlfriend is differently inappropriate than, using the most contradictory example I could think of at the time, talking about going to a strip club. Our exchange is striking.

"Right. I think the strip club wouldn't really—I think more inappropriate in that situation would be talking about your girlfriend," Isis says. "And the strip club, well, straight people go to strip clubs."

"So, it would be more appropriate in that situation . . . ," I begin, but trail off.

Isis completes my sentence, "To talk about a strip club than talk about your girlfriend." Whether or not the coaching staff would actually find it more appropriate for the team to take a recruit to a strip club than to discuss their same-sex relationships is not as important as is Isis's perception of it as true.

(Mis)recruiting: The Down Side of Toning It Down

The lengths to which programs like MWSU go to present false or incomplete images to recruits could have the unintended consequences of swaying queer-identified recruits who are looking for, hoping for, an inclusive team context in which they can be supported as fully themselves.

As some of the MWSU players outlined, coaches try to anticipate or interpret the sexuality of recruits and match them with players who share that
sexual orientation. Doing this not only ignores the fluidity of sexuality but
also, as its foundation, assumes that players want to associate only with
individuals who are exactly like them. Reflecting on her own experience
when deciding which school to attend, Prince notes,

> Yeah, like what if it's a gay kid and you're sending them to a straight en-
> vironment, you know what I'm saying? Like a gay kid and you're putting
> them on a team with all straights, what about that? You know, how do
> they feel? Who they gonna go out with? You know, they don't know no-
> body. You know what I'm saying? Like, you kinda gotta look at it in that
> way and I think that's what I kinda looked at, too, when I was coming in.
> Like, is there at least somebody gay that I know I can get along with kind
> of thing? And you know, just trying to get a feel out for who I was going
> to be around for the next four years of my life. You know what I'm saying?
> So that played a big factor.

For Prince, who identifies as gay and was searching for a welcoming
team, the presence of gay players at MWSU actually influenced her decision to attend. Jizeal similarly tells me, "Half of the time that's why they
[queer recruits] come. Because they see people that they can relate to."
Sophie, continuing her story of the time she put on a skirt just to appear
straight for a recruit, tells me, laughing, "She [the recruit] turned out to
be the gayest of all, you know?! She actually committed." She went on, "I
played with her, and she was all, 'Why did y'all do that?' 'We don't know,
we were told.' We were told, the coaches actually told us, like, 'Okay,
make sure you take her to someplace straight. Don't do anything crazy.'"
When I asked Sophie why she felt the coaches tried so hard to get the
team to appear straight when the recruit was gay, she told me matter-
of-factly, "They didn't know it at the time, and they didn't want to risk
it." For the MWSU coaching staff, appearing as they actually are (a team
with some queer players) to a straight recruit was more of a risk than
appearing as they thought they should (a completely straight team) to a
queer recruit. Focusing so intently on constructing a heterosexual image
might win over some recruits, like Rowan, Tiffany, or the top recruit in
Sophie's example, but it might also result in the loss of others who are

themselves queer or are merely looking for a place in which difference is embraced rather than shunned.

The irony in a highly sought-after recruit being "the gayest of all" after MWSU went to such great lengths to present the program as heterosexual is something that was acknowledged by many of the players. Additionally, most of them recognized that even when they tried to present an image of compulsory heterosexuality to recruits, they were thinly veiled at best and downright lying at worst. Karolina, a freshman, laughs at the contradiction: "Yeah and like half of our team you know that they are gay by looking at them. So, it's not like Prince would walk up here and wear a dress just because a recruit is here. . . . Why should we act like we are not, but we really are? And then when she gets here, she will be in shock." Jizeal, reflecting on the difficulty of appearing like something you are not, says, "Basically, we were saying, 'How are you going to get this girl to come here when we can't be ourselves?' Because this team, half of us are gay and the other half, well, now it's like a few straight people left or whatever but you know? But then when she gets here, she's going to be like, 'Damn, all y'all gay? All y'all talk to girls or whatever?'"

Discussing the fine line between "toning it down" and "putting on a show," Isis sees the latter as problematic. She says, "But it's not like putting on a show, because if they're going to come here, eventually they're going to see anyway. So, you don't want to just outright lie to somebody." Nikki, unsympathetically commenting on the nature of the recruiting game, states:

> Yeah, I guess it's just like recruiting is just like a game you play until you get in, you know. Like with the interview, if you got a job, you gone fake it till you make it and as soon as you get the job, that's when you just become who you are. So, we trying to get who we can get, and then when they get here, they get a taste of reality. It's the way it is.

Obviously, there are numerous negative consequences of the type of policing MWSU does around its players' gender and sexuality within the context of recruiting. Such institutional boundary maintenance harms all potential recruits, queer players (and coaches) who are forced to closet themselves, and straight players who want to be part of a team environment that is inclusive. All the queer players at MWSU and many of the straight ones discuss the damaging effects of attempting to construct facades of heterosexuality for potential recruits. Nikki, claiming that her sexuality does not define her personality, says, "Just because I'm like that, that don't change the person I am. That don't mean I'm trying to make your child like that, or your child is going to become like that. I'm still the same person if I was or if I wasn't."

Upset while reflecting on being asked to hide who she dates for recruits, Naomi likened such requests to being asked to hide her race:

Why am I supposed to hide who I am as a person or put on? It's kind of like saying "Oh she doesn't like . . ."—I mean it's not the same thing, but— "Oh, she doesn't like Black people, so don't act Black." For me it's kind of the same thing. I feel it goes back to people thinking that homosexuality is a choice, so you can hide that. . . . I don't think people should have to change just to—and like, you seriously think—like, if you're scared that your daughter is going to be gay because she plays basketball, she's probably gay already. I'm sorry. Like, if you really think a sport is gonna influence a person's sexuality, then I mean you're kind of twisted I feel like. [Laughing] And I mean, I don't like ignorance, and I feel like that's ignorance, so that kind of pisses me off.

Other players spoke of feeling uncomfortable and, like Sophie, admit that pretending to be straight wasn't a good feeling. Of course, like all individuals working within a structure, the MWSU players have agency and arguably could choose not to engage with pressures to present a heterosexual image to recruits. They could, in theory, sag their pants, show up with their girlfriends to team BBQs, and talk only about "gay things." But, as Jizeal admits, "We don't say anything to them, because I mean we have no say-so obviously."

"So, you just got to do what they tell you?" I ask.

"Yeah," she replies. "Basically."

There are several striking things worth highlighting about MWSU's recruiting rules—no men's clothes, no girlfriends, no "gay things."[45] First, they illuminate the extent to which gender and sexuality are conflated in this context and, as a result, the extent to which these rules were applied disproportionately. It is certainly true that there were players on the MWSU team who were queer and feminine-presenting. These rules were not made for them. These rules were for Prince, Nikki, Kyle, and the other MWSU players who were both queer and masculine-presenting. Second, such rules made clear that securing a highly sought-after recruit was more valuable than creating a context in which the players already on the MWSU team could be free to truly be themselves. While the players generally talked about these recruiting rules with indifference or at worst annoyance and inconvenience, I had to wonder about the larger effects of such explicit hostility. What does it mean to be thought of as valuable only in their abilities to successfully convince others they are not, in fact, who they are? Finally, the ideological underpinnings of the phrase "tone it down" are important to unpack in order to fully grasp its power within the MWSU context. It is at once a phrase that invokes cultural narratives about gender, sexuality, and race. When the coaches tell the players to "tone it down," they are asking them to obscure their sexuality, mostly as indicated through their gender expressions. It is also a phrase with deeply racialized dimensions, specifically reminiscent of stereotypical perceptions of Black girls and women as too loud or unladylike.[46] It is a phrase that indicts a particular kind of racialized gender expression and sexuality. Indeed, the players were not told what kinds of clothes they had to wear but they were explicitly told what *not* to wear—baggy jeans, exposed boxer shorts, Converse shoes, *and* a fitted cap. Seemingly simple requests to "tone it down" are in fact complex requirements that implore ideologies of race, gender, and sexuality in nuanced and complicated ways. The disciplinary moments embedded within "toning it down" are ultimately about bodily regulation—which bodies are perceived to be capable of representing MWSU appropriately and with the greatest opportunity for securing top recruits and which bodies, however temporarily, are disposable. The MWSU players who were queer and embodied legible forms of Black masculinity were the targets of especially harmful discipline—they were regulated from expressing their full selves, from representing the program as who they genuinely feel themselves to be. While it is clear that many of the players found these practices troublesome, they became so deeply embedded in the culture at MWSU that most of the players did not actively resist. Behind closed doors, the players laughed about these rules or balked at pictures of themselves wearing skirts. But at the end of the day, they did what was expected of them. Doing so reinforced not just the toxic "don't ask, don't tell" culture at MWSU but also reinforced larger structures of White supremacy and heteropatriarchy.

3

"Everybody Knows That One"

Racialized Lesbian Stereotyping and the Dyke Discourse

Rowan Dawson stands at just over 6' tall and weighs 185 pounds. She wears her shoulder-length, dark brown hair straightened and tied low in a pony-tail just above the base of her neck. She has numerous small tattoos located in inconspicuous places like her wrists and ankles. Rowan possesses a muscular body that is both physically strong and clearly defined. The con-tours of her arms highlight her broad, dense shoulders and high-peaking biceps. Distinct striations separate each one of her abdominal muscles like tiny boulders splayed across her stomach. Her legs are thick and powerful. In terms of pure physical strength and well-developed musculature, all of her teammates and most of her competitors pale in comparison.

Nikki Randall is a 5'6" guard with a quick first step and impressive ball-handling skills. She is relatively muscular for players her size, and sweeping tattoos cover her arms from shoulder to elbow. She wears her short black hair in thin tight braids. During practice, Nikki wears her jersey loose and her shorts baggy, hanging low on her waist and falling slightly below her knees. After workouts, she leaves the gym usually wearing a fitted backward baseball cap, loose MWSU t-shirt, and large, baggy sweatpants, bunched at the ankles against her brightly colored high-top sneakers.

Nicole "Prince" Davis is a lean 6'2" forward with long muscular arms. She has long black dreadlocks that she often pulls up high on top of her head. Often described as "extra" by her teammates, she has a strong, bois-terous personality and is almost always dancing, joking, or otherwise entertaining. Prince has a loud, raspy laugh that can be heard echoing throughout the locker room. The most aggressive player on her team, she is not afraid to knock over an opponent during competition. Her athleti-cism and enthusiasm make her a noticeable presence on the court.

* * *

These Midwest State University (MWSU) players—Rowan, Nikki, and Prince—are different in many ways. Rowan and Nikki are shy whereas Prince enjoys being the center of attention. They have different interests, friend groups, and ways they enjoy spending time. Rowan identifies as straight, and Nikki and Prince identify as queer. What brings them together, and why I chose to highlight them here, is that they are all Black women who embody and express masculinity in ways that uniquely shape their experiences on and off the basketball court, particularly within the context of what I call the "dyke discourse" in women's basketball. Each player described above embodies and enacts masculinity in one way or another, and often in multiple ways simultaneously. Rowan embodies masculinity through her musculature and physical prowess; Nikki performs it through her clothing choices and tattoos; and Prince enacts it through her confidence and demeanor. Whether any of them identify as queer—only Nikki and Prince do—is irrelevant; their masculinity and simultaneous "failures" at performing idealized femininity as well as their Blackness subject them to lesbian stereotyping and a particular form of the dyke discourse. This is because "the perks of 'being good at being a girl' also draw on Whiteness, affluence, heterosexuality, and other axes—even though they may be packaged and interpreted primarily in terms of gender."[1]

The Dyke Discourse

In her book *Dude, You're a Fag*, C. J. Pascoe argues that use of the word "fag" highlights the powerful relationship between gender and sexuality or, more specifically, the connection between masculinity and homophobia. Boys are called "fag" not because they are actually gay (although sometimes also true) but because they lack a certain amount or type of masculinity. All boys are subject to the fag discourse based on their performance of hegemonic masculinity (and rejection of femininity) because masculinity for men is synonymous with heterosexuality.[2] Like the fag discourse, the lesbian stereotype in sports—or, as I describe it here, the dyke discourse—is used to assess and regulate the femininity of women athletes. Women athletes are perceived to be lesbians not because they identify as such (although many do) but because they lack a certain amount or type of idealized femininity. Put simply, masculinity in women is read as lesbian. And, although some athletes may experience lesbian stereotyping more than others, all women athletes are subject to the dyke discourse based on their performance of an idealized femininity.

Moreover, the specific sport context fundamentally alters how the dyke discourse plays out, with some contact and team sports more likely to be perceived as lesbian than others. Team and contact sports, like basketball and hockey, are perceived to be more masculinizing than individual and noncontact sports like tennis or gymnastics, both because team and contact sports are more likely to be played by men and because of the physical contact involved. These sports, as a result, are more likely to be labeled "lesbian."[3] It is not, of course, that women athletes who participate in contact sports like basketball are inherently more masculine than women athletes who play other sports. But the "constellation of behaviors" involved in playing basketball is read as varyingly masculine and then superimposed onto women athletes. As Pascoe argues, "It is important to attend to the manipulation, deployment, and enactment of varieties of masculinity, not just as what men do, but as how respondents recognize it."[4] The dyke discourse is as much about women athletes' performances of masculinity as it is about how those behaviors are recognized by others.

All the athletes I interviewed, current and former, spoke at length about the existence of lesbian stereotyping in women's sports, supporting decades of research on the topic. As I will argue in this chapter, no woman athlete is immune from such stereotyping, from being wrapped up in the dyke discourse. To be sure, things like sport type, hair, and clothing matter in the severity of such stereotyping, but all athletes contend with it ultimately. "Um, you're gay. That's the biggest one. If you're good at sports, you must be gay!" former athlete Christina tells me, laughing, when I asked her if there are any stereotypes about women athletes. Former athlete Denise says similarly, "They think that everybody that plays basketball is gay. Every female that plays basketball is gay."

Former athlete Tiffanie and I had the following exchange when discussing stereotypes of women athletes. "So, do you think there are stereotypes about female athletes?" I asked.

Tiffanie replied, "Mm, probably. Yeah. I mean I would totally say so, yeah."

I added, "What are they? What's the most prominent one?"

"The most prominent one?" she asked. "I would say that the biggest thing when you say 'Oh, I'm an athlete' or whatever, the first thing that comes to mind I would think to most people is that you're probably gay." But, while all the athletes I spoke to commented on how women athletes are stereotyped as lesbian, such stereotypes are not applied uniformly. And, perhaps most importantly, the policing of athletes' expressions of gender and sexuality as a result of such stereotypes is racialized, leading to disparate experiences within and outside of the sport context. The dyke discourse is not just a mechanism to police women athletes' gender performance. It is also an important tool of racialized boundary maintenance, a way to regulate the MWSU players' Blackness. In this way, the dyke discourse perpetuates anti-Blackness through the containment of the athletes' gender and sexuality. The racialization of the dyke discourse draws on historical tropes of Black lesbian predators that stem from controlling images of Black women as sexually deviant and masculine.[5]

Women Athletes and the Lesbian Stereotype

There is no shortage of scholarship documenting the existence of the lesbian stereotype within sports.[6] In the late 1970s, Patricia Del Rey wrote about the concessions women athletes make to counter lesbian stereotyping due to the supposed masculinization of sport participation—a process known as "apologetics"—and scholars are still writing about it today.[7] "Without exception," according to Kerrie Kauer and Vikki Krane, "the idea that female athletes are lesbian was the first stereotype recognized" by the women athletes in their study.[8] The superimposition of woman/athlete/lesbian is so deeply engrained in our collective societal imagination that it has become an almost universal aspect of women's sports. Indeed, when I asked former athlete J. F. about the lesbian stereotype, she stated plainly, "Everybody knows that one."

At a very basic level, basketball, like other team-based contact sports, requires athletes to express characteristics of masculinity: aggression, toughness, competitiveness. It is also the case that the most successful women athletes—those small percentage of high school athletes who go on to play in college—tend to be those who are strong, tall, and fast: players like Rowan and Prince who possess large defined muscles and players like Nikki who, though smaller, are so fast they can easily run circles around their opponents. When embodied by women, such physiological characteristics—particularly when they are accompanied by above average height and weight—are often perceived as masculine.[9] Additionally, the sport itself is exceptionally physical. Players are in almost constant contact with each other and most of the basic techniques—boxing out for rebounds, picking a defender, and driving to the basket through a sea of opponents—require a high degree of physicality.

This type of physical play, an essential element of the sport, was something many of the athletes highlighted as a reason for the lesbian stereotyping of basketball players. "Basketball is a very physical sport," MWSU player Naomi tells me. "So, you need to be very physical and tough to play, and I guess that's what [other people] zoom in on." Professional basketball player Carmen similarly tells me, "In basketball, we're allowed to beat each other up basically. It's tough in a game. Eighty percent of the time you're in physical contact with your opponent in a more rough than not-so-rough way. And I think that just the nature of the sport calls for more of a masculine player." As Carmen plainly states, athletes need to be willing to engage in physical contact with opposing players because that is what is required of them. Basketball players are not only "allowed to beat each other up," as Carmen notes, but such a high level of physicality is unavoidable based on the structure of the sport. Basketball is "not consistent with traditional feminine expectations of appearance and performance," ultimately leading to lesbian stereotyping of women basketball players.[10] "I think it's more of a physical sport," a former athlete, Beckett, tells me. "You know men are supposed to be strong and powerful. Women aren't supposed to. They're supposed to be petite and thin and feminine."

The power and strength exhibited by women basketball players are not aligned with normative understandings of how women *should* behave (gender prescriptions), and this "failed femininity" leads to lesbian stereotyping. Moreover, as Rowan argues, failed femininity leads to assumptions that women athletes want to be men. "Females are portrayed to act like a dude, play basketball like a dude, or want to be a dude, you know?" she tells me. "I don't know, I guess it's just the feminine side gets pushed to the side because they play basketball." Playing basketball "like a dude," something that is unavoidable based on the requirements of the sport and societal constructions of gender, gets equated with perceptions of women athletes wanting to *be* dudes. In their study of women athletes, Kauer and Krane found that "the other dominant stereotype acknowledged by all of the athletes was that they were considered masculine, 'manly,' 'boyish,' 'butch,' or 'like a guy.'"[11] The mere practice of playing basketball subjects women to assumptions that they want to be men and the presumption that if women athletes want to be men, they must be lesbians—a logic that not only conflates gender and sexuality but also erases the existence of trans people altogether.

Former athletes Sofia and Kat discuss how highly valued athletic behaviors are interpreted as masculine. When asked why she thinks basketball players face a stigma that other women athletes do not, Sofia tells me,

> Well, I mean I think in some sense, you know, you're talking about like exhibiting traditional masculine—whatever those are—traits. And I think that threatens people. They don't really know how to make sense of it. And then okay, obvious explanation is you just don't fit the traditional notion of what it means to be a woman. Well, then you must be gay. Right? Because that's the only alternative.

Here, Sofia clearly articulates how "failed femininity" becomes synonymous with lesbianism. Women athletes who enact masculinity through sport participation by being aggressive and powerful contradict dominant ideals of what femininity should look like. This violation of womanhood is threatening because it disrupts widely held narratives about what women should and shouldn't do. While Sofia mocks the simplified way that women's masculinity gets read as queer—"because that's the only alternative"—the connection is important because it highlights how commonsense understandings of gender continue to support ideologies of gender as essential, dichotomous, static, and, perhaps most importantly, unidirectionally connected to sexuality. Kat makes a similar argument to Sofia, illustrating how behaviors become gendered within the sporting context and result in differing perceptions of sexuality: "Women aren't supposed to be aggressive. Women are supposed to be passive and nice and pretty. So, to be able to be really strong, that's a masculine thing. To be delicate, that's a feminine thing. And so, when you have women that are doing masculine things, because of people's fucked-up understanding of sexuality, they think 'Oh, they must be a lesbian.'" Kat clearly outlines how the relationship between gender and sexuality plays out in the sporting context, with women's expressions of masculinity resulting in perceptions of them as lesbians. MWSU captain Eve further illustrates how women athletes are not only perceived to be lesbians but also often thought of as wanting to be men:

> I feel like most people think that female athletes are these butch dyke lesbians when that's not the case. Although there are a lot, that's not the case and I feel like that's a stereotype that you almost have to overcome. And like I think a lot of people think that female athletes want to be like guys but that's not the case. We just, we love sports, like we're competitive. And [other people] feel like all female athletes are arrogant and cocky like most men are.

Perceptions of women athletes as "acting like guys" engage beliefs about what is normative and legitimate for women and, as such, lead to lesbian stereotyping. As all these examples illustrate, the demands of the sport require the embodiment and enactment of masculinity. Therefore, when women basketball players abide by the demands of their sport in order to succeed as athletes, they are perceived to fail at femininity and heterosexuality.

"I've Never Seen a Butch Volleyball Player"

Performing masculinity through sport-specific clothing represents another important element of the lesbian stereotyping of women athletes. Much like the way women athletes must enact masculinity through aggression and competitiveness within the sporting context, they must also embody masculinity through sport-specific clothing, especially for athletes in sports dominated by men such as basketball. Some of the athletes I interviewed spoke of being read as masculine in certain clothing in a general sense, like Jizeal who discussed how others call her a "stud" (a common term referring to Black lesbians who are masculine or butch) when she wears cargo shorts. Most of them, however, referenced how basketball uniforms and other athletic gear like sweatpants signify lesbianism. For instance, Kyle talks about how just wearing basketball shorts, especially if you are not about to compete, leads to the perception of queerness:

> I know a lot of people who aren't gay and they grow up and they're more comfortable with walking around in basketball shorts and sweatpants because that's what they've always been in. And people automatically think they're gay. Which most of the time, sometimes it is and a lot of times it's not the truth. And then they just automatically looking at her and saying, "Oh, she's gay. She plays basketball and she has on basketball shorts and she's not about to play."

Beckett similarly discusses the connection between gender and sexuality through clothing. When I asked her why she thinks basketball players are so often stereotyped as lesbian, she tells me, "I don't know if it's because we wear baggy shorts and clothes. Obviously, I think when you look at tennis or volleyball, they wear skirts and [in] volleyball they wear spandex. You know, men are supposed to wear baggy clothes. Women aren't supposed to wear baggy clothes." Because our construction of gender prescribes men to wear baggy clothes, women basketball players who wear baggy shorts, even required of them as part of their uniform, are performing masculinity and subsequently stereotyped as lesbian.

Importantly, many of the athletes who mentioned clothing or uniforms as an important part of the lesbian stereotype drew on volleyball as their counterexample, as Beckett did. That is, compared to basketball players who enact masculinity through their loose-fitting, often long, below-the-knee shorts and big jerseys, volleyball players embody femininity through their form-fitting, often spandex shorts, and tight shirts. "I don't know if it just coincidentally is the uniforms," former athlete Danielle tells me. "But I've never heard volleyball players referred to that way. 'Cause it just happens to be that they're in super-tight, super-short shorts, little tops, whatever." Former athlete and coach Jackie tells me similarly, "I mean, comparing even just the uniforms for women's basketball versus women's volleyball. We have longer, baggier shorts. You know, it's not the stereotypical feminine look, showing off the figure, that type of junk." MWSU player Sara affirms, "Volleyball is more girly. It's more acceptable for men because you're wearing tight spandex that ride up. I've never seen a butch volleyball player. I've seen plenty of butch basketball players." Volleyball uniforms represent successful displays of femininity compared to masculinizing basketball uniforms and, as such, volleyball players are perceived to be successfully heterofeminine.

"If They Have Short Hair"

In addition to the gendered meanings attached to their uniforms, many of the athletes I spoke with talked about the importance of hair and hairstyles to lesbian stereotyping. It was almost unanimously agreed upon that performing masculinity through short hair and certain racialized hairstyles leads to lesbian labeling. "Always wearing your hair in a ponytail," Rowan tells me, is one way to be quickly stereotyped. Interestingly, for women athletes with long hair, wearing their hair in a ponytail, or tied back in some way, is practically the only option during sport participation. While this is understood as an aspect of the game, however, wearing a ponytail outside of the sporting context is read differently.

At the other end of the spectrum, former athlete Tiffanie argues that lesbian stereotyping of women athletes most often comes from having short hair: "I would have to say like the biggest reason [the] majority of the females get judged upon is if they have short hair. It's like an automatic to a lot of people. I mean you can go to a game, and you can look at somebody, and this girl will have short hair, and probably every single person that you're with would be like, 'Yeah, she's probably gay.'" As Ingrid Banks writes in *Hair Matters*, there is "a scale in which long hair (read: feminine) and short hair (read: masculine) exists at the extremes. 'Mannish' is associated with 'looking like a boy' and long, flowing hair becomes a powerful feminine trait."[12] The athletes I spoke to talked about how wearing their long hair in ponytails too often outside of sport competition was an indicator of lesbianism. Even so, having long hair made them less likely to be read as lesbian than their short-haired counterparts.[13]

Gendered perceptions of hair are, importantly, racialized in ways that further complicate the connection between hair length/style and presumptions of lesbianism for women athletes. Long, flowing hair—unencumbered by a ponytail or not—is White women's hair. The standard by which these athletes' hair and hairstyles are being judged is one that is steeped in White supremacist, patriarchal constructions of beauty, only attainable by some White women. As Patricia Hill Collins writes,

> Because femininity is so focused on women's bodies, the value placed on various attributes of female bodies means that evaluations of femininity are fairly clearcut. Within standards of feminine beauty that correlate closely with race and age, women are pretty or they are not. Historically, in the American context, young women with milky White skin, long blond hair, and slim figures were deemed to be the most beautiful and therefore the most feminine women. Within this interpretive context, skin color, body type, hair texture, and facial features become important dimensions of femininity. This reliance on these standards of beauty automatically render the majority of African American women at best as less beautiful, and at worst, ugly.[14]

Black athletes who wear their hair long and straightened may be less likely to be perceived as lesbian than their short-cut-wearing counterparts, but they still remain locked out of the hegemonic White feminine ideal.

Hairstyles, in addition to hair length, are gendered and racialized, leading to varying perceptions of lesbianism among women athletes. Dreadlocks, cornrows, and fades, for example, are perceived to be masculine. Athletes who wear those styles are more likely to be thought of as lesbians than those who don't. Although short styles are generally perceived to be more masculine than long hair, the athletes in my study discussed how "Black hairstyles" such as fades or cornrows are seen as more masculine than White players' typical short haircuts. Brenee, a former athlete who now plays semiprofessional basketball and wears her hair in cornrows most of the time, told me that she thought predominantly Black teams were thought to be more masculine than White teams. "They look at how [Black athletes] carry themselves or how they hair is or how they might act," she says. "They might talk a little masculine or if they got a fade or you know, just different aspects that people look at." In her response, Brenee brings up multiple ways in which individuals become stereotyped—including hair but also language and behavior—and articulates how other people use such signifiers to make judgments about a given athlete's sexuality. Dee Dee, a former player and MWSU coach, tells me similarly, "If you see a girl that might have some braids or whatever or a low-cut fade, you just automatically think she gay. Just because of what she look like." Laughing a bit uncomfortably, she goes on. "But I think like—and I don't want to sound racist—but with some of our White girls on our team, really pretty, always was cute and they was gay. But people would never assume that about them because of what they see." In just a couple of sentences, Dee Dee unearths the power of intersecting systems of oppression to shape our understandings of ourselves and each other. She articulates not only how Black women, particularly those who embody masculinity, are perceived to be lesbians but also how Whiteness and idealized standards of beauty work in tandem to protect White women from those same perceptions. At the same time, she highlights the often-used homophobic assumption that some women are too pretty to be queer as if queerness, especially for White women, is the begrudging result of not being attractive enough to garner the affection of heterosexual men.

That people would never assume the pretty, White MWSU players were queer but are quick to pin such a label on Black players with low-cut fades is both about the dearth of diverse representations of queerness available to most people and also about the powerful ways that ideologies of race, gender, and sexuality get mapped onto people's bodies. In her book *Thick*, Tressie McMillan Cottom reflects on coming to understand through her interactions with classmates and teachers how "beauty's ultimate function is to exclude blackness."[15]

> All girls in high school have self-esteem issues. And most girls compare themselves to unattainable, unrealistic physical ideals. That is not what I am talking about. That is the violence of gender that happens to all of us in slightly different ways. I am talking about a kind of capital. It is not just the preferences of a too-tall boy, but the way authority validates his preferences as normal.[16]

Indelible histories of White supremacy, patriarchy, and heterosexism coalesce to construct images of beauty incompatible with some women and images of queerness irreconcilable with some women. That these athletes articulate with ease the complex meanings of race and sexuality attached to particular embodiments of gender—through hair, for example—demonstrates clearly how we all are bound to these histories, images, and expectations.

"Girls Who Play Basketball Are Obviously Bigger"

The embodiment of masculinity through body size, namely musculature, represents another key feature of lesbian stereotyping of women athletes. Former athlete Elise told me she thought basketball players have "a pretty bad rap." When I asked her why, she said, "The girls who play softball and basketball are obviously bigger than your gymnast and your cheerleader." While being bigger is a trait that generally helps athletes in competing in their sport, it does not align with idealized notions of femininity and, as a result, makes women athletes more susceptible to lesbian stereotyping.[17] Clarke, a former athlete who competed at two different Division I programs, similarly tells me why basketball and softball players seem to be perceived differently than women in other sports:

> I think that a lot of softball players, everybody thinks they're gay. They have a certain body type that everybody thinks—and I think a lot of people think that somewhat of basketball players, too. You know like, volleyball is more of a girl sport I feel like. I feel like people stereotypically think that volleyball players are these tall, skinny, more feminine girls. I don't know. For whatever reason like, basketball and softball players, I feel like more people see as like, more masculine. Like, bigger girls.

Again, Clarke highlights the disconnect between athletes' actual bodies and perceptions of what their bodies *should* look like based on normative understandings of femininity. In this way, gender pre/proscriptions apply to our bodies just like they apply to our behaviors. "Bigger girls," as Clarke puts it, are therefore perceived to be more masculine, and masculine women are perceived to be lesbian.

The presence of muscle mass on women's bodies goes against normative understandings of femininity that are deeply tied to sexuality and hegemonic ideals of attractiveness. Bigger bodies are perceived to be unfeminine bodies, and unfeminine bodies are presumed to be both unattractive and lesbian. The athletes I spoke to often referred to differences between basketball or softball players and volleyball players in degrees of "cuteness." Volleyball players, in part because of their feminine bodies, were "cute" whereas the masculine bodies of women athletes in other sports were not. "I guess just looking at our basketball team and looking at our volleyball team, I don't know if it has to do with training or what but we [basketball players] were all a lot more muscular compared to them," Clarke tells me. "And they were probably like, a lot prettier, which doesn't really mean anything, but I don't know why that is." Differential perceptions of attractiveness do, in fact, mean a lot when it comes to the experiences of women athletes, particularly when such perceptions are connected to harmful stereotypes. Whether the volleyball players at Clarke's university were somehow objectively prettier than the basketball players is unknown and somewhat unimportant (especially since objective attractiveness does not exist). What is important, however, is that they are *believed* to be prettier because they do gender in more normative ways. And because the volleyball team more successfully performs femininity, they are less likely than their counterparts on the basketball or softball teams to be stereotyped as lesbians. Gender performance is constructed, complex, and varied and is not an indicator of sexuality or sexual preference; feminine-presenting women can be and are queer just as masculine-presenting women can be and are straight. Shared cultural narratives, however, continue to conflate gender and sexuality, leading to the assumption that one's sexual orientation can be inferred by their gender performance.

The relationship between body size, perceived attractiveness, and sport type is, of course, racialized. Black women, and Black women athletes in particular, have always been constructed as more masculine and less heterosexually attractive than their White counterparts. At the same time, Black women are more likely to participate in basketball—a sport that carries its own association to masculinity—than volleyball. Black women made up 45 percent of all National Collegiate Athletic Association (NCAA) Division I women's basketball players in 2019 compared to just 15 percent of volleyball players.[18] That volleyball is perceived to be more feminine and its athletes more attractive while it is also a majority White sport is instructive in understanding how ideologies of race, gender, and sexuality map onto particular sports and shape the experiences of the athletes in those sports. Although perceptions of attractiveness have nothing to do with sport ability and, in theory, should be irrelevant to women athletes' experiences in sport, they have everything to do with their everyday lived experiences as women navigating the complex and contradictory demands of sport, gender, race, and sexuality.

All the athletes I spoke to, current and former, identified the many aspects of lesbian stereotyping of women athletes, particularly basketball players, and my time spent with the MWSU players highlighted the specific ways such stereotyping manifests itself in the sport context. Lesbian stereotyping of women athletes—the dyke discourse—is used to police the boundaries of sexuality and is most often accomplished through two primary mechanisms: (1) the imagined contagion of lesbianism and (2) the role of jokes.

"You'll Get Turned Out"

Like how the MWSU players' expressions of gender and sexuality were policed by teammates and coaches in the previous chapter, the players also experienced policing by family, friends, and strangers, albeit somewhat differently. The MWSU players talked to me about how others attempted to enforce and reinforce boundaries of idealized heterofemininity by invoking both the notion of being "turned out" and by the imagined contagion of lesbianism. In contrast to the "don't ask, don't tell" culture of recruiting at MWSU, the dyke discourse used here is more explicit and aggressive.

The idea of getting "turned out" and the imagined contagion of lesbianism are distinct, yet related, concepts. Both refer to straight women becoming lesbians, either by being explicitly "turned gay" by others or somehow "catching it" as a result of being in an environment where there are lesbians and/or in a sport context that is *perceived* to be more likely to have lesbians. When I asked Rowan to tell me what stereotypes exist about women athletes, she said plainly, "If you play basketball, you're gay."

"Really?" I asked.

"Yeah. And if you're not gay, then you're bi. And then on top of that, if you're not gay, you will get turned out."

For Rowan, the pervasiveness of the lesbian stereotype is three-fold. First and foremost, women athletes are perceived to be lesbians whether or not they actually are. Further, if they are not lesbians, then they are perceived to be at least bisexual. If neither, it is assumed they will eventually get turned out, ultimately confirming the original stereotype. Sara, who expressed being occasionally bothered by the lesbian stereotype, talks about how men she encounters often believe that spending enough time with queer teammates will turn her: "Like it's funny. Most men when they find out I play basketball, the first question is am I gay? Like all gay girls play basketball. I'm like, 'No.' It's like, 'Oh, you gonna get turned out. Don't go there. Don't do this. Hang out with your teammates long enough, you're going to be gay.' And it's like, 'No, those are just the people I'm surrounded by 24/7.'" As Sara's experience highlights, the dyke discourse is utilized by strangers attempting to police her behavior in order to pressure her into performances of heterofemininity. The mansplained warnings given to Sara—"don't go there, don't do this, don't hang out with your teammates too much"—represent explicit attempts at policing her (and others') sexuality by instilling a fear of becoming queer.

This type of policing was expressed by other MWSU athletes, like Tiffany, who told me that her cousin often asked her questions about whether she had been turned out:

> I have a cousin who lives near Charleston State, and you've seen their basketball team. Like fits the stereotype perfectly. So, she came to my game [against Charleston State] and I just felt like she was like, looking to make sure that I was still feminine. You know what I mean? And not that I feel like I have to prove anything. I just don't want to be given the same label that—you know what I mean? Like, I don't want basketball to define my identity.

Tiffany's experience precisely illuminates the complexity of the dyke discourse. Her cousin explicitly asks her whether she's been turned out but, more than that, her cousin's presence at games, especially against teams with players who "fit the stereotype perfectly" (read: are masculine-presenting), provokes a fear response. Although she says she doesn't feel like she must prove anything, it's clear that Tiffany experiences pressure from her family member to express femininity to signal her heterosexuality and to prove that she hasn't been turned out. Tiffany struggles with the lesbian labeling that comes with playing basketball and, in this way, polices herself as much as her cousin polices her. Jizeal, too, has a cousin who monitors her sexuality by checking up on her. "My cousin calls me all the time," she says. "'Oh, you better not be a . . .'—I hate this word—'bull-dyke' or whatever like that." Jizeal goes on to tell me how her cousin has questioned her about her sexual experiences with other women. "My cousin asked me when I went home, 'Oh, so have you ever kissed a girl before?' I'm like, 'Why is that any of your business?'" By calling and questioning Jizeal about whether she has ever kissed a woman and warning her that she better not be turning into a "bull-dyke," her cousin is engaging in aggressive policing of her gender and sexuality.

While many of the athletes I spoke to talked about presumptions of their getting turned out by lesbian teammates, others spoke more specifically about the imagined contagion of lesbianism specifically as a result of playing basketball. "I finally came out to my dad two and a half years ago and he blamed it directly on my mom because she put me into basketball all my life," former athlete Christina told me. "Well, obviously he thinks that I was—he's probably stereotyping saying, 'Oh yeah, basketball players are gay. You're surrounded by a few of them at least on each team.' So, you know, rubbed off on me or whatever." Christina's father, like Tiffany's and Jizeal's cousins, believed that playing turned her gay. He believed that if Christina's mother had not encouraged her to play basketball at an early age, she would not presently be gay because she wouldn't have been exposed to, and converted by, lesbianism.

How the boundaries around gender and sexuality are enforced through the use of concepts like being "turned out" and imagined contagion is important because these concepts highlight how gender/sexuality boundary maintenance can be both explicit and aggressive. The use of these ideas to police gender and sexuality is also meaningful because the ideas illuminate how commonsense understandings about sexuality are both complicated and often contradictory. On the one hand, these examples provide support for understandings of sexualities as fluid, social constructions (though this typically isn't the view held by those doing the policing). If lesbianism is perceived as a contagion, capable of permeating institutional contexts like sports and turning unsuspecting straight women gay, then sexuality must not be an essential, biological quality of an individual. On the other hand, the close association between women's masculinity and lesbianism in these examples (e.g.,

Tiffany's cousin looking to see if she was still feminine) supports a dichotomous, essentialist, and congruent sex/gender/sexuality system.[19]

The concept of straight women being "turned out" by lesbians is grounded in historical perceptions and representations of queer people as pathological, predatory, and criminal.[20] As Lynda Hart argues, "Lesbians in mainstream representations have almost always been depicted as predatory, dangerous, and pathological . . . historically inscribed both as 'not-woman' and as violent."[21] Importantly, narratives of the lesbian predator are both gendered and racialized. Historical fictions of Black women as sexually deviant and masculine that have been perpetuated in the media over time result in tropes of Black lesbian predators. Such controlling images of Black lesbians proliferated within the prison system throughout the twentieth century, with Black women being portrayed as masculine aggressors and their White partners as "normal" feminine women "who would return to heterosexual relationships upon release from prison" (i.e., "gay for the stay," as depicted in contemporary carceral narratives like the television show *Orange Is the New Black*).[22] Within these interracial relationships, it was presumed that Black women took on the role of "husbands" or "daddies" and White women "wives"—presumptions founded on racist and sexist ideologies labeling Black women as mannish with uninhibited sexual proclivities, and homophobic theories of queerness as a form of gender inversion. As Estelle Freedman notes, "Assigning the male aggressor role to Black women and preserving a semblance of femininity for their White partners racialized the sexual pathology of inversion."[23] The fear was that lesbians would spread "moral contagion," a panic ultimately focused on protecting White middle- and upper-class heterosexuality.

Fears of Black lesbian criminality and predaciousness have persisted over time, with several high-profile media scandals as illustrations. In 2006, a group of young, queer, Black women were harassed by a man as they walked through New York City's West Village. According to the women, the man called them "dyke bitches" and spit at them before a physical altercation ensued. The man ended up getting stabbed (he survived) and four of the women were convicted on felony charges. The media referred to these women as the "lesbian wolf pack" and common news headlines read "Attack of the Killer Lesbians" and "The Case of the Lesbian Beatdown." In addition to publicizing ideas of Black women as violent criminals who attack heterosexual men, the media has also perpetuated false narratives about Black lesbian "gangs" that prey on young heterosexual girls in bathrooms and schools through ambiguous "underground networks."[24] Media imagery of Black lesbian criminals out to violently inculcate unsuspecting heterosexual girls is "deeply rooted in historical narratives stemming from slavery, framing Black men as violent sexual predators and Black women as sexually degenerate seductresses, whose depravity is further twisted in the context of sex-segregated prisons against members of their own sex."[25]

The archetype of the Black lesbian predator is about narratives of both Black masculinity and Black femininity. That is, the embodiment of Black masculinity by queer, Black women lives at the center of sensationalized media representations of Black women as predatory. Moreover, the racialized and gendered tropes of Black lesbians as predacious rely on the deeply rooted historical fear of Black men enacting violence against White women; the predator is often "imagined as a Black man or woman, and their unsuspecting victims White heterosexuals."[26] More than that, the particular conflation of Black lesbianism with Black masculinity coupled with the fear of Black men assaulting White women exists at the intersection of these archetypical constructions of Black lesbians as violent and seeking to "turn out" other women. Ultimately, the dyke discourse and the specific subnarrative of lesbian contagion that is used to control women athletes' expressions of gender and sexuality are made possible by the gendered and racialized construction of queer people as pathological and predatory. That it took the athletes I spoke to just seconds to identify the stereotypes associated with women athletes—and only a few more to illuminate the mechanisms through which these stereotypes are employed to constrain them—highlights just how powerful they are. Rather than feeling nervous to perform well when her family attends games, Tiffany is instead focused on making sure she performs femininity well enough to convince her cousin she hasn't been "turned out" after all.

"I Thought It Was Funny"

The dyke discourse, perpetuated through the use of jokes about lesbians, is a second mechanism by which others, specifically heterosexual men, enforce boundaries around women athletes' expressions of gender and sexuality.[27] Although similar in many ways to the narrative of lesbian contagion, joking about lesbianism is a separate mechanism by which women athletes are policed. Only some of the athletes I spoke to told stories about being explicitly checked up on like Jizeal or Tiffany, while many others told stories of how close friends or significant others would joke with them about turning gay. Jokes about getting turned out discipline women athletes in the same ways that explicit directions do, but, instead, the boundary maintenance is enforced in a more playful, passive-aggressive way. Former athlete and current coach Danielle, for instance, talks about how her high school friends would joke about her becoming a lesbian when she went to college to play basketball:

People in college never said anything to me, but in high school, my friends—especially my guy friends—used to give me a hard time. And I know it wasn't intentionally mean. I didn't take it personally and I thought it was funny. But once it was clear that I was going to play college basketball, they would always give me a hard time like, "Oh man, Danielle, don't spend too much time with girls, they're gonna make you turn, they're gonna make you switch." We'd be joking like senior year, who's gonna be the first to do this, who's gonna do this and it was all, "Danielle's gonna be the first one to turn lesbian, that's for sure." Comments like that. Obviously, I didn't take it personal, but that is the stereotype that's out there—college female athletes are considered majority gay.

Even though Danielle claimed to find them funny, her friends' jokes represent clear attempts to regulate her sexuality. Encouraging her not to spend too much time with other women so she doesn't "turn gay" perpetuates narratives of lesbian contagion. Perhaps Danielle didn't take such commentary personally because she identifies as heterosexual and expresses her gender in a hegemonically feminine way. Since the jokes make it clear which identities are stigmatized (e.g., lesbianism), Danielle does not feel personally attacked by the comments. While her friends' lesbian jokes do not threaten Danielle as a straight woman, they do contribute to the persistence of homophobia within the sporting context.

Former athlete Elise experienced joking about her sexuality from the men's scout team during her collegiate career and continues to experience such jokes in the present moment. "You know, some of my friends would joke about it," she told me. She added:

> We had a men's scout team that we would practice against. And we ended up getting like super close with them and being really good friends with these guys. Like, they would just joke about it like lightheartedly. Nothing serious. But I feel like it happened more so like after I was done playing, you know? Like, I would be like, "Oh yeah, I played basketball in college" and then my friends would be like, just like lightheartedly say, "Oh, you must be a lesbian then." You know, I'm like "Okay, that's a stereotype." . . . It bothers me when they take it to a different level. If they're just joking about it lightheartedly, and I know they're just messing with me, that's fine. But if they're like—I mean, I never really had, I mean most of the time people are just messing around. I've never really had anybody who's actually said it to me and meant it, you know. I guess if I met somebody who actually said it to me and actually meant it, I maybe could see where that would infuriate me a little more.

Elise illuminates something important here about the mechanism of the joke. Although cloaked as lighthearted or playful, jokes about being "turned out" serve the ideological function of reinscribing long-standing homophobic rhetoric about women in sports and particularly about lesbians as predatory.[28] As Elise says, she's not bothered by lesbian jokes because she knows her friends are just "messing with her" and, probably, because she is not actually a lesbian. If she was *actually* confronted by someone who meant it, Elise admits that she would be bothered. That Elise might not be bothered by her friends' jokes, of course, doesn't mean she isn't impacted by them. What's more, there are larger consequences to such jokes. "Disparagement humor," according to Thomas Ford and Mark Ferguson, "communicates a message of tacit approval or tolerance of discrimination against members of the targeted group."[29] Jokes are powerful tools with which to regulate gender and sexuality— and uphold larger structures of inequity—because they act to deliver a serious message (e.g., don't become gay) under a guise of playfulness.

Another former athlete, Jackie, told me about how she gets joked with presently about being gay when people in her life, typically men, find out she was a collegiate athlete:

I mean, I will occasionally get, people make the remark, "Oh, you play basketball. Oh, you must be gay" type thing. It's more like that's the joke to make. Like, for some reason that's like, an acceptable joke to make. Like, "Oh, you played college basketball?" or "Oh, you played college softball?" "Oh, you're gay." So it's not necessarily they're like, questioning, coming out and questioning, but it's more like they think that's an acceptable joke to make, knowing that I played basketball in college.

Here Jackie highlights another important aspect of using jokes as a tool to police gender and sexuality. She notes that when others joke about her being gay because she played basketball, they are not actually questioning her sexuality, like Jizeal's cousin who told her directly that she better not turn into a "bull dyke." Under the guise of a joke, others can attempt to control Jackie's sexuality without having to actually question her sexuality. Clarke, a former athlete and teammate of Jackie, also talks about experiencing questions about her sexuality posed in a joking manner. Interestingly, as she is telling me about this experience, she begins to wonder out loud if, in fact, people were joking at all. "I mean, I've had people joke with me before, too, and like, maybe it was just because of like, basketball and stuff. Or maybe they were joking to like, really be serious?"

"What?" I ask her.

She explains, "Well, you know how like, people joke around about stuff that they're really actually like, not really joking about? They're really like, trying to ask you questions, but they like, make it into a joke." After saying this, she laughs.

I ask, "So, that's happened to you before?"

"Yeah, like, just about basketball and, you know, if I was a lesbian or something."

"Okay, and who asks you these kind of things?"

"Um," she tells me, "I would say probably, you know, mostly guys." Clarke recognizes that questions about her sexuality posed as jokes, while appearing not to be serious, may represent actual concerns from others about the possibility of her being or becoming queer. She is aware of how making such questions into a joke often covers for serious inquiries and serious efforts to regulate her gender and sexuality and shores up heterosexual men's masculinity in the process.

Notably, the athletes I talked to who told me about their experiences with lesbian jokes all self-identified as straight (or at least identified as straight when the joking occurred), further reinforcing the notion that these types of jokes are a means to police sexuality. None of the athletes who self-identified as queer were joked with because the jokes would have not served their dual purpose of maintaining the boundaries around gender and sexuality while simultaneously stigmatizing queer people. That is, a joke becomes a useful tool with which to maintain boundaries and enforce discipline by having the power to impact thought and behavior. Lesbian jokes are unnecessary and ineffective when used with queer athletes; they would merely come across as what they are—homophobic sentiments. Used in this way, lesbian jokes seem most necessary and effective in attempting to prevent straight athletes from falling outside the boundaries of heterofemininity.

Interestingly, only MWSU players Prince and Kyle, both of whom are queer and out, offered criticisms of the notion of being "turned out" and of jokes about being "turned out." "I mean, if you gay, you gay," Prince says. "But don't try to blame it on, 'Oh, it happened because I was around a whole bunch of gay girls.' I mean, you're either gay or you're not." Kyle similarly tells me, "It wouldn't be the players on our team or coaches that would make your child gay. If she's going to be gay, she's felt that way obviously before." Notably, both perspectives, while critical, rely on essentialist and static understandings of sexuality (e.g., you're gay or you're not). Most of the athletes, however, seemed to take jokes about lesbianism or being "turned out" in stride, being vaguely critical (e.g., stereotypes are wrong) yet ultimately accepting that such jokes come with the territory of being a woman athlete. For instance, even as Elise says "I tell them it's not funny anymore" she also admits that "if they're just messing with me, that's fine."

The lack of more critical reactions to others' jokes about getting "turned out" or lesbian contagion reflects how many women athletes become desensitized to lesbian stereotyping because of its pervasiveness within the sporting context. The consistent and persistent regulation of their gender and sexuality over time has resulted in many athletes feeling as though such experiences were routine and unavoidable. Given their everyday experiences with lesbian stereotyping, that more women athletes are not expressly outraged by the policing of their gender and sexuality points to a generalized form of resigned acceptance.[30] This resigned acceptance can be so deeply ingrained that, in some cases, athletes who do not experience excessive forms of lesbian stereotyping actually feel lucky.[31] While lesbian jokes may seem harmless, in reality they serve to perpetuate vitriolic messages about queerness and serve as a mechanism of the dyke discourse used to constrict and constrain women athletes, even long after they've hung up their jerseys.

The Impact of Lesbian Stereotyping

Stereotypes are powerful not merely because they exist but because of their ability to impact individuals' lives, even for those who claim not to care or believe in them.[32] The MWSU athletes, as well as the former athletes I talked to, spoke at length about how lesbian stereotyping of women athletes, particularly basketball players, affects them. Their responses were varied and contained important nuance; lesbian stereotyping bothered some athletes because they felt stereotyping was wrong generically while others had more specific reasons. Although only a few of the athletes felt personally offended by being stereotyped, the majority identified feeling bad about others—their friends and teammates—being stereotyped. Whether or not the athletes feel personally bothered by lesbian stereotyping, however, they are still negatively impacted. A player's sexuality is irrelevant to their ability to perform athletically, yet most of them spend a significant amount of time defending their sexuality, reassuring others, and navigating the emotional uncertainty that comes with stereotype threat—the fear of confirming negative stereotypes about one's group.[33]

"I Hate That!"

Many of the athletes I talked to mentioned that lesbian stereotyping bothered them either because an inaccurate identity was being placed upon them or because they were being associated with the stigmatized identity of lesbian. Many of them felt as though they needed to defend themselves against the lesbian label. "I really don't like it," Tiffany told me. "And I don't have anything against gay people. Some of my closest friends are gay. I just don't want to be put under that same label if that's not who I am." Feeling as though her identity was under constant threat of misrepresentation caused Tiffany to reject lesbian stereotyping of all women athletes. Tiffany's dislike stems not from her feelings about queer people—many of her friends and teammates are queer—but from her desire to be seen for who she is, a heterosexual woman. Kameron, an MWSU sophomore, told me she hates being stereotyped. "I think the biggest stereotype with female basketball is that we are all extremely masculine or lesbians," she told me. "I personally hate that statement just because I know who I am, and it's not that." Like Tiffany, Kameron wants to be perceived as her authentic self, not viewed through the lens of a stereotype that is incongruent with how she identifies. When I asked her if she's had people say those things to her, she exclaimed, "Well, yeah! I've had people say, 'Y'all play basketball? Y'all all lesbians!' Or I have guys who talked to me saying, 'I was scared to say something to you or scared to really try to talk to you because I figured you might be a lesbian.' Because I play basketball. I hate that!"

Curious, I asked, "What do you say to people when they say that to you?" Kameron replied, "I say, 'Really? Really? Seriously?! Not every girl that play basketball is a lesbian. Or, you know, is masculine or whatever.' You know?" Like Tiffany, Kameron rejects lesbian stereotyping of women athletes for at least two reasons. First, the stereotype is inaccurate—as she says, "I know who I am and it's not that." Second, being attached to the stigmatized identity of lesbian has seemingly made some heterosexual men scared to try and talk to her, potentially limiting her available dating pool.

Tiffanie, a former athlete, tells me how she also gets upset when confronted with lesbian stereotyping. "Well, I just hate being stereotyped. I don't like that, you know?" she says. "I've had people question me, and I don't like it. I've had people question other people, and I don't like it."

"Like your friends or something?" I ask.

"Just people that don't necessarily know me," Tiffanie replies. "I mean, yeah, my friends, but at the same time people that don't necessarily know anything about me. Like maybe I just met them a couple of times."

I go on: "And they're assuming things about you?"

Tiffanie continues, "Right, right. Or they assume something about somebody else just 'cause, you know, we play a sport and the sport that we play, you know? I don't understand that, and yeah, that does bother me. But, unfortunately, that's just the society that we live in right now."

"How do you respond to people?" I wonder.

"Um, well, I usually don't respond that well." Like Kameron, Tiffanie admits hating being personally stereotyped, something she sees as assumptions being made by people who don't know her very well, and she rejects the stereotyping of other women athletes. Tiffany, Kameron, and Tiffanie all express feelings of anger and annoyance with lesbian stereotyping, feelings like those experienced by women athletes in other studies.[34]

Although unintentional and subtle, these players' rejection of lesbian stereotyping is ultimately rooted in the presumption that there is something wrong with being a lesbian. Their desire to center their authentic identities is co-occurring alongside the unintentional reinforcement of negative stereotypes about lesbians. For them, being perceived as lesbian is not just wrong because it's inaccurate but because it's a stigmatized identity. When Tiffanie tells me that she doesn't "usually respond that well," it's not because she's offended that other people are perpetuating the stigmatization of a minoritized sexual identity, but because she is being presumed to be a lesbian and therefore a part of that stigmatized group. This is bolstered by the fact that Tiffanie gets most upset when lesbian stereotyping comes from people she doesn't know that well, like the comments Kameron gets from men whom she doesn't know but may be interested in dating her. If these athletes weren't partly concerned about what it meant to be presumed to be a lesbian, one might imagine they would spend less time trying to convince others the stereotype is not true—if they even bothered to correct them at all—and might do so with less emotional vigor.

Clarke, while not angered by being stereotyped like Kameron or Tiffanie, admits that being stereotyped makes her feel negatively about herself because of the inherent meaning behind those stereotypes. When asked if lesbian stereotypes about women athletes bother her, she told me, laughing, "Um, a little bit. Like, so I was out the other week and this guy told me that he thought I was a softball player. So . . ." When I asked Clarke to explain why being thought of as a softball player bothered her, she responded, "'Cause I was like, 'Well, like, am I really stocky for a person? Like, is that what you're trying to tell me?' Because like, that's the picture that comes to my mind." For Clarke, being asked by a man if she played softball conjured up a host of stereotypes that she interpreted as him perceiving her to be stocky—a masculine characteristic—and presumably unattractive.

Interestingly, Clarke conflates being asked if she plays softball to being asked if she's a lesbian, further solidifying perceptions that certain sports, like softball and basketball, are seen as "lesbian" sports. She takes it one step further by then equating lesbianism with masculinity, particularly through body size. It's, of course, impossible to know if the man who asked Clarke whether she played softball was implying that he thought she was a lesbian, but that's irrelevant. What is relevant is that with one simple question, commonsense understandings of gender, sexuality, body size, and sport context coalesced in Clarke's mind, causing her anxiety about how she is perceived by others. This is perhaps an unsurprising reaction in a culture that frames women as objects rather than subjects, and trains them to be hyper-aware of how they are being viewed by others.[35] But, Clarke's anxiety—like the anger other athletes felt when confronted with lesbian stereotyping—is still tied to the perception that there is something to be upset about when someone incorrectly assumes you are a lesbian. That a question about softball invoked such concern for Clarke speaks not only to the power of the sport type/sexuality link, but also to the power of stigmatization in general and the persistence of the stigmatization of queer identities specifically.

Even athletes who self-identify as queer felt bothered by lesbian stereotyping, not because the stereotype was an inaccurate reflection of their identities but because they feel as though stereotyping is wrong. "Even though I am a lesbian," MWSU captain Eve says, "I don't want you to assume that I'm one just because I play basketball." Prince similarly admits, "It bothers me, and I mean, I'm gay. . . . I just don't think it's right." Naomi adds, "I mean I don't like ignorance, and I feel like that's ignorance, so that kind of like, pisses me off." Dee Dee asks rhetorically: "Why you can't just enjoy playing a sport because you want to play the sport? Why does it have to be an underlying type thing?" Like Eve and Prince, Naomi and Dee Dee dislike the idea of overarching stereotypes on principle—a belief that it's wrong to be ignorant and make assumptions—rather than because they feel personally harmed by them. While different from those of the athletes above, these players' responses don't challenge the assumption that there is fundamentally something wrong with being a lesbian. Eve's and Prince's rejections of lesbian stereotyping might be rooted in some broader value about judgment, but such rejection doesn't question the basic premise that to be perceived to be a lesbian is wrong because to *be* a lesbian is wrong. Even Dee Dee, who rightly asks why women athletes can't just play sports without having to contend with outside distractions, is critiquing the necessity of navigating lesbian stereotyping within the sport context, not the inherent stigmatization of lesbianism.

"She's Not Gay"

Interestingly, many of the self-identified queer athletes I interviewed told me that lesbian stereotyping of women athletes bothered them because of its negative impact on others, especially their straight teammates. Eve, for instance, tells me, "I mean it bothers me because I have teammates and friends who aren't gay and that's how all women are perceived. But all women aren't like that. It's a lot of women who love men but play basketball and are great at it, you know. But it's just a stereotype that's placed on 'em." Nikki, an MWSU point guard, tells me that while she does not care about the lesbian stereotype personally, she is bothered because such assumptions hurt her straight friends. "Nah, honestly I don't care," she says. She then adds, "It does bother me, because like I have a lot of friends who is not gay, and that plays basketball, and it's sad that as soon as you hear that they play basketball, somebody say, 'Oh, they're gay' or something. And you know, I don't really like that because everybody's not like that. And it hurts people that are like that to hear every time they turn around, people think that they're gay or whatever. Like, I'd be upset just because I play basketball, you think I'm that way."

"But it doesn't really bother you?" I wonder.

"Nah, it doesn't because I mean it is what it is. It's my life, so."

Nikki doesn't feel personally upset by lesbian stereotyping because she identifies as queer. She believes, however, that such stereotypes are hurtful to those who are not queer and are forced to hear those comments "every time they turn around." Kyle similarly tells me that she doesn't care personally about being stereotyped but is bothered when it's applied to other people:

> It like, used to bother me when people used to say stuff about people I knew weren't gay and they would say, "Oh, she's gay. Look what she has on. She has on baggy shorts." You know, I would be like, "She's not gay, she's just comfortable, just like you're comfortable in what you wear. Because you don't play sports and you're used to wearing clothes all the time. We don't, that's not what we do. Our paid job 24/7 basically is to play basketball."

All these players' varied rejections of lesbian stereotyping, whether out of a desire to be seen authentically or a result of defending others, are complex examples of how efforts to counter stereotypes can reinforce their ideological backing. Lesbian stereotyping of women athletes gets its power from and relies on heteropatriarchal ideologies that perpetuate messages about gender nonconformity and queerness as negative, wrong, or other. Lesbian stereotyping hurts players' straight friends—and hurts queer players themselves—because of the perception that there is something wrong with being a lesbian in the first place.

"Regardless of What You Tell Them"

Several athletes I spoke with approached their feelings about being stereotyped from a place of resigned acceptance. Because they think they do not have much control over whether they are stereotyped, they think it is not worth worrying about. In their minds, people are going to think what they want, so even if being stereotyped initially upset them, they quickly realized there was nothing to be done about it. During our conversation about stereotypes, Rowan expresses contradictory feelings, initially pissed off and ultimately concluding she doesn't care. "Every guy that comes to me, is like, 'Oh, you like guys?'" she says. "Like what type of question is that? 'Oh, you sure you're not bi?' 'I'm positive.' It really pisses me off, but then again, it's just like 'Okay, whatever.' Just brush it off." When I asked Rowan to tell me more about how she deals with these perceptions from men, she adds, "I don't know. It's just, if I know I'm not something, I won't get mad about it. He think I'm gay, let him think what he wants. I could care less."

"You don't care?" I wondered.

"No," she replies. "People are going to think what they want regardless of what you tell them, so . . ." Rowan is ambivalent about how to feel; she is clearly bothered yet frames the situation as one in which she has no control, believing that people who hold stereotypical views will not change their minds even if she attempts to confront them.

Brenee discusses a similar sentiment when she tells me, "People are gonna say what they want regardless, and the ignorant mind can't be changed." Dee Dee told me how she used to be bothered by stereotypes when she was playing but eventually became accustomed to hearing them and stopped feeling negatively impacted. Laughing as she reflects on how long she's been involved in sports and dealing with stereotypes, she tells me,

> I mean at first it did, but after a while I just was like, "whatever." Because honestly, I feel like people gonna think what they want to think about you regardless. Because honestly, to this day, like I still, you know some people still may stereotype me in that group and I just be like, "whatever!" Honestly, I might have felt that way when I was younger, but I don't care now. Because I'm so used to it, I guess.

"Ten, eleven years is a long time to be dealing with stereotypes . . . ," I interject.

Dee Dee then adds,

> I don't want to say I'm to a point where I don't care, but I do, I am. And I'll just be like, "whatever." There used to be a time where I used to be like, "I'm not gay, but just because I play sports, you gonna automatically assume that about me?" But now I just got to a point where I just be like, "Whatever, nobody got time for that," you know? "I've got other things that I need to be worried about, aside from you. And you, one little person that I don't really care about." So, I'd be like, "whatever."

After a decade of dealing with stereotypes, Dee Dee has decided it is no longer worth her energy to try and change others' perceptions. Like

Rowan, Dee Dee used to attempt to defend herself, but she has been worn down by the persistence of the stereotype.

"I'm Comfortable with Myself"

Many of the athletes I spoke to told me that they were not bothered by lesbian stereotyping because they had self-confidence and were comfortable with themselves. Like Rowan and Dee Dee, these athletes claimed to not be affected by what others thought of them but took a more subjective approach. Rather than focusing on changing others' minds, these athletes turned their perspective inward and spoke of feeling self-assured and secure with their own identities. "I'm comfortable with myself," MWSU senior Isis tells me. She goes on:

> So, I know what I am, and I know what I can do. And anybody that knows me or any man that's ever going to try to come into my life, he's going to know that, right? Or I'm going to let it be known. And it's never bothered me, because some of my teammates, you know, we all live different lifestyles and being that I'm comfortable in mine, I don't mind embracing theirs or what they're doing. Because they're still, we're all just human. We play basketball, but we still women, regardless of our lifestyles or what we know how to do and what we don't know how to do.

For Isis, her self-confidence in her own identity acts as a buffer against lesbian stereotyping so much so that she believes that any man who might attempt to date her will automatically know she is straight or, as she says, she will "let it be known." In this way, her personal comfort is reassuring for her and for others who might have questions about her sexuality. Being comfortable in her lifestyle also allows her to more fully embrace her queer teammates. Interestingly, Isis's comment "we play basketball, but we still women" puts the identities "athlete" and "woman" in direct contrast and, in doing so, she is not only highlighting the cultural contradiction between athleticism and femininity but also acknowledging the perception of women basketball players as somehow not fully women (read: lesbian).

Elise, a former athlete, echoes Isis's belief and tells me that she's not bothered by stereotypes because she's "comfortable in her own skin":

It doesn't really bother me because I'm confident with who I am. And, you know, I've been playing sports since I was little. Like, I am very proud of who I am and what I've done and what I've accomplished. And just because I might be a little boyish and, you know, I might have muscles, but you know I've grown up with that, and I actually like being athletic. I enjoy working out and, you know, I'm very comfortable in my own skin. And if people make comments like that, I just look at them and I'm like, "You're being stereotypical. That's not true." I just kind of brush it off. I'm not worried about what people think about me just because I played basketball. You know, like, it's made me who I am. I went to college for free. Not a lot of people can say that. I got a great education, and it's made me a better person I feel like. So, if you're gonna judge me based on that, it sounds like a you-problem.

Elise acknowledges the negative perceptions of women athletes who, like her, might be "a little boyish and have muscles" but engages her self-confidence by stating that she "actually likes being athletic." Elise's use of the word "actually" highlights her awareness of the pervasiveness of lesbian stereotyping; contrary to how she feels about herself, she knows that there is a possibility that others will read her athleticism and masculinity as lesbianism. Elise is able to brush off what others think of her because she is proud of who she is and what she has accomplished through playing sports.

Having or expressing self-confidence does not mean that the negative stigma associated with lesbian stereotyping does not matter. Rather, self-confidence and feelings of being comfortable with oneself become important buffers against the potentially debilitating effects of near-constant policing of gender and sexuality. Unfortunately, not all athletes may be in the position to exert their self-worth in such a way. Younger athletes and those in more vulnerable positions—athletes living with more unfriendly teams or in hostile regional climates—may not have self-confidence at their disposal. More importantly, women athletes should not have to be comfortable or confident in their sexualities in order to navigate the sporting context freely. That the sport and our larger societal context is one of hostility and inequality is the problem, not whether women athletes possess enough self-worth or resilience to guard against the negative impact of lesbian stereotyping.

"There's Nothing Wrong with Gay People"

A small subset of the athletes I talked to offered progressive viewpoints on lesbian stereotyping when I asked them if being perceived to be a lesbian bothered them. For these athletes, the real problem with lesbian stereotyping of women athletes is the presumption that there is something fundamentally wrong with being gay in the first place. Karolina tells me she does not care about lesbian stereotypes because she is secure in her identity and, importantly, does not see being gay as a bad thing:

> I don't really care 'cause I know what I am. I know some people on our team, too, are mad about it. If people think I'm gay that don't really matter to me because, so what? 'Cause I don't see like—it's not a bad thing to be gay. So, if people think I'm gay then, well, they'll probably find out that I am not. I have nothing against gay people, so I don't see it as a bad thing.

While expressing feelings of self-confidence, similar to Isis and Elise, Karolina also removes much of the power within the stereotype by turning it on its head; if there is nothing wrong with being perceived to be gay, then it is irrelevant if someone thinks that you are. When asked why she is not bothered by stereotypes, Danielle makes a similar point, while highlighting the similarities between her straight and gay teammates:

> I think because I don't see a huge difference between gay and straight female athletes. I don't take it—some people take it personally like, "Oh, you can't, I'm not gay," like saying it like it's a bad thing or getting defensive about it. Me and my gay teammates, if no one knew they were, you would not be able to tell the difference between us whatsoever. There is no difference. We don't play any differently. We don't talk any differently. We care about the same things. And to me, I think because we're always on the same team and had the same goals and we're working towards the same thing, it does not make any difference whatsoever. And so to me, if someone called me that or referred to me that way, it was like, "So what if I am?" I don't see how that's a bad thing or any different.

Interestingly, Danielle is expressing both her own perception of the normalcy of being gay and her general feelings about queerness. Like

Karolina, asking "so what if I am?," she highlights a more progressive perspective than offered by most of the other women athletes. Former athlete Jackie offered a nuanced perspective when I asked her why lesbian stereotyping bothered her for her teammates:

> In terms of maybe not the stereotype, but in terms of just the reality of them [gay teammates] being masculine or them being gay, that that had to somehow interfere or even come into play into athletics. I just think it's ridiculous. I mean, I know it's a reality but the fact that it's somehow used as a negativity. When people joke about basketball being, "Oh, you must be gay," they don't do that in a positive light. So, for my teammates, it's something that's actually real. To me, it's just not right 'cause I didn't have to deal with that. No one jokes about, "Oh, you must be heterosexual." No, you know? I can just go out and play. Big deal. Like I didn't, none of that added stuff had to factor into once I got out on the court.

Lesbian stereotyping bothered Jackie because of its homophobic premise. Jokes about basketball players being lesbians are harmful to players who are lesbians. Jackie recognizes her heterosexual privilege and finds unfairness in the way that queerness is used as a negativity, as something to be joked about and judged for. More than any other player, Jackie articulates the larger structural context in which women athletes must navigate their identities and others' attempts to police them. She acknowledges the inequity inherent in the lesbian stereotyping of women athletes and the emotional toll it takes to manage, as she says, "that added stuff." The reality, though, is that Jackie does contend with that stuff—the mental and emotional energy involved in constantly treading the waters of persistent and pervasive regulation of one's identity—because all women athletes do. Regardless of whether they reject lesbian stereotyping due to internalized homophobia or progressive views, they are all constantly coming up against the hard choice of letting people assume what they want or attempting to change the narrative to more accurately reflect their identities. Of course, the experiences of straight, White players like Jackie, Clarke, and Karolina are fundamentally different than for queer, Black players like Prince, Nikki, or Kyle, but they all still share a common experience as athletes contending with the seeming inter-minability of the perception that "if you play basketball, you're gay."

Within the context of sport, the dyke discourse serves to constrain women athletes' gender and sexuality in myriad ways. Perceptions of women's masculinity, read through sport-specific clothing and hair-styles, blanket athletes' experiences as does the imagined contagion of lesbianism. The dyke discourse is, importantly, racialized; idealized no-tions of femininity are constructed through the lenses of White suprem-acy and anti-Blackness, disparately shaping the experiences of Black and White athletes. The dyke discourse also relies heavily on the women/ath-lete paradox and women's embodiment of masculinity through muscle mass—the subject of the next chapter.

4

"Not a Lot of Leading Ladies Have Muscles"

The Cultural Contradiction of the Woman Athlete

The buzzer sounded, signaling the end of the drill, and the Midwest State University (MWSU) players made their way off the court for a quick water break. Some sat, rehydrating and high-fiving each other over made shots and clever passes. Others refastened headbands and tightened shoelaces, shaking out their arms and legs to stay loose. I sat at the scorer's table, midcourt, tallying statistics from the drill, carefully calculating how many shots Kyle took, whether Jizeal secured at least five rebounds, and how many steals Nikki made.

As I counted the final numbers and prepared to hand the sheet to one of the coaches for review, Rowan Dawson walked over to me. Sticking her arm out in front of her, she glanced at it briefly and casually asked, "Are my arms getting smaller?"

I smiled, taken aback by her question and, after looking at her arm for a second or two, said, "No. Do you want them to be?"

"Yeah!" Rowan quickly exclaimed.

"Why?" I asked, confused.

Rowan replied, "I look too manly. Like when I get dressed up and wear a shirt like this, . . ." pointing to just above her bicep, ". . . it doesn't look good."

I stared at Rowan quizzically and shrugged. "Isn't that the point, to be big?" I asked.

"No. I gotta look sexy."

The buzzer sounded again to signal the end of the water break. Coach King blew her whistle and motioned for the players to line up for the next drill. As Rowan walked away, I shouted, "You can't be both?" Rowan turned, looked back at me, and with a slight, almost pitying grin on her face, shook her head from side to side as if to say "no."

* * *

With one shake of her head, Rowan summed up the essence of an idea that gender and sport scholars across disciplines have been grappling with since the 1970s: the cultural contradiction of women's athleticism or the woman/athlete paradox.[1] In her 1978 article "Apologetics and Androgyny," Patricia Del Rey contends that

> what should be evident is that the characteristics necessary for sport performance are those which match the masculine model in our society; feminine characteristics are dysfunctional for achievement in sport. Since femininity is dissonant with the qualities necessary for sport participation, a woman who deviates from the norm or rejects the concept of femininity will experience dissonance between her own desires and her motivation to fit into society.[2]

Simultaneously expected to perform traits characteristic of hegemonic masculinity (e.g., toughness, competitiveness, aggression) as *athletes* while retaining traits characteristic of heterofemininity (e.g., passivity and attractiveness to men) as *women*, women athletes are culturally required to walk an impossibly thin tightrope. These competing priorities, what Vikki Krane labels "dual and dueling identities," create a state of cognitive dissonance for women athletes in which they must engage in near-constant identity negotiation and management in order to succeed at their sport and still be viewed as appropriately feminine (and, for heterosexual women, attractive to men).[3] Failure to successfully balance their athletic and gender identities—to look "too manly" in sleeveless shirts, as Rowan fears—leads to gender policing and lesbian stigma.[4] There is ample research evidence for the cultural contradiction of women's athleticism, with scholars identifying how women athletes across sport type and social identity characteristics such as age experience the woman/athlete paradox.[5] While most prevalent in contact and team sports, women athletes in basketball, soccer, softball, gymnastics, weightlifting, swimming, golf, ice hockey, track and field, tennis, rugby, and volleyball experience pressures to reconcile their embodiment of masculinity, primarily through muscle mass, with societal expectations of the feminine ideal.[6]

It is certainly true that definitions of femininity have changed over time, and with them societal expectations of bodily ideals have evolved.

Physical strength is not only accepted but also encouraged in girls and women, particularly for those who participate in sports.[7] Popular fitness activities like CrossFit have played a large part in this reshaping, touting slogans such as "strong is the new sexy" and featuring women with clearly defined musculature in their advertisements. Research on the transgressive potential of CrossFit, however, demonstrates that while it does offer space for women to embody strength in new ways, it also (re)constrains them within heteronormative and hegemonic ideals of beauty.[8] We must not confuse a change in form with a change in substance. In this contemporary moment, women have more latitude to embody traditional characteristics of masculinity, but they are still very much working within limited boundaries. In my time spent with the MWSU women's basketball team, and in my conversations with former elite-level women athletes, it became clear to me that despite shifting societal perceptions, most of the athletes grappled with the woman/athlete paradox. Besides, even if they did not feel constrained by it in similar ways, all of them could easily articulate the nature of the contradiction in the same ways they could tell me, without hesitation, "if you play basketball, you're gay."

"Caught in the Middle"

Several athletes I talked to discussed a near-textbook experience with the woman/athlete paradox, a direct conflict between their athletic and gender identities and how those identities are expressed. When I asked former athlete Danielle, for instance, whether she ever felt tension between her identities while she was a college athlete, she said, "I definitely think so. I mean, just like culture and society, and the way you see girls on TV and movies. Like, there's nothing about female athletes out there. It's not something that when you're born as a little girl that you will think—you dress up as a princess, you don't dress up in a basketball uniform." Laughing a little, she continues: "It's not the norm. And it's hard to balance it because you do want to maintain femininity and you want to still be considered a girl but at the same time, sports—you can't change what you love to do." Danielle expresses feeling a personal dilemma between maintaining her femininity so that she will still be "considered a girl" by others and performing masculinity through playing basketball. She acknowledges the role of the media and the lack of representation of women athletes in the media as contributing to this tension. Danielle also importantly highlights the lack of available options she perceives in resolving this tension. When she says "you can't change what you love to do," she is making clear that the tension is inherent to sport and opting out of the woman/athlete paradox by leaving sport is not a viable option for her. Clarke, another Division I former athlete, discusses feeling a similar conflict between her identities as an athlete and a woman:

> I always felt like I was caught in the middle between like—I loved wearing sweats and showing up sweaty to class, but like, that's not really the typical female, you know? And then you're caught between. I also like to be more feminine and dress up and like, look nice, too. But you're kinda caught in the middle because of what people expect you to be like as a female, which is not wearing long shorts and basketball shoes and cutoff t-shirts. You know? Most of my friends were like that. That's just how we were. But also like, I wanna look nice as a person, you know? I'm obviously not gonna wear that like, to work. You're just kinda caught between, in the middle.

Clarke paints a clear picture of the difficulties existing in those in-between spaces, attempting to embrace athleticism and the perceived masculinity that accompanies it while also embodying normative aspects of femininity that others expect and, importantly, that make her feel good. The tension Clarke feels prohibits her from feeling nice and from truly enjoying the times when she was wearing sweatpants and showing up sweaty to class, despite her admitting that she likes doing those things. She can only feel good when she is presenting an acceptable type of femininity through dressing feminine, something she also enjoys doing. Rather than view these two aspects of her identity as congruent, two parts of many that make her whole, Clarke repeatedly mentions feeling caught, wedged between incongruent identities and expectations. Former athlete J. F. echoes Clarke's experience when she tells me, "To be a strong athlete somehow diminishes you as a female or makes you more masculine. I've definitely experienced that." J. F. goes on to elaborate on the nonsensicality of the woman/athlete paradox: "If

I walk like an athlete and I play like an athlete, like just an athlete, then that's considered masculine, which is weird for me. Like, I'm a basketball player. I'm supposed to wear basketball shorts when I play, you know? It's kinda weird. So, I think that's always an issue." Here, J. F. locates the contradiction of the woman/athlete inherently within the definition of athlete. As she says, playing like "just an athlete" is considered masculine because athlete is synonymous with men and masculinity. Just doing what she's supposed to do, wearing basketball shorts when she plays basketball, she invokes a clash of expectations and a conflict of identities. The woman/athlete paradox is weird for J. F. as someone who has spent her whole life playing sports and, as a result, her whole life experiencing this contradiction. "You know, sometimes it's a source of anger and frustration. It's just sometimes you just get sick of it, of always having to feel like you have to break down all of these barriers just to play."

There is an exhaustion inherent in what J. F. is saying; balancing on the cultural tightrope of conflicting expectations for woman athletes is time-consuming and requires mental, emotional, and physical energy. To be a woman athlete within a society that continues to define athletes through the lens of masculinity means that for J. F., and for all women athletes, breaking down barriers is simply a requirement to play. By any measure, J. F. was an incredibly successful athlete, playing both Division I basketball and softball. When the seasons would overlap, it was not uncommon for J. F. to get off the bus after traveling from an away basketball game and go straight to her shortstop position on the softball field for a double-header. Even still, I find it worth wondering what more J. F., Clarke, Danielle, and so many others like them could have done had they not had to also spend time and energy thinking about whether they looked nice enough while playing the sport(s) they loved (and being really good at them, too).

"Big Fucking Man Legs"

When describing their experiences with the woman/athlete paradox, the embodiment of masculinity through musculature and muscle mass was a central focus for many of the athletes I spoke with. Developing bulk from weight training and sport participation was of particular concern, with many of the athletes connecting muscle mass with feeling unfeminine and unattractive to men. Former athlete Kat, for example, tells me, "I did not like having really big muscles. And I just didn't feel it was beautiful to have big fucking man legs." Embedded in Kat's pithy response is the essence of the ideology behind the woman/athlete paradox. An increase in muscle mass is read as an embodiment of masculinity because muscle mass is a physical trait of hegemonic masculinity. The embodiment of masculinity in women, even women athletes, contradicts normative understandings of heterofemininity and notions of what is beautiful. Society tells us that big muscular legs on women are simply not beautiful. The dilemma for Kat, and for all athletes to some degree, is that the development of muscle mass is a natural result of sport-specific types of training and is one measure of physical strength, an important contributor to sport success.

Danielle situates the barriers of bulk even more firmly within understandings of and expectations associated with heterosexual attractiveness to men: "If you want attention from guys, you look at what they pay attention to, and they don't pay attention to Serena Williams and her big muscles everywhere. They, I mean, it's just natural. You see the girls that most guys look at or are drawn to or talk about . . . and even in movies, not a lot of the leading ladies have muscles." It is not surprising that Danielle draws on Serena Williams to explicate the problematic nature of muscle mass for women athletes. Despite being arguably the greatest tennis player of all time, Serena Williams has been relentlessly criticized for her body, particularly its size and musculature. Of course, while Danielle does not acknowledge it, Serena's Blackness has been central to her marginalization.[9] Danielle also invokes essentialist understandings of gender and heterosexuality to explain expectations of normative heterofemininity—for her, it's "natural" for men to not be attracted to women with muscle mass who, as a result, resemble men, but to be drawn to the "leading ladies" popularized in the media. As Shari Dworkin argues, muscles have become a "popularly acquired paradox of gender."[10]

> On the one hand, "commonsense" ideologies tell everyday women in fitness not to fear the weight room because natural, biological difference from men prevents them from getting "too big." At the same time, many women *can* and *do* experience gains in muscle mass when lifting weights,

particularly women who do so regularly. The tension that results from the difference between common sense and knowledge of one's own bodily experiences is compounded by widespread bodily ideologies about what women's bodies *should* do.[11]

Rowan, Kat, and Danielle are not the "leading ladies" of the movie screen; they are highly talented, elite women athletes who have engaged in specific forms of body work that give them a competitive advantage against other athletes. Building muscle mass is a key part of such body work and has likely contributed to their success in sport. This is what I was essentially asking when I questioned Rowan as to whether getting big was the point—in order to succeed at her sport, which I presumed she had the desire to do (and did exceedingly well at), she *had* to possess muscle mass. The point, however, for Rowan was to look sexy, likely not at the expense of her athletic success but certainly in spite of it. Despite being high-achieving athletes, Rowan, Kat, and Danielle felt that their muscular bodies made them less successful women.

During my interview with Rowan, I recalled the exchange we had about her arms and asked her about it. I was curious to see whether her thoughts had changed, especially as she was about to embark on a career in the Women's National Basketball Association (WNBA).

"I remember you said once, you said something about your arms are getting big, in the season, and that you didn't like it 'cause it didn't look sexy."

"It doesn't!" Rowan replied. "It's so, like, unattractive." She went on to use her teammate Kameron, as an example. For context, Kameron, though shorter than Rowan, possesses equal if not more muscle mass, giving her a stocky, chiseled appearance. Rowan explains, "I'm not tryin' to knock Kameron's hustle but like, when she dresses up, it's just so bleh. It's just not cute at all."

"Why?" I pushed.

"Because she's so muscular and it's like, it's not cute. And so, I don't want to . . . ew, it's just nasty." For Rowan, musculature is not cute, especially when considered in combination with feminine-gendered clothing. When these athletes are barreling down the court, sinking three-pointers, or jumping two feet in the air to secure a rebound, their musculature is nasty in a good way. But when they attempt to dress up and embody normative heterofemininity, those same physical characteristics that served them well on the court seemingly let them down off of it. As Vikki Krane observes in her work with women athletes, "The athletes considered their muscular bodies as the primary hindrance to being perceived as heterosexually feminine in social settings. When they considered their athletic bodies in comparison to 'normal girls' or the culturally ideal body, the athletes felt 'different.' They were larger and more muscular, and they did not fit into trendy clothing."[12] The glass ceiling on women's muscular strength seems then to apply to all women, even high-performing athletes like Rowan, Kat, and Danielle.[13]

"I Don't Care If I Look Masculine"

While many of the athletes I spoke to expressed clear and powerful conflicts between their athletic and gender identities, many also did not. MWSU players Kameron and Jizeal, for example, did not have trouble balancing femininity and athleticism because they did not see themselves as possessing the "masculine drive" that they believe is crucial to being a successful athlete at their level. As Jizeal tells me,

> I'm not the aggressive type and I don't like contact when I play and stuff like that. But that's obviously a problem. My coach doesn't like that. And then there's things I want to do, like I want to get my nails done. I want to get my hair done. But because of basketball I can't do it because it wouldn't make no sense. I'd just sweat it out, you know, and mess up my nails and stuff like that. But like some people it doesn't matter. Because I'm like really girly. If you're not really girly and you don't want those things it really doesn't matter, I guess.

The source of the tension for Jizeal, and for Kameron who says "I am not masculine at all," is located in a lack of identification with or aversion to masculine-gendered behaviors such as aggression and physical contact. It is also associated with a desire to engage in feminine-gendered behaviors such as getting nails and hair done, which they are practically prevented from doing because of their roles as athletes. While Kameron still acknowledges that "female athletes are severely stereotyped as these grungy, masculine people," she can extricate herself from such a perception because she does not identify with traits characteristic of masculinity. Similarly, Jizeal's lack of identification with the core aspects of athleticism makes her experience of the woman/athlete paradox untraditional.

Perhaps the lack of a strong athletic identification—at least in terms of normative conceptions of what it means to be an athlete—contributes to Jizeal's and Kameron's lack of experiencing the woman/athlete paradox, as compared to athletes like Rowan or J. F. who strongly identify with their athletic identities. Research on stereotype threat—"the social-psychological threat that arises when one is in a situation or doing something for which a negative stereotype about one's group applies"—demonstrates that "individuals are more susceptible to stereotype threat when they identify strongly with their social group and value the domain."[14] While it is beyond the scope of this book to tackle whether and how athletic identification influences how athletes experience the woman/athlete paradox, it is a possibility worth considering.

The other athletes I spoke to who did not feel a tension between their athletic and gender identities offered two primary explanations: self-confidence/not caring and socialization/social context (or a combination of both). "I think it is hard to balance if you're not comfortable, if you're trying to live up to whatever people may think," Isis, an MWSU senior, tells me. "Because I think along with women's basketball comes a lot of stereotypes. Like if you are comfortable with who you are, I think other people will be just as comfortable with that." Isis acknowledges the stereotyping of women athletes but argues that being comfortable in her sense of self shields her from the negative perceptions of others. Former athlete Brenee echoes a similar sentiment when she says, "I don't really care how other people perceive me. And that's all on you. And that's how I felt going into college. This is life, you know, and if you don't like it then you don't have to deal with it." Tiffanie, another former athlete, also articulates how not caring insulates her from the negative impact of the woman/athlete paradox:

> I mean, I really never put too much thought into all that. I mean, mainly I don't really care what people think about me. I'm gonna be who I wanna be and act the way I wanna act. I mean, I'm an athlete and yeah, I'm a female, but I don't need to be all dainty. Like that's how basically I think

society pretty much wants females to be for the most part. But yeah, I just don't. I didn't have an issue with it. But I mean, I'm sure there are plenty of females out there that struggle with that.

In her explanation for why she doesn't feel any tension between her athletic and gender identities, Tiffanie rejects normative expectations of women in society, the foundation of the woman/athlete paradox. Even Denise, who, like Rowan and Kameron, embodies masculinity through significant muscle mass, never felt as though she was conflicted in her identities. "In my junior year, I got really big . . . but it never occurred to me like 'this is not feminine.' Everybody [men] always said they liked it. I mean, I ain't never heard anybody ever say otherwise."

Social context and family socialization additionally mediated some athletes' experiences with the cultural contradiction of being athletic women. Jackie attributes her lack of felt tension between her identities to her family, in particularly her parents' support of her sport participation:

> Once you get on the court, I don't care if I look masculine. That wasn't even in my kind of frame of mind. Like, that wouldn't even come into play. But I think obviously my parents and my family encouraged sports so much, and basketball in particular, that I didn't really feel ever bad about myself or have that struggle between being masculine and being feminine because it was so acceptable in my family. So, if my mom was more maybe traditional and wanted me to, you know, play ballet or something then I could see it being more of an issue. But it was just like, I'd come home from basketball, and she'd be just as interested in how it went as my dad. It was just kind of like accepted.

Jackie's family support contributed to her embracing her athletic identity, even if it meant she looked masculine while on the court. Former athlete Elise grew up in a small town and she credits that social context, particularly its support for sports, for her ability to avoid conflict between her athletic and feminine identities:

> I was very fortunate 'cause I went to Western State. It's a small town but it's very supportive. The whole community loves sports, and if you were an athlete at WSU, everybody in the community knew who you were.

Our posters and stuff were up all over, you know, in shops and whatever. It wasn't like taboo. It was like the cool thing to be an athlete or whatever. I never really had a problem with fitting in or trying to maintain like, my feminism I guess at the same time as being an athlete. I never really felt conflicted with that at all in college. I guess I'm fortunate looking at it that way. I never really felt like I had to work at both, being an athlete and being a female.

Elise's ability to not feel conflicted was aided by the support of her community and the fact that sports in her small town were celebrated. Context also mattered greatly for Jackie, who discussed never feeling a tension between her athletic and gender identities until she left her college atmosphere where she spent most of her time around other athletes:

So, I can honestly say that I never felt any sort of conflict probably until being done with sports. I was obviously always surrounded with other athletes and so taking kind of behavior from the floor to the classroom to, you know, a social event, it was very just kind of fluid, and I never noticed anything. . . . Just even, for instance, like what I'll wear around. Like right now I have on long shorts and, you know, a bigger t-shirt. And on the weekends if we're around I'd put on sweats and like, kinda saggin'. I don't even think twice about that, you know? And, yet, people will notice it and will comment on it like, "Oh my god, you're sagging!" I would never even recognize that my shorts are long or that my pants aren't pulled up to my waist. And I think that's more just acceptable throughout athletic culture, and I don't know if that's a masculine trait per se. I see it more as like an athletic trait. But I think other people outside of athletics view that more as a masculine-type behavior, I guess. Like, I'll just be in whatever, like sweats and stuff. And yeah, it's more like, "Oh. Your pants are falling down," almost like they're trying to help me out. And I'm just like, "No, that's just how I wear 'em. I'm okay with this." More like catching people off guard, I think. 'Cause you know, when people study at the library, they'll wear sweats, but it's more like, you know, stretch pants and stuff and I've just never been into that.

Being immersed in a sporting context surrounded by other athletes who all wore sweatpants that sagged, baggy shorts, and t-shirts contributed to the normalization of masculine-gendered behavior, which only became noticeable to Jackie after she left college and attempted to engage in those same behaviors in new contexts. Others' intervention strategies or subtle acts of gender policing—"your pants are falling down"—signal to Jackie that what was once acceptable for her as an athlete is no longer acceptable as a former athlete.

"Girls Love My Body"

The cultural contradiction of women's athleticism, at its core, is about dominant understandings of gender and sexuality. Women athletes experience a contradiction between being athletic and appropriately feminine because it is prescribed that women do not engage in masculine behaviors or embody masculinity because to do so would make them unappealing to men. As a result, the woman/athlete paradox is fundamentally heteronormative and cisnormative; that is, it presumes that women athletes are heterosexual and cisgender.[15] For the athletes who identify as queer and especially those who are queer *and* express gender nonnormatively, the woman/athlete paradox became almost nonexistent.

I asked Eve, an MWSU captain, if her athletic body ever presented her with identity conflicts, to which she replied, "I never struggled with it because like really, I don't like men, so their opinion doesn't really matter much. And girls love my body." Eve's response underscores important ways sexuality might mediate how the woman/athlete paradox impacts athletes. First, she highlights the meaningful relationship between gender and sexuality in that pressures to conform to idealized conceptions of femininity are not just about expectations of gender but also about heterosexuality and attractiveness to men. Eve's queerness then does two things: it eliminates her need to engage in body work that would make her appear feminine by, for example, not having lean, defined muscles, and it opens up possibilities for gender expression that go beyond the gender binary. Second, Eve's admission that women love her body illustrates how normative cultural understandings of "sexiness" are fundamentally heteronormative; queerness, therefore, may allow for greater variation in gender expression and in perceptions of attractiveness.

Sexuality also mattered for former athletes Carmen and Christina who expressed how the tension they initially felt between being athletic and appropriately feminine dissipated once they came out as queer. For them, the tension existed before coming out because they felt unable or unwilling (or both) to conform to the expectations of hegemonic heterofemininity. As Carmen describes in her story about preparing to go on a team trip,

> For instance, my freshman year, we had a tournament. We were going to Hawaii for a tournament, and my coach was like, "Okay, everybody has to dress up." You know, we had to be presentable and what not. So, I was like, "Crap! What am I supposed to do? Am I supposed to be comfortable? Or . . ." You know, 'cause my really close friend in college was straight, and she was like, "Oh, I'm gonna wear a skirt cause it's comfy" and blah blah blah. And I'm like, "Hell no! I'm not traveling anywhere, let alone walking out of the house in a skirt!" For me, I definitely struggled with "Do I need to portray being feminine? Do I need to portray being, you know, the girly girl even though that's not comfortable, that's not who I am?" And I think that, especially in the beginning, I definitely struggled with that.

I asked Carmen how her experience changed after she came out and whether this tension was still an issue for her. "It was definitely not an issue," she said. "I was out. I was comfortable with myself. The people who mattered to me and cared for me were comfortable with it. So, it was never—the femininity issue was never an issue." Christina similarly told me she "had the hardest time in high school but not in college" because she came out in college. After she came out, her queerness negated many of the gender expectations she received when she identified as straight. Christina also expresses gender androgynously—what she calls a "half-and-half-type deal"—which again frees her from normative expectations of femininity.

The experiences of Eve, Carmen, and Christina suggest that the cultural contradiction of women's athleticism may be mediated by sexuality, and there is research evidence to support such a claim. Coming out for women often brings with it changes in appearance, particularly as it relates to normative gender signifiers such as hair, clothing, or makeup.[16] Indeed, for many lesbians "the theme of 'freedom' from heterosexual appearance norms after coming out was a unifying factor."[17] Queer culture, and lesbian culture in particular, may allow a protective space for women to feel more freedom related to their appearance in theory, but dominant ideologies about gender may make it hard to do so in practice. A number of studies, for example, point to the fact that lesbian and bisexual women are no less impacted by social pressure to conform to heterosexual beauty ideals than their heterosexual counterparts.[18] It is possible then that out, queer women athletes, especially those who express gender nonnormatively, are less constrained by the woman/athlete paradox than straight women because they have a different imagined audience. At the same time, "despite the fact that lesbian-feminist ideology challenges conventional standards of female beauty, lesbians still grow up as women in our culture and are exposed to and internalize cultural beliefs about female beauty."[19]

Indeed, while sexuality seemed to mediate the tension experienced by Eve, Carmen, and Christina between their athletic and gender identities, it did not do so for other queer athletes. For example, J. F. may not buy into normative gender ideologies but that did not prevent her from seeing them as a barrier to her ability to "just go out and play." In this way, cultural expectations around gender operate distinctly from sexuality in shaping women athletes' experiences with the woman/athlete paradox. In many ways, I was glad to know that for a number of these elite-level athletes, the contradiction of women's athleticism was not perceived as a hinderance in their everyday lives. At the same time, as Heather Widdows argues, "rejection is a far cry from being immune to the demands of beauty."[20]

Beauty Ideals and the Body

The cultural contradiction of women's athleticism operates within a larger framework of beauty ideals rooted in notions of womanhood, femininity, and sexuality that are deeply racialized. The very construction of the category "woman" and ideas of beauty cannot be separated from ideologies of race—they are mutually constitutive and "evidenced at every historical turn."[21] Womanhood was created to be synonymous with Whiteness, and the exclusion of Black women from the category of "woman" has been enforced legally and embraced culturally throughout history.

Sarah Haley's work on Georgia's chain gangs in the nineteenth and early twentieth centuries meticulously illustrates this process. With few exceptions, White women who committed crimes were exempt from laboring on chain gangs whereas Black women were routinely not only forced to perform this brutal form of labor but also forced into domestic servitude in White homes.[22] Given work designed both for men and for women yet kept outside of either category—indeed, outside of the boundaries of humanness—represented a dual positioning that solidified Black women's otherness while simultaneously reinforcing the "singular status of White womanhood."[23] Importantly, gendered and raced ideologies of beauty and the body were central to these processes. Justifications for the placement of Black women on chain gangs were buoyed by narratives of them as being too ugly to be considered women and therefore unredeemable and undeserving of the protections from grueling and violent forms of labor afforded to White women.

> Perceived ugliness was one attribute that defined black women's deviance from the category "woman" and justified their imprisonment and assault during the nadir of American race relations. . . . In the white imaginary "black woman" was an oxymoronic formulation because the modifier "black" rejected everything associated with the universal "woman." The black female subject occupied a paradoxical, embattled, and fraught position, a productive negation that produced normativity.[24]

Black (un)womanhood was crucial to the construction of White womanhood, White femininity, and White beauty. White womanhood was designed in response to and in relation to Black (un)womanhood and nonbeing—purity, submissiveness, and frailty deserving of the protection of White men take shape most clearly when juxtaposed with criminality, lasciviousness, and grotesquery. In this way, "it was black female otherness, their dehumanization, that made 'white women' possible as a subject position" and that created the "aesthetic standard that reinforced the hierarchy of races."[25] White womanhood became true and White femininity beautiful as a result of the peripheral positioning of Black women to the category of woman itself.

Body size has been particularly important to the construction of gendered and raced ideologies of beauty and the body. During colonization, body size came to be associated with character traits such as rationality, self-control, and intelligence.[26] "The depiction of colonized black women . . . represented them as having monstrous, 'unwomanly' bodies that were not beautiful and admired as were the delicate bodies of their White counterparts."[27] The controlling of White women's bodies and eating practices in the nineteenth century was thus a direct result of attempts to distinguish those who were free from those who were slaves and in doing so uphold White supremacy. As Sabrina Strings asserts, "It was important that [White] women ate as little as was necessary in order to show their Christian nature and also their racial superiority."[28] Racial ideologies that constructed Black people as self-indulgent and sensuous and Black women as intemperate and immoderate coupled with perceptions of them as "too fat" served as justifications for the exploitation of their bodies through slavery and racial sexual violence.[29]

The legacy of this gendered project of White supremacy remains in contemporary manifestations of beauty ideals and expectations of femininity. As Ruby Hamad notes, "What is common about the experiences of women of color is an unspoken assumption that we always lack a defining feature of womanhood that White women have by default."[30] While research has shown that Black women have a preference for resisting cultural ideals of beauty centered on Whiteness and thinness by valuing thickness and fuller body figures, normative standards of beauty writ large are still defined by Whiteness, and White women serve as the benchmark by which all other women are measured.[31] The centrality of blondeness to the feminine beauty ideal is important in that "many Black and Brown women are categorically excluded."[32]

> Black women, by definition, cannot achieve the idealized feminine ideal because the fact of Blackness excludes them. Dominant gender ideology provides a social script for Black women whereby everyone else needs Black women to be on the bottom for everything else to make sense. Just as hegemonic White masculinity occupies the most desired social script, an equally hegemonic Black femininity organized via images of bitches, bad mothers, mammies, and Black ladies coalesce to mark the least desirable form of femininity.[33]

The ideology of the "thick Black woman" persists, perpetuating conceptions of Black women as less beautiful and less feminine than White women.[34] Indeed, perceptions of Black women's bodies—either because of size or other characteristics such as skin tone—continue to situate them closer to Black masculinity than to White heterofemininity. This historical and contemporary exclusion is perhaps nowhere more obvious than within the institution of sport.

"I Am a Woman and I Am Fast"

The institution of sport has been intricately tied up with structures of White supremacy and heteropatriarchy in constructing and contesting the womanhood of women athletes and in the policing of women athletes' expressions of gender. International governing bodies such as World Athletics (formerly the International Association of Athletics Federation, or IAAF) have specifically used pseudoscientific ideologies of race and gender to not only draw a dividing line between men and women in sport but also demarcate *which* women are woman-enough to compete at the highest levels. Using arbitrary signifiers of competitive advantage with little to no medically rigorous backing—most notably testosterone levels—these governing bodies have subjected women athletes to a variety of "sex tests," including physical exams (known in the 1960s as the "nude parade") and hormone testing. Importantly, the impetus for such testing need only be the questioning of an athlete's sex based on their outward appearance or gender expression.[35]

Although not the exception, the most famous woman athlete impacted by these racist policies is undoubtedly South African track and field runner Caster Semenya. Semenya is a two-time 800-meter Olympic champion and a three-time 800-meter world champion. In 2019, in what many speculated would be her last race, Semenya sailed past her competition to win the 800-meter at a time of 1:54:98, faster than any other woman had run in over a decade.[36] Ten years prior, at the age of eighteen, Semenya burst into the spotlight by winning gold at the 2009 World Championships in Berlin. Her dominance in the race coupled with her physical appearance inspired "experts," the news media, and her fellow competitors to question whether Semenya was a man. Italian runner Elisa Cusma was noted saying, "These kind of people should not run with us. For me, she is not a woman. She is a man."[37] Canadian runner Diane Cummins said, "Even if she is a female, she's on the very fringe of the normal athlete female biological composition from what I understand of hormone testing. So, from that perspective, most of us just feel that we are literally running against a man."[38] Suspicions about Semenya's sex prompted World Athletics to put her through a "gender verification process," including hormone treatment and, importantly, to adopt new policies to set restrictions for women athletes with naturally higher-than-average levels of testosterone.[39] When the first policy—limiting women athletes' testosterone levels to 10 nmol/L—failed to hamper Semenya, World Athletics lowered the upper limit of these levels to 5 nmol/L, effectively banning Semenya and others from competition unless they took medically unnecessary, hormone-altering medication or underwent invasive medical procedures.[40] Coincidentally, this policy applies only to the 400-meter, 800-meter, 1,500-meter, and the mile events—events in which Semenya runs—because World Athletics argues that those are the races in which high levels of testosterone would give a woman the most advantage.

The link between testosterone and competitive advantage is dubious, with many experts insisting that it is but one of many factors—physiological, social, and environmental—that contribute to high performance.[41] As Katrina Karkazis and Rebecca Jordan-Young have argued about Semenya, "Observers have attributed her athleticism to a single molecule—testosterone—as though it alone earned her the gold, undermining at once her skill, preparation, and achievement."[42] Semenya appealed the World Athletics decision to the Court of Arbitration for Sport (CAS) and lost. She appealed again in 2020 to the Federal Supreme Court of Switzerland and lost again. Importantly, both CAS and the Federal Supreme Court of Switzerland acknowledged the discriminatory nature of the policy; CAS argued that while discriminatory, the policy was "necessary" and "reasonable" in order to achieve World Athletics' goal of "preserving the integrity of female athletics."[43] In a statement challenging the initial World Athletics ruling in 2019, Semenya articulated two things that are and will remain true, whether or not she is ever allowed to compete again: "I am a woman and I am fast."[44]

Semenya's story is, of course, about the deeply troubling ways in which false, pseudoscientific conceptualizations about sex and gender endure: that there are only two dichotomous biological sexes, male and female, and that sex is a natural predictor of one's gender identity, behavior, and expression.[45] It is the story of an international sport governing body drawing arbitrary boundaries around sex and gender to police women athletes into conforming to hegemonic ideals of femininity. That an investigation of an athlete's sex can be instigated solely based on their physical appearance or their gender expression makes this abundantly clear. If Semenya appeared more feminine, she might not have drawn the ire of her fellow competitors, despite beating them consistently and thoroughly.[46] Semenya's story, however, is about much more than this. As Moya Bailey has argued, it is a story of misogynoir at work: "Semenya's appearance prompted the gender testing she endured and the public notoriety she experienced in popular media. Her physically fit body and athletic prowess were the source of medical speculation about her 'health' and furthered media representations of athletic Black women as less than appropriately feminine."[47] Semenya's sex was questioned, but it was done so through archaic yet enduring tropes about Black women as unfeminine, "mannish," and aggressive, tropes that resulted from imperialism and colonization and disproportionately affected women of color in the Global South.

> World Athletics remains committed to a centuries-old, white supremacist notion that defines "womanhood" in terms of the white, cisgendered female body, rendering everyone else, especially women of African descent, socially unacceptable abberations [sic]. . . . And while some might dismiss the relevance of these concepts today, chalking them up to a long-ago historical era of "overt" racism, they nonetheless helped Europeans institutionalize racism in areas like sports. As a result, the medical knowledge that informs society and World Athletics' standard of womanhood is deeply rooted in racism, to the extent that black women like Semenya, Niyonsaba, and Negesa never really stood a chance.[48]

The specific pathologizing of Semenya's body, something done routinely to those with differences of sexual development who do not fit neatly into our commonsense understandings of "normal" bodies, was done through the lens of anti-Blackness, in which Black bodies in and of themselves are seen as not "normal" (i.e., through depictions of Black athletes as superhuman and animalistic). Semenya's Blackness provides the cultural frame in which debates over her body, her womanhood, and her livelihood play out.

Ideologies of White supremacy, patriarchy, and imperialism intertwine to shape Semenya's story. It is not just Semenya's perceived unfeminine Blackness on display, but the White femininity of her competitors who variously took up rallying cries of "unfairness" by accusing Semenya of cheating. In an article for the *Guardian*, British runner Jemma Simpson is quoted saying,

> It's obviously a human rights issue but human rights affect everyone in the race, not just one person. The rest of the field just gets ignored. No way is it a personal issue but it's a debate about what is right and fair for everyone. It's a really tough subject and a lot of people are very careful about what they say. You have to be. You have to be diplomatic and keep your opinions to yourself but sometimes it is so frustrating.[49]

Diane Cummins, the Canadian runner quoted earlier, professes similarly,

> As athletes we feel frustrated because everyone is allowed to give their opinion except us. If we give an honest opinion, we're either seen as bad sports or we're not happy because we're being beaten. But that's not the case. Jemma and I have been beaten tons of times by athletes who we feel are doing it in the realm of what is considered female. . . . It is certainly frustrating to be running against someone who seems to be doing it effortlessly. We all believe that Caster Semenya, pushed to her full potential, could break the world record. That's 1.53, and that's what college guys are running. From that perspective, she's far superior to any female 800m runner we've ever had.[50]

Both Simpson's and Cummins's comments follow a predictable pattern in which, under the guise of protecting the integrity of women's sports, these athletes are able to turn their disappointment of losing, badly, into a referendum on the "true" nature of Semenya's sex. Rather than being sore losers—as Cummins argues, they've been beaten "tons of times" by athletes "considered female"—they are merely calling attention to the highly touted values of integrity, justice, fairness, and equality. If Semenya is not *really* a woman, then it is unfair for her to participate in women's sports. Their comments also, importantly, center themselves and their White femininity. The "what about us?" slant coupled with their pushback against what they seem to think is political correctness gone awry—"you have to be diplomatic . . . but sometimes it's so frustrating"—centers their own White femininity and, in doing so, invokes tropes of damsels in distress, White women in need of protection from the unfairness that they would lose not to any woman but to *this woman*—a Black, masculine-presenting, queer woman. Their frustration and sense of having been wronged becomes the focus. It is not Semenya they are concerned about, whose life has been torn apart in the media and whose career has been stripped away from her, but their perceived entitlement to compete against women who cannot beat them so effortlessly.

Simpson's and Cummins's commentary falls in a long line of examples of how White people's, and specifically White women's, emotions have been used to perpetuate racist violence against Black people and generally exempt them from confronting their own racial advantages. A large body of writing from women of color has articulated how White women's tears can be weaponized in uncomfortable or painful situations to silence people of color or, worse, flip scripts in which *they*, not the person they have harmed, become the victims in an uncomfortable racial encounter.

> White women tears are especially potent and extra salty because they are attached to the symbol of femininity. These tears are pouring out from the eyes of the one chosen to be the prototype of womanhood; the woman who has been painted as helpless against the whims of the world. The one who gets the most protection in a world that does a shitty job overall of cherishing women.[51]

As Shay Stewart-Bouley argues, "White women tears are multipurpose: they derail conversation, they emotionally bully others (particularly people of color), and they are almost never questioned—which only adds to the power of a white woman and her tears."[52] Historical and contemporary examples of the ways White women's tears have been used as a tool of White supremacy abound; they were the catalyst for the brutal murder of Emmett Till (as just one example) and embolden the "Karens" and "Beckys"—entitled White woman who believe everything they're doing is right—of today who are quick to call the police on Black people who are sitting in coffee shops, having a BBQ, or birdwatching.[53] These incidents, and the countless others that have not gone viral on social media, illuminate the power of White women's tears: "Karen is no longer the sort of annoying person who, like, wants to see your manager. She's the one who's willing to mobilize violence against you because she can."[54]

Importantly, White women's tears manifest in numerous ways, not always as actual crying. White tears, rather, refers to the numerous emotions that arise—anger, frustration, sadness, embarrassment, fragility—when White people feel as though their dominance is questioned, when they perceive (usually incorrectly) that their safety is being threatened, when their comfort is not prioritized, or when their sense of the way the world should be is otherwise interrupted (i.e., seeing Black people in a predominantly White neighborhood).[55] White women's tears, as Stewart-Bouley writes, are about emotional angst leveraged to idolize White womanhood.[56]

The reactions of Semenya's competitors—Simpson and Cummins certainly, but also the reactions of many others, including the media and World Athletics—to her athletic dominance are all examples of White tears on display. Their reactions are the collective emotional angst levied at a young, queer, masculine-presenting Black woman who dared to be athletically dominant while simultaneously disrupting archaic, normative expectations around race, gender, and sexuality. That Semenya is now banned from competing unless she utilizes medically unnecessary interventions to place her back within the acceptable, if not appropriate, boundaries of womanhood is perhaps the purest demonstration of the power of White tears, of the possibilities when White people feel wronged simply because they were not the best.

The cultural contradiction of women's athleticism is grounded in a definition of sport as masculine and presents women athletes with a challenge: demonstrate heterofemininity to prove your womanhood. But because definitions of womanhood have been defined "through a lens of whiteness," the presence of Black women athletes in sports was historically taken for granted.[57] That is, if sports are fundamentally masculine and Black women are perceived as being masculine, their participation in sport is not a paradox to be solved in the way it is for White women. The suitability of Black people for athletic participation based on racist ideologies about essential physiological differences between Black and White bodies has long been used to explain the overrepresentation of Black athletes in certain sports.[58] These ideologies compound the belief that Black women are inherently more masculine than White women and serve as a justification for Black women's participation and success in sport. Such assumptions, however, have their limits. As Semenya's case illustrates, assumptions about Black women's inherent masculinity and aggressiveness only go so far in protecting them from the woman/athlete paradox, particularly when they are competing against White women and competing for widespread popularity.

Numerous scholars have documented the unrelenting ways that women athletes' bodies are sexualized and their images strategically crafted for consumption by a White, male, heterosexual audience.[59] Again, inherent in the cultural contradiction of women's athleticism is the directive to women athletes to be feminine in a way that makes them heterosexually attractive. A Google search of "sexy female athletes" yields White athletes almost exclusively. Some Black women athletes, such as basketball players Candace Parker and Skylar Diggins, whose gender expressions align more closely with White heterofemininity, are "imagined outside the margins of blackness" so as to achieve commodification status similar to their White counterparts.[60] Those who remain unable and/or unwilling to conform to White standards of femininity and womanhood, whose Blackness cannot be transcended for the sake of the White imagination, find themselves caught in a state of constant surveillance and potential erasure.

Returning to Rowan

Exploring the woman/athlete paradox was what brought me to the MWSU women's basketball team. I wanted to understand whether contemporary women athletes still experienced "dual and dueling identities" between being athletes and being women who are perceived to be appropriately feminine. Most importantly, I wanted to understand how this experience is racialized, impacting Black women athletes differently. My time spent with the MWSU players, as well as my interviews with elite-level former athletes, demonstrates that the woman/athlete paradox continues to shape the everyday lived experiences of women athletes in important, albeit different, ways. For many, this means that they acutely feel caught in between conflicting expectations with little recourse. For others, it means that while they are aware of this paradox, it is not something that alters their individual behaviors. This is especially true for athletes whose identities explicitly do not align with heterofemininity—queer, masculine-presenting athletes. Race matters in athletes' experiences with the woman/athlete paradox because race is central to its construction, not because there are racial differences between athletes. The woman/athlete paradox lives at the intersection of ideologies about race, gender, and sexuality, meaning that athletes will experience its effects differently based on their intersectional identities. What is most important about understanding this nuance within the cultural contradiction of women's athleticism is that women athletes are thinking about this, consciously or otherwise. And every second a woman athlete thinks about whether she appears feminine enough is a second wasting limited cognitive resources that could be used to do something better.

In 2020, marine biologist Ayana Elizabeth Johnson penned a powerful op-ed in the *Washington Post* in which she describes the mental and emotional toll of racism on Black people and the corresponding loss of what could have been:

> Even at its most benign, racism is incredibly time consuming. Black people don't want to be protesting for our basic rights to live and breathe. We don't want to constantly justify our existence. Racism, injustice and police brutality are awful on their own, but are additionally pernicious because of the brain power and creative hours they steal from us. I think of one black friend of mine who wanted to be an astronomer, but gave up that dream because organizing for social justice was more pressing. Consider the discoveries not made, the books not written, the ecosystems not protected, the art not created, the gardens not tended.[61]

Whenever I read this quote, I think about Rowan and about how, in the middle of practice, she was thinking about whether her arms were getting "too big." She might have also been thinking about sport-related things—her shooting form, how her knee was feeling, whether she made a good decision during the last drill—but she was also thinking about her arms and likely the rest of her body, too. In some ways, this is what it means to be a woman in the world, the gaze of others incessantly thrumming in the background of our lives. But in other ways, Rowan's mental meandering seems especially troubling. I'm not suggesting that Rowan should not have been thinking about anything else except basketball during basketball practice. I am suggesting, however, that of all the things she could have been thinking about, wondering whether her body still looked sexy despite her muscular arms should not have had to be one of them. Rowan Dawson was one of the best players to go through the MWSU women's basketball program. Across all players in the program's history, Dawson is ranked in the top ten in points scored in her career, three-pointers made, and rebounds. She is quite literally one of the best players to have ever stepped foot on the court in an MWSU uniform. Yet, she is not immune to the perniciousness of the woman/athlete paradox and the energy required to battle it.[62] Quite often I wonder what more Rowan, or any woman athlete for that matter, might have accomplished were she not hemmed in by White supremacist and heteronormative expectations of her body. Perhaps she wonders sometimes, too.

5

"We Don't Want You Looking All Beat Up"

Gender Strategies of Women Athletes

The room was cold and dark, except for two large spotlights shining against a giant green screen in the center of the room. Video cameras, lighting umbrellas, and boom mics were placed strategically at the front and sides of the screen. The Midwest State University (MWSU) media team walked around hurriedly, checking microphone volume and testing lighting brightness. Assistant coach Johnny Jacobs stood at the entrance of the room, directing the players as they entered one after another. Some of them were already wearing their jerseys while others rushed into the bathroom to quickly change, having just come from class. After all the players gathered together, Johnny explained the nature of the video shoot. The MWSU women's basketball team would be filming a series of short clips to be used during timeouts at their games. The clips were designed to make the atmosphere of the game more entertaining and interactive by giving the fans an opportunity to connect with the individual players. The players were to stand in front of the green screen and be filmed doing a variety of things, such as dancing, showing off their muscles for the "flex cam," and doing the limbo.

First up was Jizeal, who was wearing her hair down and straightened, bright eyeshadow, blush, lipstick, giant gold-hoop earrings, and several thin gold bracelets on each wrist. When she walked in front of the screen, the bright lights revealed her hot-pink nail polish, which matched her bra straps that were conspicuously peeking out from underneath the top of her jersey. Right before the camera started rolling, Jizeal turned to Johnny, pointed at a small blemish under her left eye, and asked if he thought it was noticeable or if the editors of the video could "do something about it." Johnny reassured her that she looked fine. "They'll take care of it," he told her. Jizeal then put on headphones, turned on a pop song and swayed back and forth, smiling and singing along. When this clip was shown during the games, a chosen fan would watch the video of Jizeal singing and when the video paused, they would have to guess the next word in the song to win a prize.

Next was Rowan, who was perhaps unsurprisingly asked to do the "flex cam." Although not wearing any makeup, Rowan's hair was also down and straightened and she was wearing two pairs of small gold hoops in her ears and two gold necklaces, one of which had a basketball hoop charm attached to it. Rowan stood in front of the screen and hesitantly performed a series of poses in which she flexed her arm muscles, playfully imitating the way a bodybuilder might show off their muscles in competition. In between poses, she would dance a little, smile, and say into the camera "Now YOUR turn!" while continuing to flex. While Rowan flexed for the camera, her teammates giggled on the sidelines. Rowan looked down at the floor, smiled bashfully, shook her head slightly, and then continued flexing. During the games, the camera would pan over the audience and stop at individual fans who would be encouraged to imitate Rowan by flexing their own muscles while the rest of the crowd cheered them on.

Isis walked onto the platform next, her hair down and straightened as well, wearing one small pair of gold hoops in her ears. Her makeup was subtle, barely visible even under the drastic camera lighting. Isis was handed a basketball and filmed shyly tossing it back and forth and smiling. Then she began slowly clapping and shouting "de-fense, de-fense, DE-FENSE!," with each chant louder and more excited than the last. Next, she exclaimed to the camera, "MAKE SOME NOISE!" while raising her hands higher and higher to encourage fans to keep cheering. In between, she would clap, say "Yeah! Keep going!" and "Come on! You can get louder than that!," and pump her fist in the air. These clips were often played during the games to motivate fans to cheer loudly during crucial moments, like when MWSU needed to stop their opponent on defense or when the game was tied close to the finish.

Other MWSU players like Nikki were filmed doing clips such as "three things I can't live without," where a fan would guess the third thing from a list of options to win a prize. Some of the players were filmed in pairs or groups of three, leading chants like Isis, while others opted out altogether. Tiffany refused to be on camera because she had a swollen lip from getting elbowed by an opposing player in a game the weekend before. Although at times the players seemed embarrassed or shy—often apologetically giggling in between takes—they all completed their respective clips and promptly went to the gym to start practice.

Gender Strategies

Initially, I didn't think anything of the video shoot. At the time, it reminded me of my collegiate basketball days when our team would take our yearly photo—usually in front of fire trucks or construction equipment to apparently symbolize our toughness—for a poster that would be displayed across campus and in a handful of bars and restaurants around town. While we all had to wear our uniforms, many of my teammates would come to these photo shoots with their long hair down, often straightened (even if they never wore it that way otherwise), and wearing makeup and jewelry, exactly like the MWSU players did for their video shoot. At a basic level, this makes sense. Media promotion is a crucial part of elite-level sports, and the players are often asked to do things such as signing autographs after games, having their photos taken, and filming promotional videos like these. Of course, the players want to look their best, and for many of them that means wearing makeup and doing their hair a certain way. At a deeper level, however, what was on display during the MWSU video shoot was much more than athletes simply putting their best selves forward: it highlights the cultural contradiction of women's athleticism, and the strategic ways women athletes engage in various forms of body modification— attempting to change the ways their bodies look or prevent their bodies from becoming a certain way—as they navigate this contradiction. This behavior, originally labeled "apologetics" by Jan Felshin in the 1970s, has been well documented within gender and sport scholarship over the last four decades.[1]

Although the form has changed somewhat, apologetic behavior has remained stubbornly consistent over time.[2] In their early 1990s studies of women athletes, Elaine Blinde and Diane Taub demonstrated that women athletes engage in a complex set of strategies to mediate the tension of the woman/athlete paradox and particularly to avoid lesbian stigma.[3]

Athletes were interested in adopting an acceptable public appearance consistent with societal expectations of women. For example, several respondents made a conscious effort not to wear athletic attire, especially in situations where they would be interacting with faculty and students. Others indicated that they used accounterments [sic] such as earrings and makeup "to appear feminine." Athletes also stated that they (or other athletes they knew) accentuated certain behaviors in order to reduce the possibility of being labeled a lesbian. Being seen with men, having a boyfriend, or even being sexually promiscuous with men were commonly identified strategies to reaffirm an athlete's heterosexuality.[4]

Scholars studying women athletes across sport type have similarly found that athletes engage in various "compensatory actions" to (over)emphasize their femininity and heterosexuality, including wearing feminine clothing, makeup, and jewelry; disassociating with their athletic identities or their lesbian teammates; and monitoring their muscle mass by limiting the amount of weightlifting they do.[5] Many women athletes resist engaging in these compensatory behaviors in a variety of ways, and others have argued that contextual factors such as age and sexual orientation impact whether and to what degree athletes utilize such strategies.[6]

Women in male-dominated fields other than sports have also been found to utilize apologetic behavior to counteract their perceived gender transgressions. As Linda Carli details in her overview of gender and social influence, "Women, but not men, are disliked for criticizing others, disagreeing with others, being highly successful in a male-dominated profession, or being immodest" in addition to merely being competent.[7] In order to be perceived as likable and exert social influence, women must "display a blend of agentic and communal qualities."[8] By utilizing "social softeners"—smiling and expressing agreement, warmth, and communality—women can dilute the negative impact of their competence and assertiveness and then potentially be judged less harshly.[9] Perceptions of women's competence, likability, and likelihood of getting hired are also mediated by how they embody femininity through gender signifiers such as clothing, hairstyles, and makeup. Jennifer Klatt and colleagues found, for example, that pants, makeup, and jewelry increase perceptions of competence in women, but wearing makeup makes women seem less warm and more arrogant than not wearing makeup. They also found that different combinations of hair, makeup, and clothes influenced a woman's perceived warmth.[10]

Departing from previous scholars' use of the terms "apologetic behavior" or "compensatory actions," I utilize Arlie Hochschild's concept of gender strategies to better understand the complex negotiations of gender expression that women athletes engage with within the context of sport. Hochschild defines a gender strategy as a "plan of action through which a person tries to solve problems at hand, given the cultural notions of gender at play."[11] Gender strategies are rooted in ideologies of gender and can be engaged in consciously or unconsciously. In other words, when an individual applies their ideas about gender to their life circumstances, they are pursuing a gender strategy to align ideology and circumstance. What makes the concept of gender strategies particularly useful is the importance of emotion to one's strategy. According to Hochschild, "To pursue a gender strategy a man draws on beliefs about manhood and womanhood, beliefs that are forged in early childhood and usually anchored to deep emotion. He makes a connection between how he thinks about his manhood, what he feels about it and what he does. It works the same way for a woman."[12] Rather than apologizing for their athleticism or compensating for a perceived lack in femininity, women athletes utilize gender strategies—conscious and unconscious plans of action—to align both their own gender ideologies *and* the gender ideologies at play within the institution of sport (e.g., ideologies of their coaches, other players, administrative staff, the public). This is notably true with elite-level athletes. The cultural contradiction of women's athleticism—the clash between gender ideology and circumstance—requires athletes to develop various courses of action that will neutralize the tension that such a context creates.

I wasn't necessarily surprised by how the MWSU players enacted gender strategies such as fixing their hair a certain way, shaving their legs and underarms, or wearing makeup during games. When I was an athlete, I witnessed my teammates doing these same behaviors and I engaged in some of them myself. Why, I thought, put on a face full of makeup only to immediately wipe it off once you start sweating? That, I know now, is the wrong question altogether, a point I'll return to at the end of this chapter. What did surprise me, though, was how other

people's ideologies about gender exerted power over individual players' decision-making around whether and how to enact gender strategies. Athletes like Rowan, Jizeal, and Isis are constantly negotiating with
themselves and their own identities as well as with the expectations of
others, all of which is happening within a sport context not designed
with them in mind. Moreover, along with gender, these strategies are
informed by race and sexuality in undeniable ways. Ideologies around
gender, race, and sexuality are mutually constituting and reinforcing.
Behaviors that attempt to reconcile the discrepancy between gender ideologies and circumstance are also about reconciling with ideologies of
race and sexuality.

"It's Just Unladylike": Tattoos

"Do people ever say anything to you about your tattoos because you're a
woman?" I ask Rowan as we sat together in a small MWSU conference
room for our interview.

"Oh, no, no. Not at all," she replied matter-of-factly. Then, after a
pause: "But like, my [future Women's National Basketball Association
(WNBA)] coach asked, 'How many tattoos you got?' I said fifteen. She
said, 'Where they at?' I said, 'That's good that you can't see them, huh?'
She's like, 'Yeah, that's great. See most girls they have them on their forearms, everywhere.' I'm like, 'Nah, I'm not like that.' She's like, 'Good,
good, good.'"

Curious, I asked Rowan whether she intentionally chose not to make
her tattoos visible.

"Yeah, I don't like that," she told me.

"How come?" I added.

"It's just unladylike. Like, I understand, I see, you know, getting a tattoo is unladylike and you shouldn't. But having it all over like, come on.
You do have to get a job in the future."

"Right," I replied. "So, you're kind of like, 'Well, I'll just get them kind
of strategically small . . .'"

"Yeah, to where I can make sure they are able to be covered up," she
replied.

My exchange with Rowan reveals several important things about how
women athletes utilize and negotiate gender strategies. Rowan's decision

to get only small tattoos that are not visible is a way for her to reconcile that she has tattoos with her belief that tattoos are "unladylike" and unprofessional, evidenced by her comment "You do have to get a job in the future." Rowan's plan of action was affirmed by her soon-to-be WNBA coach who made explicit her belief that women should not have tattoos on their forearms, if at all. The conviction that tattoos are unladylike is rooted in gender ideologies that associate tattooing with masculinity and, in particular, "male dominated subcultures (e.g., military groups, prisoners, street gangs, motorcycle clubs) as a mechanism for creating and confirming aggressively strong, or 'dangerous,' masculinities."[13] Tattooing has also historically been associated with criminality, mental illness, and sexual deviancy. As Beverly Yuen Thompson notes, "While men appear more masculine, tough, and potentially criminal with their extensive tattooing, tattooed women report being treated like prostitutes or as sexually adventurous women by strangers."[14] Rowan's explicit decision-making around her tattoo placement is thus a clear attempt at navigating a complex landscape of conflicting identities and ideologies, further complicated by a sport context that is inherently masculine. For Rowan, a Black woman whose body does not conform to White heterofeminine beauty standards, her tattoos must be tempered by their invisibility.

Prince, who is also tattooed, did not talk explicitly about being strategic with their placement but did acknowledge that others' perceptions of women athletes with tattoos play into stereotypes. "[Other people] assume every female athlete is gay," she says. "And they assume that all of us got tattoos and all of us are ghetto and all us were brought up in probably bad neighborhoods and stuff like that." In one sentence, Prince clearly articulates the dynamic associations among gender, sexuality, race, and class that work to inform women athletes' experiences and decisions around engaging in gender strategies. Women athletes' masculinity is, in Prince's view, a shortcut to a plethora of resulting stereotypes, including lesbianism, enhanced by deviant embodiments of masculinity like being tattooed, as well as racist and classist assumptions of being "ghetto" and from "bad neighborhoods." Through this lens, the balance Rowan attempts to strike by having tattoos but keeping them hidden is a method of self-preservation and of mitigating the negative impact of others' perceptions.

"I'm Not Trying to Prove Anything": Makeup

"Do you put makeup on before the game?" I ask Jizeal.

"Eyeliner."

"Just eyeliner?"

"And mascara," she replies.

"Yeah. Like, is that because you know you're about to be on TV or you want to look good?" I ask.

Jizeal confirms, "Yeah. Yeah, basically."

I continue: "So do you think that you feel like you need to look a certain way when you're playing?"

She replied, "When I'm playing, I know I look a mess. But if I'm sitting on that bench, I want to look presentable. So, I mean, I make sure my eyes is done, my hair is done. But I mean when I play, I know I'm just gonna look a mess. I know it, regardless. Nobody wants to sit over there looking a mess."

Jizeal's comments reveal the power of gender ideology in shaping women athletes' use of gender strategies. She knows that "looking a mess" (e.g., being sweaty) is an unavoidable result of engaging in a competitive contact sport like basketball. Yet, she still chooses to engage in the highly gendered practice of putting on makeup only to almost certainly sweat it off. Few players, however, are on the court for all forty minutes of a game. Wearing eyeliner and mascara and making sure her hair is done are the gender strategies Jizeal uses to look "presentable"—gender-coded language—while on the bench where she is on display for others.

"You never know who's watching. You want to be cute. They do it because they want to be cute," MWSU center Sara tells me when I ask her why she thinks many of her teammates choose to put on makeup before games. She then adds, "And it's a natural thing. It's like, I don't know, putting on makeup for them is like brushing your teeth in the morning. It's repetitive. It's like embedded in their system."

"So, can you be cute and not have makeup on during the game?" I asked.

Laughing, she replies, "I hope so. If not, then I'm in a world of trouble."

Sara sees her teammates' use of gender strategies as merely partaking in normalized routines like brushing their teeth. Such a perspective makes sense of both her teammates' gender strategies and also her own. Sara's decision not to wear makeup is the result of her just being herself in the same way that her teammates' decisions to wear makeup are reflections of their natural, essential selves.

"I don't know," MWSU freshman Karolina tells me. "I always wear mascara because my eyes just look so tired if I don't. That's what I feel like. I mean, of course, I want to look good or whatever, but it's not like I'm doing . . . I'm just . . . yeah."

"You're not doing anything extra that you wouldn't normally do?" I asked. " 'Cause I notice that sometimes it seems like people really try." She responded:

Yeah, I know that people are. But like, when I go out, I don't do that much. So, what I am doing for the games I couldn't do a lot more 'cause I don't want to overdo it. But I know a lot of people want to look good when we have like TV games. I guess a lot of people are watching and people are coming to the game, and you want to look good. I mean, the people that does that are probably the same people who do that outside of basketball, too.

"You don't think anybody does it just for the games?" I wondered. Karolina responded:

Maybe they do it a little bit more, yes. I don't know. Yeah, I mean, I don't feel like it's that much on this team. I had one girl on my team back home she would like always flat-iron her hair hours before the game and put on makeup and everything. It's probably a lot of people that does that, but I don't really feel like on our team it is such a big deal. I mean everybody is doing their hair and all that, but it's not too much.

Our back and forth is revealing on several levels. In describing her own use of gender strategies, Karolina is drawing intricate boundaries around what can be considered "natural" or a part of a typical routine and what can be considered overdoing it. For Karolina, her use of mascara is about not looking tired as much as it is about looking good. Like Sara and Jizeal, Karolina acknowledges the importance of televised competition on athletes' felt need to engage in the particular gender strategy of wearing makeup. But even in this context, Karolina draws a line between her former teammate's flat-ironing her hair and what most of her MWSU teammates do before games, which she believes they would do outside of basketball as well. The ability to argue that these practices are merely a part of her (and others') everyday routine seems to be an important justification for her decision-making.

Most of the athletes at MWSU do not interpret wearing makeup or styling one's hair as conscious attempts at appearing (extra) feminine. Most explain these behaviors as merely a result of their normal routines or as part of their individual personalities and what feels natural. The degrees to which MWSU athletes engage in such behaviors create distinctions between what is purposeful and what is natural, and that allows the athletes to separate themselves and their behaviors from others who are doing "extra" or doing things "on purpose." Whether or not Karolina and her teammates are doing more for a game than they would otherwise (or more than other players on other teams) is not the point. Each of these players, in similar and unique ways, engages in micro-level decision-making to strike a balance between their and others' ideologies about gender (especially in regard to appearance) and their realities as athletes whose athletic behavior inevitably contradicts those expectations.

More than just being "natural," a number of MWSU athletes explain that their decisions to engage in certain gendered practices before games is not an effort to "prove" anything. Tiffany, for example, tells me, "I mean, I think if there's a TV game, somebody might make an extra effort to go get their eyebrows arched, but that's just because you want to look nice on TV, not because you want to fit some mold or trying to go against the grain, you know what I mean?"

Naomi similarly tells me that she wears makeup because it's part of her personality. "I don't know how to explain it. It's weird. . . . I mean I put makeup on before a game. I do that. I did that back home, too. But that's just like how I am as a person. But I don't really care about how people see me on the court."

I ask, "So you don't do it because you want to look a certain way for . . ."

She goes on: "No. No. I mean, I put makeup on all the time. That's just like how I am as a person. But I don't know. It's weird. I'm not going to like—if I want to wear heels, I'm going to wear heels today. But that's not because I'm trying to prove to you that I'm feminine. Or if I wear baggy clothes and stuff like that, that's because that's just how I feel, and that's not because I'm a cool athlete or something like that."

"You're not trying to like, demonstrate anything."

"Yeah," Naomi continues, "I'm not trying to prove anything to anyone."

"Do you think that other people do things like that though?" I ask.

"I think so, yeah."

Tiffany and Naomi illustrate the intentional boundary work that goes into their utilization of gender strategies. They explicitly delineate their behavior as basic efforts to look nice, to do things they would normally do all the time rather than as attempts to prove something or "fit some mold." They also, particularly in Naomi's case, highlight the often significant ambivalence that comes with attempting to interpret their gender strategies in real time.

With the exception of Rowan, all of the MWSU athletes who talked to me about engaging in gender strategies such as wearing makeup, rationalized their behavior in several overlapping and sometimes contradictory ways: (1) as basic attempts to look presentable, (2) as natural extensions of their essential selves and behaviors they would engage in within or outside of the sporting context, and (3) as highly contextualized (e.g., for TV games). These athletes uncritically believe they wear makeup for games solely as an individual endeavor, engaged in because it reflects their personalities outside the court and their desires to look a certain way. They don't, importantly, question why they wear makeup outside the court either. These behaviors are part of larger systems that create the conditions for their decisions to wear makeup or not. Although their individual decisions may feel highly personal, they are not isolated occurrences existing outside of the larger societal context that rewards women for heterofemininity. The cultural contradiction of women's athleticism sets the stage for athletes like Karolina, Jizeal, Sara, and Tiffany to have to make such decisions—decisions that will either bridge the gap between gender ideology and circumstance or widen it.

"You Don't Want to Look Rough": Hair

"No, um, I don't know," Rowan tells me when I ask her if she feels like she needs to look a certain way when she goes out on the court. "The most important thing I worry about is my hair. I don't know why but . . ."

"Like having it look good?" I ask.

Rowan adds:

> Uh, just not trying to go out there and be all nappy-headed like a thug. Like be decent, just have your hair done. Like I don't want to go out there and [others] be like "Ugh, look at her. Like, do you see her hair? Like, she looks tacky." Like, no, I need my hair done. Some guys have to gel it down. I have to have my hair done. But like, if it's for practice, okay, whatever, like, my team is the only one that's goin' to see me. But if it's a game, no. There's millions of eyes out there so I have to have my hair done.

"Do you think other people feel like that? Or do you think that's expected of you?" I ask.

Rowan thinks, and then says, "I wouldn't say it's expected of me, but it is expected that I carry myself well. Other people, I don't know. I don't know. 'Cause some people go without doing their dreads, just nappy-headed. I don't know."

When I ask Kyle the same question, she similarly tells me, "No. As long as I'm not looking a hot mess. I mean as long as I'm fine, my hair is okay, it's not perfect, but, you know, I throw it back in a ponytail and put on my headband. I mean I wear headbands, so you're not really going to see much."

Prince, too, offers a parallel perspective. "I don't think it's so much as trying to look a certain kind of way. I think it's just kinda cleaning up for the game, you know? You don't want to go out there hair all nappy and stuff like that. It's more like I want myself to be presentable kinda thing whether I'm playing or whether I'm on the bench kinda thing. You know?"

Sara talks about looking presentable when she tells me, "The only thing I worry about is my hair." She goes on:

> That's probably the most girliest I would get. My hair has to be at least presentable when the game starts. Because if I'm wearing my real hair

out, by the time the game ends, it's horrible. That's why I keep braids all the time, because after workouts I like to look somewhat presentable. Because you know there are guys around this campus that you're going to have to be around all the time and sometimes you'll see right when you get out of workouts and you don't want to look rough because, you know, that's what you're attracted to. You don't want to look too bad.

For Rowan, Kyle, Prince, and Sara, having their hair done becomes synonymous with carrying themselves well, being presentable, and not looking a "hot mess." The conflation between not having their hair done a certain way and being a "hot mess" is perpetuated by gendered and racialized standards of beauty. Rowan is aware that failing to tend to her hair might mean others—the millions of eyes out there—perceive her as "nappy-headed like a thug," a sentiment that is steeped in anti-Blackness and heteropatriarchy. Focusing on their hair is a gender strategy that athletes like Rowan, Prince, Sara, and Kyle use to safeguard against others' perceptions of them as unfeminine, perceptions that are fundamentally different for them because of their Blackness.

Other MWSU players, like Karolina, for example, also told me that she always puts her hair in a braid before games. "When I sweat, my hair gets stuck on my face, and it gets in my eyes and stuff. So, I always like to put either a braid or a scrunchie in. I guess I make a braid before the games because that looks better than just putting like a scrunchie, but I really don't care," she says. Karolina's decision to braid her long, blonde hair is both practical (it would otherwise get in her eyes) and symbolic (a braid looks better than a scrunchie). Karolina is not, however, concerned that if she doesn't braid her hair, she will look like a "thug" or "nappy-headed," descriptors that are strictly anti-Black. Even though all these players spoke of thinking carefully about their hair and deciding what they want their hair to look like before games, their experiences of making such decisions are fundamentally different. As gender ideologies inform and are informed by ideologies of race and sexuality, Karolina's gender strategies are filtered through the lens of her Whiteness, just as the gender strategies used by athletes like Prince, Rowan, Sara, and Kyle are filtered through the lens of their Blackness, necessarily altering the intentions and decisions they all make around their hair.

The MWSU athletes' fear of being judged by others for their hair looking like a "hot mess" is a uniquely racialized concern, as Black women
athletes across sports have long had to navigate criticism of their hair.
Serena and Venus Williams were condemned for wearing beads early on
in their careers; in a 1999 match against Lindsay Davenport, the umpire
penalized Venus for "distracting" her opponent when a few of her hair
beads fell on to the court. More recently, US gymnast Gabby Douglas
faced a torrent of disparagement about her hair at the 2012 Olympic
Games in London and again at the 2016 games in Rio de Janeiro. Despite
being styled in accordance with the general expectations for gymnasts
while in competition—tightly secured away from the face—countless
Twitter users took it upon themselves to call out Douglas for the way
her hair looked. Tweets such as "Who let Gabby Douglas out the house
with her hair lookin like that" and "I know this isn't important, but can
someone get Gabby Douglas a hair stylist? Looking crazy on TV right
now" were commonplace, as were those specifically making fun of her
clips and use of hair gel (i.e., "I just want to do Gabby Douglas' hair. Like
stop gelling that babygurls hair. Omg"). A twenty-two-year-old woman
named Latisha Jenkins was quoted in the *Daily Beast* saying, "I love how
she's doing her thing and winning. But I just hate the way her hair looks
with all those pins and gel. I wish someone could have helped her make
it look better since she's being seen all over the world. She representing
for black women everywhere."[15]

It is worth noting that many people took to Twitter to defend Douglas and admonish those who chose to focus on her hair rather than her
athletic success—she was, after all, at the *Olympics* her supporters right-
fully pointed out. The critiques of Douglas's hair are problematic, however, not just because they take away from her athletic achievements
but because they are a continuation of decades-old White supremacist, heteropatriarchal standards of beauty that reinforce hierarchies of
womanhood and femininity—hierarchies that consistently place Black
women at the bottom in large part because of their hair.

> Black women exist within a complex set of sociohistorical, structural, and
> affective body politics, particularly around concepts of beauty. Perhaps
> one of the best-known ways in which hegemonic beauty standards are
> mapped onto Black women's bodies is a long-held dichotomous under-

standing of "good hair" and "bad hair." "Good hair" is a term that has been ascribed to women of color whose hair most closely fits a Eurocentric standard of beauty—loosely curled, rather than kinky or coily.[16]

Douglas is an Olympic athlete, but she is also a Black woman navigating the realities of misogynoir, realities that constrain how Black women, even world-class Black women athletes, can show up in the world. The institution of sport is embedded within a larger societal context of White supremacy and heteropatriarchy. As a result, it is not enough for Douglas to be an Olympian. Douglas must be an Olympian with "good hair" who conforms to standards of beauty fundamentally not meant for her. As Renee Martin writes in an article for *Medium*,

> Gabby may be the amazing athlete who represented her country in two Olympic games and won three Olympic medals, but she's also the young woman who had the temerity to appear on an international stage with her so-called bad hair on display for all to see. In the eyes of far too many, that means Douglas is not someone to be lauded, but someone who failed in the most important task a Black woman has: Never let them see you sweat. And while her treatment on social media brought Gabby to tears, in the years to come it will be the little girls who watched her compete who pay the price. What they will take away from this lesson is not that hard work breeds rewards, but that they will forever and always be less.[17]

In September 2020, Douglas posted a photo of herself on Instagram accompanied by a caption about her struggles with her hair. In it, she documents how years of wearing her hair in tight ponytails damaged it so badly that she had bald spots and she eventually had to cut it all off, causing her embarrassment and self-consciousness. "Fast forward to both Olympics and my hair was the topic of conversation [sad face emoji]," she continues. "Now here I am today—no extensions—no clip-ins—no wigs—no chemicals—all me."

"I Don't Want to Get Freaky": Body Modification

Loud rap music played from the speakers inside the MWSU weight-training room, a small space adjacent to one of the practice gyms with one wall of glass and another of floor-to-ceiling mirrors. Brandon Gray, the MWSU strength and conditioning coach, was guiding a handful of players through a series of exercises. The mood was serious yet relaxed. The players rotated through stations of dumbbell squats, bench press, leg curls, bicep curls, and other exercises while dancing and singing to the music in between sets. Rowan, Kameron, and Prince were the most focused, lifting far more weight than their teammates. Their faces strained and their lips curled around their teeth as they focused on breathing in and out slowly and methodically with each repetition. Sweat was dripping off their foreheads and glistening on their arms and legs as their muscles flexed throughout each exercise. In between stations, Prince took her shirt off and began lifting only in her sports bra. "Come on, Prince," Brandon pleaded. "It's hot in here," she replied as she begrudgingly put her shirt back on. Sophie, a former MWSU player and current coach, was in the weight room doing her own exercises while the team worked out. "I used to be big when I was playing but I'm not anymore," she told me as she took a break in between sets. "I wanna stay that way."

"You're playing professionally now though. You don't want to lift more and try to get big again?" I asked.

Picking up a pair of dumbbells for her next set, Sophie replied, "I don't want to get freaky."

Sophie's concern over getting "freaky," or having muscle mass that could be considered "bulky" or "manly," was one that many of the MWSU athletes shared. They employed body-modification gender strategies in an attempt to mediate those concerns and align their bodies more closely with the heterofeminine ideal. Many of the MWSU athletes were ambivalent about their bodies, and they expressed competing and unresolved feelings about how weight training specifically changed their bodies. They were simultaneously empowered by their strength and hindered by how that strength was perceived.

After the MWSU season was over, I asked many of the players whether they consciously attempted to alter their workouts so that they didn't put on muscle mass. "Did you ever try to, like, do anything so that you didn't put on muscle?" I asked Rowan, who was continuing to train in preparation for her first season in the WNBA.

"Yeah, now," she told me.

"Now you do?" I asked, somewhat surprised.

She explained, "Now I don't lift. I don't do anything upper body. I tried to lose my arms, but they keep saying, 'No, you're still big.' I try to do everything lower body."

"But if it was up to you, you just wouldn't lift arms ever again?" I pushed.

"No. I haven't yet. Since my last game, probably. I guess I took a week off and then I started back that full week and did a couple upper body workouts. But other than that, after that one week I was like, 'No.' But it's still not gone so . . ."

"So, you want your muscle mass to be gone completely?" I reiterated, half assuming she wasn't serious.

Gesturing to her arm, Rowan replied, "I mean just flat, like . . ."

"No muscles?" I interrupted.

"Oh my god, yeah!" she added, laughing.

After a pause, I asked, "Do you worry about how you look in that way?"

"Hmm, no," Rowan said. "It's whatever, I don't really care."

"But you don't want big arms . . . ," I offered.

"Yeah, I don't want big arms at all. I mean if it's there and if it's going to happen, then okay, I'll have to deal with it. But other than that, no, I don't want big arms if it was up to me."

Our exchange illuminates the specific gender strategies that Rowan utilizes to negotiate the conflict between her gender ideology and her current circumstance. It also underscores the emotional difficulty that athletes like Rowan have in not only justifying their decisions but also accepting the reality that they may not be successful. At 6' with 185 pounds of pure muscle from over a decade of training, Rowan knows that it will be difficult for her to have flat arms, especially as she continues to play professional basketball. She nonetheless is committed to trying, and she seems to understand that if she doesn't succeed, she will have to accept it.

Next to Rowan, MWSU junior guard Kameron is the most muscular on the team, so much so that her teammates nicknamed her "Tank." When I asked Kameron whether that nickname ever bothered her, she tells me, "Yeah. I feel like the bigger I get the less feminine I look." She goes on:

That always bothers me. Like "Oh, you're so ripped!" When a guy tells me "Oh, you're bigger than me," that just bothers me to the point where I have had conversations with our weight trainer and I am like, "Yo, you need to give me less reps or something. I cannot keep getting this big." So, I guess that's me, my psyche on that. I really don't like the name Tank, but it stuck. I don't allow anybody to call me that besides my teammates. You know? At the same time, too, though, although I don't really like it just because I feel like it takes away from my femininity, I also look at it like, "Well I could be fat and sloppy, but yet you're making fun of me because I'm strong and I'm athletic and I'm fit."

"Yeah, I mean, you obviously have clearly worked very hard to have that kind of body. But you would prefer not to have muscles?" I ask.

"Just not as big," Kameron replies. "If I could still be strong and still be a great athlete and not be like as physically or visually ripped or as big as I am to the point where I've been deemed 'Tank.' Like I really don't want to be a huge muscle woman."

Kameron and I continue having the following exchange:

Michelle: At what point did you start feeling like, "Okay, I like my body and I like the way it looks. I'm fit" to "Okay, maybe this is a little bit too much"?

Kameron: *Well, I got the nickname "Tank" like literally my freshman year, so I was already pretty strong, definitely the strongest out of the freshmen who came in with me. But I guess I really didn't express this concern until this year with Brandon, when I started to get feedback from people like, "Oh, you're bigger than me."*

M: From men in particular?

K: *Yes, in particular. They will see a picture and say, "Dang you need to stop lifting weights." And I think to myself, "I would if I could but I can't. This is what I do."*

M: Right. So, do men have a problem with that?

K: *This is funny because I just had this conversation with one of my good guy friends. I think he wanted to make sure I wasn't hugely insecure about it. But I'm not insecure. It's just weird. I will definitely use it to my advantage. Yeah, I'm bigger and I could beat you down or catch me on the court and I'll muscle you. In the weight room I'm competitive because that is who I am, but when it comes to being feminine or when it comes to men then it's kind of like, yeah I don't really want to be this big. Yeah, I would say it's just with men in particular. I just feel like in that stereotypical man-woman relationship, the woman shouldn't be as big, or bigger than the guy. And like some of the guys I've encountered recently, it bothers me when they continue to point it out all the time. I don't think they do it to poke fun. I have had a guy tell me he loves my body; he loves the fact that I'm so fit and muscular to the point where he's like "I gotta get bigger than you," so he's hitting the weight room every day, too. I think he likes my body, but I personally don't like it when I continue to hear about it. Or, you know, I already get called "Tank" every day. I don't need my guy friends to say something about it every day.*

M: You know, friends say things to each other all the time, that's one thing, but then does it become something else then if you're just out in the world and people are commenting?

K: *Yeah, it does become something else.*

M: It's harder for you in that way?

K: *Yeah, but I don't want to give you a sob story, like I'm just, "Oh my gosh, I just hate when people . . ." I'm stronger than that. It doesn't bother me that much, but it is something that kind of bothers me.*

M: It just gets you a little bit?

K: *Yeah. "Shut up! Stop talking about my body. Stop talking about my muscles. Don't grab my arm!" I hate when boys go like this [squeezing arm motion]. "Don't touch my arms!"*

M: Like strangers?

K: *Not strangers, but like guys I talk to. But I'm not insecure. It's just weird. I will definitely use it to my advantage.*

M: Do you think other people on the team feel that way as well?

K: *Honestly, on this team I don't think anybody else deals with it like I deal with it.*

Kameron's deep ambivalence about her body stems from persistent monitoring and policing, by teammates who call her "Tank" and men who compare their bodies to hers. She embodies masculinity through her muscle mass, feeling disempowered in social situations with men while simultaneously feeling empowered by her strength and athleticism.[18] Kameron can use her strength to her advantage and easily push around weaker opponents but is hindered by her muscles when it comes to interacting with and dating men. Men who are friends and acquaintances regularly and explicitly police her gender and sexuality by claiming she is "too big." In some cases, these men physically touch her body and, in doing so, enact an especially aggressive form of policing. By telling Kameron she should stop lifting weights because she possesses more muscle mass than they do, men send messages that Kameron's muscular body is not heterosexually attractive because it is masculine (even more masculine than their own bodies). The dissonance between Kameron's body and her ideology of gender (i.e., women shouldn't be bigger than the men they date) left her pleading with MWSU's strength and conditioning coach, Brandon, to change her workout routine, a body-modification gender strategy she hoped would keep her from continuing to gain muscle mass and fall further outside of the boundaries of heterofemininity.

In fact, both Rowan and Kameron participated in different weight-training workouts than their teammates because they expressed so much distaste with their muscle mass and embodiment of masculinity. Brandon tells me:

> You hear it all the time . . . and obviously it's different between the women and the men. Women, they get nervous: "I'm getting too big and bulking up too much." And there is a fine line, don't get me wrong. For example, Kameron, and especially right now, she's really getting kind of big. Not in a bad way, but for her, she would be better off if she leaned up a little more. Some people literally get too muscle bound. It doesn't help their game, especially with something like basketball and their shooting and things like that.

"Do you think they're thinking that though?" I ask him. "When Kameron comes to you and says to you, 'Brandon, I'm getting too big,' is that because it's messing up her shooting?"

"No, I don't think so," he replied. "It's more about the look. 'I'm looking manly, I'm getting too muscular.'"

As a strength and conditioning coach, Brandon is focused on training athletes to be the most successful they can be in their sport. He does acknowledge, however, the perceived need for balance between what is deemed appropriate athletically and what is acceptable socially. I asked Brandon where he thinks the pressure for women athletes not to be too muscular comes from. "It comes from the public, the general public. Looking at magazines, you see all these pictures. Parents. I can't tell you how many girls I've had send me text messages that they went home . . . ," Brandon pauses mid-sentence and nods to an athlete walking past. He continues:

> There's one right there. She went home and her mom said, "You're getting—your traps are getting too big," you know. And so, parents have a lot to do with it because they have no clue. They don't know, and so they make comments or people in the general public make comments. I had a girl text me the other night, she went to, I don't know, to eat somewhere, fast food or something like that and the guy behind the counter made a comment about, "Man, your quads are bigger than mine." Women don't want to hear that. Whether he means it good or bad, women don't want to hear that kind of thing. So that, yes, it comes from the public, from comments, and then from the pictures you see in all of the magazines with ladies and their dresses, and everybody wants to look nice and this and that and look feminine. They want to look healthy, but they want to look feminine. They don't want to look too big.

Brandon ultimately supports athletes in their employment of body-modification gender strategies because he understands the complexity of what they are up against. He adjusted Rowan's and Kameron's workout routines by having them do exercises that focused solely on lifting their body weight or by doing fewer repetitions or sets of a given exercise, making it less likely that they would continue to develop significant muscle mass. Brandon's support of the gender strategies utilized by Rowan and Kameron is meaningful because it highlights just how much pressure these athletes feel to not look masculine and to what lengths they and their coaches will often go to maintain their heterofemininity. Even someone like Brandon, a coach who has dedicated his life to training athletes to craft their bodies into tools with which to accomplish athletic feats, finds it difficult to resist helping women athletes who are struggling to mediate the cultural contradiction of women's athleticism.

Other MWSU athletes, although not specifically engaging in body-modification gender strategies themselves, told me that they understood why their teammates would feel ambivalence about their bodies. They often expressed an intense desire to make sure their own bodies would never look like their teammates' bodies. Senior and team captain Eve explained, "Yeah, like it was at a point when we was doing weight lifting, where Brandon didn't have Kameron or Rowan lifting anymore 'cause they didn't want to get anymore ripped."

"Why?" I asked.

Eve replied:

I mean because like I guess they still want to feel like women. And you know like, once you lift so much like, . . . Rowan has pecs. Like, she doesn't have breasts anymore but like she has pecs. So, like, once you lift so much like, you stop having breasts, and that's very disturbing. But, yeah so, I mean, it takes off the womanly characteristics, I guess, because you become so muscular. And they don't wanna be—like, they want to be toned but they don't want to be muscular. Which is so stupid to me, 'cause like, if you toned or muscular, same thing. Of course, you don't want to look like a bodybuilder, however.

Eve's discussion of Rowan's experience with weight training and her changing body is illustrative. She acknowledges that the reason Rowan (and Kameron) stopped lifting was because her body was developing so much muscle mass that she no longer felt like a woman. Eve's focus on Rowan's pectoral muscles is perhaps the most striking example; not only was Rowan's body unfeminine, but it was bordering on becoming unfemale since her body was developing male characteristics such as "pecs." Importantly, while Eve is quick to dismiss Rowan's and Kameron's gender strategies as "stupid," she simultaneously describes their musculature as "very disturbing" and admits that "you don't want to look like a bodybuilder." Scholars who have studied women bodybuilders highlight the edgework involved in balancing the conflicting demands of muscular development as a fundamental aspect of their sport with societal expectations for normative femininity.[19] As Meredith Worthen and S. Abby Baker note, "Muscularity in women goes against established Western norms about femininity. Indeed, because they are seen as violating traditional gender expectations, hyper-muscular women have been stigmatized as deviant. Researchers find that overall, women bodybuilders are perceived as less socially desirable when compared to other women simply because of their large musculature."[20]

Like Eve, Jizeal was concerned when she started at MWSU that she would develop similar muscle mass as Rowan. "When I first started, I was like, 'Oh my gosh, I do not want to look like Rowan, like, no.' Personally I wouldn't want to be walking around looking like that," she told me.

"Why wouldn't you want to get that big?" I asked.

"That's too big for me," Jizeal continued. "They [Rowan and Kameron] have like nice stomachs. I would take they stomach but they arms are like, mm-mm," she said, shaking her head back and forth. She added:

I like being feminine. You know? I like my feminine body. I wouldn't mind being cut but I wouldn't want to be big with it, too big. Like, when you wear certain things, you know, you look like a man. Which I'm not saying they look like a man, but like, you just don't look as feminine with it on. Every time we go somewhere if Kameron have on like, a little spaghetti strap shirt or something like that, people be like, "Whoa." You don't expect that from girls.

Here, Jizeal articulates the exact conditions under which athletes like Rowan and Kameron are enacting body-modification gender strategies. She not only acknowledges that their muscular bodies make them masculine, but also distances herself from them by vehemently arguing for why she wouldn't want a similar type of body. Jizeal likes her feminine body, and she calls attention to how others' bodies, particularly Kameron's, are policed in public.

Perhaps one of the most troubling aspects of body-modification gender strategies like those utilized by Rowan and Kameron—and endorsed by others like Jizeal and Eve—is that they can have a direct effect on athletes' performance. Basketball is a high-intensity contact sport. It requires athletes to jump, sprint, shuffle, change directions rapidly, and physically battle with their opponents. A player's ability to outmuscle an opponent for a rebound, explode down the court for a loose ball, and power through defenders toward the basket relies heavily on their physical strength. By engaging in gender strategies such as altering weight training, or opting out altogether, athletes like Rowan and Kameron (and their teammates who fear looking like them) jeopardize their ability to be the best athletes they can be, potentially damaging their careers. But, as Harriet McBryde Johnson argues in *Disability Visibility*, "choice is illusory in a context of pervasive inequality. Choices are structured by oppression."[21] In a societal context that punishes women, and Black women in particular, for not conforming to an unrealistic heterofeminine ideal, what choice does Rowan really have? When the options available are so limited that it's impossible to imagine oneself as anything but what others expect, what real choice does Kameron have? If every time either of them try to date or go to a restaurant, their bodies become billboards for others to gawk at and shame, is it any wonder that they risk harming their athletic potential for however fleeting of a reprieve?

"Nobody's Got Time for That": Practicality

"I mean, I ain't gonna lie. Damn, my arms are huge," MWSU director of operations Dee Dee, a former athlete herself, tells me, laughing.

"You're very fit though. You don't like that?" I say to her.

"I don't mind them, but like, for instance, I was out this weekend and ugh, and I hate when people be making comments about my arms. But I was out and like, three people stopped me like, 'Damn, what you be doing? Lifting weights?' I was like, 'Why? Stop looking at my arms!'" she explains, still laughing.

I emphasized, "So, you get people on the street, random strangers coming up to you saying your arms are big?"

"I get it all the time," Dee Dee replies. "It's not nothing. I mean I don't want to say I'm ashamed or anything, but I do, I get it all the time. It's constantly. I can't go anywhere without somebody asking me, 'You play sports or a sport?' Like, it don't matter, nowhere."

I then asked her whether she ever tried to emphasize her femininity while she was an athlete. "Nope," Dee Dee responds, matter-of-factly. "Me and my teammates, we didn't care. Because I'm sorry, nobody's got time for that. We would have practice at 6:00 a.m. sometime. Nobody trying to put on no clothes, looking cute."

It is not that Dee Dee doesn't experience the cultural contradiction of women's athleticism—she clearly does. As with Rowan and Kameron, she consistently experiences policing of her body by strangers who make comments about her size or muscle mass and, as a result, she is reminded that she falls outside of the boundaries of normative hetero-femininity. But for Dee Dee and her teammates, the demands of being athletes override their willingness to overemphasize their femininity. Other former athletes I spoke to echoed Dee Dee's sentiments. Some did so while being more critical of those who wore makeup for games or altered training regimens to modify their bodies. Former athlete Tiffanie told me, "I mean yeah, there were definitely girls on the team that would put makeup on and all that stuff like, before games and everything. And I was just like, 'What are you doing? Like, you're gonna sweat, it's gonna come off. What's the point in it?' I never understood that. I don't see the need to do that when you're about to be sweating and running around. Basketball's not a dainty sport. I don't understand it."

"You never felt compelled to put on some lipstick before you played or anything like that?" I asked.

Laughing, Tiffanie replied, "Uh, no. Not at all."

Former athlete and current MWSU coach Sophie, who engages in body-modification gender strategies, tells me that she resists other strategies like wearing makeup because she is not attempting to "look straight" and because such things are fundamentally impractical in a sporting context where athletes sweat. "Like, people putting on makeup before the game. I'm like, 'Why'? You're going to sweat it out. I don't know why people try to be so pretty when they do this. Just because they wanna make it more feminine, you know? I don't understand," she says.

"Did you ever do that?" I ask her.

"No! No!" she exclaims. "I would never do that."

"Why not?" I wonder.

"Because when I play, I don't think about what I look like. I'm not tryin' to look as straight as possible, you know?"

I add, "Did your teammates do that?"

"Yeah, all the time," Sophie replies. "You know, not like full makeup. Some mascara, I mean, a little glitter here and a little, you know. And then they'd sweat it all out, running down." Like Dee Dee and Tiffanie, Sophie resists wearing makeup while playing basketball: it didn't make sense to her if it's all going to run off when you sweat. More than that, however, Sophie sees such behaviors as fundamentally about appearing straight. As someone who identifies as a lesbian, Sophie exempts herself from that pressure.

Rowan expresses a similar distaste for wearing makeup during competition for issues of practicality and because she thinks it's "stupid." "I don't see how people can do that—wear makeup in games," she says. "You sweat too much."

"Right, but why do you think they do?" I wonder.

"I really don't know. I think they just want to look pretty on the court. I wouldn't say I care about my appearance but I'm not gonna go out there looking tacky as hell," Rowan adds.

I ask, "You think that's tacky to wear makeup?"

"No, it's just stupid. It's like, 'What are you doing?' You go out there to get rough, like you don't go out there to 'Oh, I broke a nail. Like, oh, my mascara's smearin'. Like, come on, 'Move!'" she exclaims, furrowing her brow and waving her hand back and forth. Rowan's perspective is interesting in part because while she doesn't wear makeup, she does engage in multiple types of gender strategies. She is very strategic about the size and placement of her many tattoos, attempting to appear "ladylike." She tries to modify her body by altering her weightlifting workouts to decrease her muscle mass and align more closely to the heterofeminine ideal. And she utilizes resistance strategies, criticizing those who wear makeup during games to appear pretty. Rowan's example is meaningful because it illustrates the ways women athletes can not only engage in multiple, even conflicting, gender strategies at the same time but also adopt partial strategies, selecting out the elements they feel are necessary or desirable and discarding the ones they do not.

"Drinking the Kool-Aid": Commitment

Importantly, several athletes I spoke to, including MWSU players and former athletes, spoke of how they engaged in various resistance gender strategies. For some of these athletes, their ideas about gender and their circumstances as elite-level athletes were more aligned, giving them latitude to resist practices like wearing makeup or altering training routines. For others—including those who spoke explicitly of feeling embroiled within the cultural contradiction of women's athleticism and of facing lesbian stereotyping—commitment to their identities as athletes took precedence over their desires to mediate tension using heterofeminizing practices. Some of the athletes who used resistance strategies also engaged in other forms of gender strategies. Using multiple types of gender strategies simultaneously or switching between strategies is common; it illuminates both the complexity of how athletes manage multiple dynamic constraints and also the agility with which they've learned to navigate between these constraints effectively.[22]

Many of the athletes I spoke to engaged in gender strategies of resistance though idealized notions of commitment to their sport. These athletes deeply understood the pressure placed on them to perform heterofemininity and resisted, focusing instead on doing what they felt was necessary to achieve their athletic potential. In some cases, these athletes wanted to or wished they could do things like avoid weight training but felt as though it was their duty to accept their embodiment of masculinity as a consequence of being fully committed to their sport. Former athlete Danielle tells me,

I actually got our team's Iron Woman Award for dedication in the weight room. My strength coach had me on Creatine one summer, and I got my max up, like highest girl max he's ever had. I was not afraid. I loved the weight room. I loved it. I was not afraid of it. But I did have teammates that were. Here I am like, shrugging 45-pound dumbbells and I'm not the biggest girl on the team. The biggest on the team are grabbing like 25s and 30s. And I'm like, "I know you guys can do more than that." "Well, I don't wanna get football player shoulders." And I definitely saw a lot of that. It was annoying.

Unlike her teammates, who were afraid of lifting too much weight and actively chose to lift less than they were capable of, Danielle embraced weightlifting because she enjoyed it. She seemed to revel in her success. Tiffanie told me, "I always wanted to get stronger just because, you know, I'm small, and in order for me to hold my own, I needed to be strong." Tiffanie embraced weightlifting to guarantee she could compete with bigger opponents. Former athlete and coach Jackie articulates a more reluctant form of resistance, buying into notions of commitment that she needed to do "whatever it took" to be better, even if she didn't like the way she looked as a result:

> Yeah, I mean, I think I definitely drank the Kool-Aid in terms of like, I was willing to do whatever, you know, put on weight, muscle. I drank protein shakes four times a day and then I was gonna be better and get on the court. But no, I mean, I definitely, I know I didn't look in the mirror and necessarily liked the way I looked all throughout college. But I can remember just consciously being like, "This is a sacrifice that I'm doing for basketball." And, you know, I wish that wasn't the case. I wish, you know, I was strong but also I don't think it'd be true if I said I loved the way I looked. I definitely was more concerned about, just kind of the incongruency between what was best for me for basketball versus what I wanted to look like outside of basketball. In college, number one, I wanted to do well in basketball. I also wanted to look good for, you know, guys. And for myself as well, but obviously it's also that attraction. You know, over the summer and stuff, getting in the gym and lifting and putting on weight and, you know, sprint work and stuff. That was more what was gonna get me ready for basketball, which is, you know, obviously what I did. But I didn't feel like that was what was gonna make me look my best.

What is so powerful about what Jackie shares is her acknowledgment that she actively chooses to sacrifice her own desires for how she'd like her body to be in favor of putting on weight and muscle in order to be a more successful athlete. She feels that a big, muscular body is not attractive to men, but she was so committed to doing well in basketball that she embraced weight training and tolerated the body that came with it. The cultural contradiction of women's athleticism was something Jackie struggled with, but she resisted engaging in behaviors that would mediate that tension, such as lifting less weight, choosing instead to fully embrace her training.

"Do you ever feel like that, like you don't want to lift weights because you don't want to get big?" I ask MWSU forward Naomi.

"No. Not really," she tells me. "But I mean I build muscle pretty easily, so sometimes when I lift, I'm like, 'Oh my gosh, my shoulders.' Like, I've been shaped up basically since I got here. I've never been skinny. I've been pretty big, but I've never had like, muscle definition really. And I can see it and I'm like, 'Oh my gosh, I'm getting big.' But that never stops me though."

"What are you feeling at that moment?" I add.

Naomi goes on:

I don't know. It's just like, you look in the mirror and if you put on a tank top, you're like, "Oh my gosh, I look like an athlete. Like I look strong." But then again, I'm proud of it at the same time. Of course, you want to put on a dress and feel like you're not like—people don't look at you and be like, "Oh, you're big." But like, it doesn't stop me though. And I know people say that, too, like coming to college, you're probably going to gain at least ten pounds in pure muscle weight. And this is the four years, you're just going to have to deal with it. I mean it's a part of it and that goes back to like, this is a job, and you can't hold back. I mean I don't feel like that should even be in your mindset that you don't want to do certain things because of the way you look. I mean, of course, you may get insecure and stuff or you may not like it, but you better deal with it.

Naomi laughs slightly at the end as she says "you better deal with it," highlighting the very real discomfort many of these athletes face in trying to balance the discrepancy between their ideas about gender and how their bodies should look with their reality and expectations of them as elite-level athletes. When Jackie looked at her body in the mirror in a tank top, it gave her pause—she looks like an athlete, which can be interpreted by others as looking big or masculine, something that she admits can lead to insecurity. Naomi resists partaking in behaviors that prevent her from developing muscle mass, because she sees basketball as her job. Despite her "oh my gosh" moments, Naomi is doing what it takes to be the most successful athlete she can be, even if that means putting on muscle weight and finding ways to deal with the impending changes to her body.

"I mean, now looking back on it, I'm like, 'God, I was huge in college!'" former athlete Elise tells me. She adds:

My strength coach was huge and into Olympic lifting. And we did a ton of Olympic lifting. I don't know how I fit into clothes. I was big. But I never really worried about it. I was working hard, you know. I was on scholarship. I was doing what they told me to do. You know, nobody ever, as far as people outside of the athletic community, nobody ever said anything to me about, you know, like, "Man, you're too big," you know? Anything about me being a girl and having muscles or that kind of thing. Nobody on my team was really like that either. We were always having competitions between one another to see who could squat the most, or whose thighs were bigger. We never really had any of that.

Like Jackie and Naomi, Elise saw basketball as her job and felt committed to doing what she was told to do by her strength coach. Retrospectively, she views her college body as "huge" but didn't at the time feel conflicted by her muscle mass and didn't feel the need to try and curtail its development. Perhaps most importantly, Elise's teammates were also committed to strength training, and she doesn't remember receiving any criticism from others, conditions that certainly made it easier for her and her teammates to fully embrace their athletic bodies. MWSU freshman Kyle approaches weightlifting similarly to Elise and the other former athletes who see basketball as their jobs. "Yeah, I've known females who say, 'Why do we have to lift these weights, I mean my arms are going to get big,'" Kyle tells me. "I have a friend who did that. I said, 'I mean you're not really going to get that big. It's just to get you stronger. I mean you're not ultimately going to see it unless you want to see it.' But I mean, it's kind of crazy," she added.

"What is it about getting big that people don't like?" I wonder.

"I don't know, because personally for myself, I want to get big," Kyle replies. "I do. I mean, I think because of the profession that I'm in basically, basketball, that's a requirement. You don't want to be too small, and then nobody ever knows you're strong. You'd get pushed around."

"So, you're trying to get bigger?" I ask her.

She tells me, "Yeah. I want to get bigger. I want to get more weight on me. I think it's just some people who are kind of self-conscious about getting too big. Like, they'll want to get a little bit bigger, but they don't want to get too big."

"Because then people will think what?" I ask.

Kyle thinks for a second and responds, "Maybe like, probably going back to the gay thing, or it will just be like, it doesn't look right when you throw on a dress. But if you love what you do, it shouldn't matter."

There are several important things shaping Kyle's perspective on weight training. First, she sees basketball as her profession and weight training to gain strength and muscle mass as a requirement of her job that she intends to fulfill. She is also actively trying to get bigger so she doesn't get pushed around on the court. Lastly, Kyle holds firmly to the belief that if you love playing basketball, it shouldn't matter if your body doesn't "look right" in a dress. Kyle is not dismissing that many athletes struggle with lesbian stereotyping or feeling discomfort around their embodiment of masculinity but she, like Naomi, feels as though her commitment to her sport should override those feelings.

"Save That Shit for the Birds": Identity

Several of the athletes who engaged in gender strategies of resistance were queer with nonnormative gender expressions. Their ideologies about gender were not rooted in normative standards of beauty or in heteronormative conceptions about how women should look and behave. Their queer identities and more expansive expressions of gender gave them space to be critical of the cultural contradiction of women's athleticism and of other athletes' attempts to navigate that contradiction through gender strategies such as wearing makeup or altering training protocols. These queer athletes constructed their identities outside of the narrow constraints placed on athletes. In doing so, they were able to more fully embrace their athleticism and embodiments of masculinity as extensions of their other identities. "A lot of people think they look better with makeup on," Prince tells me. "Shit, why put it on for the game and sweat pounds of it off? I never really understood it. But I would never put on makeup whether I was a girlie girl or not, you know? It's just not something I believe in. I believe in natural beauty, you know? All that extra shit, you can save that shit for the birds." Beyond criticizing the practicality of putting on makeup only to sweat it off during a game, Prince is critical of the need to wear makeup in the first place—as she says, she believes in "natural beauty."

Former athletes Rogue and Beckett expressed similar sentiments as Prince. They both invoke their commitment to basketball as reasons why they didn't engage in body modification, but they also express resistance to hegemonic notions of femininity and the corresponding devaluing of women's expressions of masculinity. I asked Rogue whether she ever explicitly tried not to lift weights so that she wouldn't gain muscle mass. "Hell no!" she responds, laughing. "That just wasn't me, you know what I mean? Like, no way. No. I was completely like, 'This is what I gotta do to get better basketball-wise.' Even before that, I made fun of the girls who did that," she added, laughing a bit more. While Rogue invokes her dedication to her sport as her primary justification, she also importantly adds "that just wasn't me" and mentions that even before she was a basketball player, she made fun of other athletes who did those things. Rogue's identity and her ideologies about gender mean that not lifting weights in order to align herself with the heterofeminine ideal was not an option. In fact, it was laughable.

Beckett, a former athlete who played on three different collegiate teams, told me similarly, "I wanted to do whatever I had to do to be the best that I could be. But I do specifically remember teammates saying that, you know, 'I can't do that, my arms are gonna get big and then I'll look like a guy and get all bulky.'"

"Why do you think they didn't want their arms to get big?" I asked.

"I think it goes back to that stereotype about what females are supposed to look like and what's beautiful, and being bulky is not beautiful in some people's eyes," Beckett added. "Not even bulky, I think, just having muscles. Some females, and males, think that muscles make you not seem feminine, which I think is totally wrong. I don't agree with that at all." Beckett's ideologies about gender, and femininity in particular, do not exclude muscular women. She acknowledges the societal expectation that feminine women are supposed to be beautiful and that to be beautiful means not having muscle mass, but she challenges that expectation head-on.

Policing Gender Strategies

The MWSU players engaged in a variety of gender strategies designed to align their own gender ideologies with their circumstances as elite-level athletes. In a sport context where many decisions are made for them, however, they must navigate others' ideologies about gender, namely their coaches, teammates, and the league conference, and the corresponding expectations of them as a result. In my time spent with the MWSU women's basketball team, I witnessed numerous explicit attempts by the coaching staff to police their players' expressions of gender and sexuality in order to enhance their femininity and downplay their masculinity and perceived queerness. I watched as players, in ways both subtle and direct, policed each other's expressions of gender and sexuality in an attempt to "look right." And I saw how the marketing approach of the larger conference promoted a particular kind of hetero-femininity grounded in racialized standards of beauty.

"Just Brush Your Hair": Coaches

It's exactly sixty minutes before the start of the game, and as expected the MWSU players start to make their way to the stadium floor to begin their warm-up exercises. As they begin to assemble on the court, lightly jogging up to half-court and back or stretching in pairs, the coaching staff gathers near the team's bench to discuss last-minute strategy and lineup changes. Rowan Dawson, MWSU star player and team captain, emerges at the top of the stadium steps, quickly and gracefully tip-toeing down, a focused but relaxed look on her face, eyes turned downward. Her hair is pulled loosely back in a low ponytail, and as she descends toward the floor, a few small wisps come loose. Unfazed, she brushes them back and continues toward the floor. Coach King looks up from her clipboard and, after a moment of watching Rowan, exclaims, "Just brush your hair!" The other coaches turn to see what King is referencing. She goes on: "I'm not asking her to do anything fancy. Just brush your hair. Why would she think it's okay to come down like that? We're playing another team. She wants to be All-League? Why does she think that's appropriate?" Without hesitation, assistant coach Johnny Jacobs walks over to Rowan, who has by now joined her teammates in a pregame layup drill, and pulls her to the side. After a brief moment of talking, Rowan walks off the floor toward the MWSU locker room. She comes back several minutes later. This time, her hair is slicked back tightly into her ponytail, not a single strand out of place.

While King uses the language of "appropriateness" to second-hand shame Rowan into redoing her hair, it enforces a certain type of feminine gender expression for someone who otherwise embodies masculinity. There were many other moments throughout the season in which the

MWSU coaching staff expressed opinions and expectations for how the players should look, undoubtedly influencing players' decisions around their clothing, hairstyles, use of makeup, and so forth. For example, during a trip to Hawaii for a large tournament, the team went to a fancy dinner at a local hotel restaurant reserved solely for them. The players were expected to "look nice," so many of them showed up wearing short, flowy dresses with sandals or high heels, makeup, and expertly styled hair. "See, you don't have to look like a basketball team. Y'all look cute!" assistant coach Erin exclaimed excitedly to the players as they entered the hotel lobby. Erin's positive reinforcement of the players' expressions of normative heterofemininity, accompanied by the larger expectation that they dress a certain way, leaves them with little meaningful choice as to how to show up in that space.

I highlight the pregame incident between King and Rowan specifically because it demonstrates how seemingly benign requests, especially when couched under the justification of helping, become pervasive and potentially result in serious, avoidable consequences. Here is Rowan, undoubtedly the MWSU's most talented player and all-around athlete, entering the stadium for competition. She should be focused, arguably, on only one thing in this moment: the game. Instead, her pregame warm-up is interrupted by her coach's request for her to go back to the locker room and redo her hair so that she "looks appropriate." If Rowan was not thinking of her gender expression before, she certainly was after that moment. If she wasn't preoccupied with wondering how her arms looked—something she's expressed dissatisfaction with before—she surely was now. And if she is thinking about those things instead of thinking about, for example, how she will defend her opponent's highest scorer, then she may not perform at her highest level.

Throughout that game I found myself wondering repeatedly whether every time Rowan sprinted down the court past her opponents or drove to the basket and was knocked to the ground for an "and one," she was thinking about her hair. Although I don't know whether this incident impacted Rowan's attention during the game, she was certainly thinking about it for as long as it took her to "fix" her hair during the pregame warm-up. There is ample evidence documenting how discrimination, even in seemingly innocuous instances such as microaggressions, has a negative effect on individuals' mental health and well-being.[23] Even if

Rowan didn't spend one conscious second worrying about her hair during the game, that's not the point. Rowan (or any other MWSU player for that matter) shouldn't have to be thinking about her hair, or any other aspect of her body, during a game unless it is directly related to how she's competing—whether her knee is feeling tight or she's having calf cramps again.

"A couple of years ago, our coaches were always like, 'Make sure you look good all the time,'" Eve tells me when I ask about her pregame routine.

"Look good, meaning have makeup on?" I reply.

"No, [Coach King] was just like, 'Make sure your hair is always done. Make sure you look alright in the face.' Like, 'We don't want you looking all beat up,'" Eve adds.

The messages that the MWSU players received from their coaches was to make sure they didn't look "beat up," code for heterofeminine expressions of gender. Even players, like Eve, who didn't wear makeup needed to be sure their hair was always done. Similarly, previous research has found that coaches attempt to promote feminine and heterosexual images on their teams by encouraging their players to wear makeup or enforcing dress codes.[24]

"That Does Not Look Right": Teammates

Coaches were not the only ones who policed the MWSU athletes' gender expressions; their teammates did as well. Freshman guard Kyle tells me:

> Our team has to be the most, in a way, honest team. Sometimes it's out of control honest. But in an honest way, they'll say, "That does not look right. Don't wear that. Don't do that." And they don't care, especially the upperclassmen, they will not care what they say out their mouth. They will tell you the worst honest truth you want to hear. If someone's hair is looking a hot mess, they'll be the first ones to tell them to take it out right there.

Like King's use of "appropriateness" or Erin's use of "cute," Kyle describes how her teammates use the language of "hot mess" to police one another's expressions of gender.

Prince similarly tells me about how she didn't care about how she looked before games until her teammates stepped in to correct her:

Like we first get here, my hair nappy before the game, everybody like, "You not gonna do shit with your hair?" and I'm like, "Well? Like I don't too much care." And they're like, "People gonna be taking pictures of you, you know what I'm saying? You want to look presentable. You don't want nobody just to come to the game and be like, "Oh my god, look at that kid" kinda thing. But to me, I didn't really care. I'm just like, "Shit, I'm here to play," you know what I'm saying? Like, "Let's go to work" kinda thing. But you know, eventually, you kinda buy into the whole like, expectation. I feel like, with picture day, everybody get like fucking dressed up all crazy and everybody's amazing. People who ain't get their hair done all year, done got their hair done for picture day. You know what I'm saying? But I think that just come with like, what team you're on. Like, my freshman year, all the seniors, all the juniors, like in the mirror, putting on makeup, putting on eyeliner, blush, foundation, mascara, all this stuff for the game and we lookin' around, we all freshman and we like, "What the eff . . ." you know? But then as the years go on, you know, sophomore year, everybody who was in my class, kinda . . . [gesturing putting on makeup and doing hair in a mirror]. Then junior year, we telling everybody, "Girl, you better put you some makeup on." You know, it's just how it worked over time. So I mean, I really don't know why it's done. It's kinda just, I guess, tradition for us.

Gender policing operates in a team context. First, Prince acknowledges that, as a freshman, she was taken aback by her teammates' use of gender strategies such as putting on makeup and doing their hair. As she said, she was there to play, and she wanted to get to work. But over time, the culture of the team—tradition, as she calls it—sank in and she found herself focusing on how her hair looked. Eventually, she policed other players as well.

"Slam Dunk Design": The League

During MWSU's conference tournament at the end of the season, the league distributed a short magazine called "League Extras" along with the standard large conference booklets that highlight the statistics for each participating program. On the cover of "League Extras" is an athlete from Prairie View State, wearing an evening gown, covered in dark eye shadow and lip gloss, and casually holding a basketball. The first page of the magazine boasts the title "Slam Dunk Design—Our Girls Have Style!" and pictures seven athletes from various schools dressed in a variety of styles, some wearing tailored suits and high heels and others wearing short cocktail dresses and diamond necklaces, all with their hair carefully styled and wearing visible makeup. Later in the magazine are players' favorite family recipes for pies or homemade shampoo.

Publication materials like "League Extras," while disconcerting, are not a new occurrence for women's athletics. Scholars have thoroughly documented how media portrayals of women athletes favor presenting them as feminine women over showcasing them as successful athletes— often being photographed in feminine-gendered clothing with their husbands and children.[25] Many collegiate programs have been known to pose women athletes in prom-style dresses or other formal wear for team posters. Moreover, popular magazines like *ESPN* and *Sports Illustrated* have promoted issues featuring professional women athletes in swimsuits, lingerie, or nude, with sensitive body parts covered with sports paraphernalia such as tennis rackets or soccer balls. Professional organizations such as the WNBA had classes for rookie players on makeup, hair, and fashion until 2016.[26] More recently, the WNBA has moved away from such practices and, as part of a larger rebranding strategy, has embraced the diversity within the league around gender and sexuality. In 2019, they entered into a formal partnership with TomboyX, a gender-neutral underwear company.[27] Despite these changes, only a small handful of women who play college basketball will go on to play professionally in the WNBA. We have yet to see similar efforts at the college level to embrace athletes' varied gender identities, expressions, and sexualities in meaningful ways.

"What's Wrong with Bows?": Agency

Many years ago, I taught a Sociology of Sport class to undergraduate students. One of the sections of the course focused on the cultural contradiction of women's athleticism and the gender strategies women athletes use to navigate their "dual and dueling identities." During one class period, I was giving a lecture on gender strategies and showing photos of professional women athletes wearing makeup, jewelry, or ribbons during competition. Photos of Jennie Finch, the former professional softball player, who was known for wearing sparkly headbands or ribbons in her hair, and Tina Thompson, the former WNBA player whose bright red lipstick became her signature, flashed on the screen. After viewing these and other photos, one of the women in the class raised her hand and asked me, "What's wrong with bows?"

My short answer to this student was: nothing. The more nuanced answer, of course, is that what's wrong isn't the bows, or the makeup, or even the body-modification strategies that athletes like Finch, Thompson, or MWSU athletes Rowan or Kameron so heavily relied on. In fact, some might argue that the gender strategies the MWSU players utilized represent specific acts of agency in a sport context that confines and constrains them and within a larger societal structure that leaves them feeling inadequate. As Cecilia Ridgeway argues, women's use of gender strategies within the workplace—what she refers to as "social softeners"—can have meaningful consequences. Such practices "allow very competent women to break through the maze of constraints created by gender status to wield authority."[28] As more women attain power and authority in the workplace, the structures in place to support traditional beliefs about gender begin to erode. The gender strategies used by athletes like Rowan and Kameron are clearly attempts to survive within multiple structures that continually take power from them.

While bows are not wrong, what is wrong is that many of these athletes, especially ones like Rowan or Kameron who embody masculinity through muscle mass, often feel as though they *must* engage in certain gender strategies in order to be seen as feminine and attractive, or, at the very least, not to have their bodies commented on or touched by strangers when they are out in public. Bows themselves are not a problem; the systems that have created a context where women athletes feel like they have to wear them (consciously or unconsciously) are indeed a problem. Gender strategies, even when individually chosen, still solidify stereotypes and require athletes to attempt to conform to idealized standards of beauty if they are to be taken seriously as women.[29]

Gender strategies can certainly represent how individual athletes enact agency in their day-to-day lives, which is important on a micro-level. But such practices do not fundamentally shift the larger structures of White supremacy and heteropatriarchy that are continually working to prevent these athletes from ever feeling enough, with or without makeup, muscles, or the perfect ponytail.

Conclusion

In July 2021, American sprinter Sha'Carri Richardson, a clear favorite for the summer Tokyo Olympic Games, tested positive for marijuana and was suspended for one month. The suspension invalidated her victory in the 100-meter Olympic trials and effectively cost her a spot on the US team. Tweeting about Richardson, sociologist Ben Carrington wrote, "Sport is about power; not the 'power' on the field but the power to decide who plays and who doesn't."[1] Carrington was referencing the rules of the World Anti-Doping Association and World Athletics, which have kept not only Richardson from competing in the Tokyo games but also several other Black women athletes like Caster Semenya, Christine Mboma, Beatrice Masilingi, and CeCe Telfer.[2] Carrington is right: sport is about the power to decide who plays and who does not play. Sport is also, importantly, about the power to dictate the everyday lives of those who play by enforcing unofficial rules related to athletes' identities. Sport, therefore, has the power to decide who can be fully themselves and who cannot. *Denied* is the story of these unofficial rules and of how they construct and constrain women athletes' identities along intersecting lines of race, gender, and sexuality.

My time spent with the Midwest State University (MWSU) women's basketball program affirmed much of what my own experience taught me about college sports—to be a college athlete is physically and mentally grueling. This is especially true at an elite-level program like MWSU where players are competing at the highest level of competition, literally against the best of the best. In these settings, the physical and mental demands of three-mile runs at 5 a.m., multiple workouts a day, constant meal tracking, daily study hall, and late-night weight sessions are commonplace. After my season with MWSU, what became clear to me, and what I have hoped to capture in this book, is that college sports are grueling in another way as well, especially for athletes with marginalized identities. To be an elite-level collegiate woman athlete is to continually navigate a complex landscape of competing expectations around identity. Players are immersed in an institution that is fundamentally shaped by larger societal structures of White supremacy and heteropatriarchy. These structures create specific conditions within the sporting context whereby the identities of women athletes, particularly those athletes who are Black, queer, and/or who embody masculinity, are surveilled and policed. But while athletes like Prince, Rowan, Eve, and Kameron are uniquely impacted, the persistent regulation of women athletes' identities harms everyone because it constrains and contains their full potential both within and beyond the context of sport. These unofficial rules do not ban players from competing in sport altogether, but they are still undoubtedly damaging. Constantly navigating whether they are too much—"too queer," "too muscular," "too sweaty," "too Black"—is a daunting task that requires tremendous mental and emotional energy, energy that could be better employed for sport, academics, relationships, and many other meaningful activities.

Throughout this book, I showed how women athletes are intertwined in a complex ideological web, caught between expectations around gender and sexuality that are informed by histories of White supremacy as well as gendered expectations around women's athletic performance. The athletes are at once constrained by narrow definitions of femininity and womanhood that have been constructed around Whiteness and heterosexuality *and* encouraged to embrace the masculinity of sport—as Coach King would say, to "be bitches and ballers." They are hemmed in by the seemingly unrelenting lesbian stereotyping of women athletes that has existed since women began participating in sport and the perceived cultural contradiction of women's athleticism—the belief that you cannot be athletic and feminine at the same time. As a result, these athletes continuously engage in attempts to reconcile theirs and others' gender ideologies with their circumstances as athletes. I showed how they use gender strategies, some seemingly benign like wearing makeup and others more consequential such as altering workout routines or deciding to stop certain forms of training altogether. These competing and contradictory expectations leave athletes in precarious predicaments, always too much and yet somehow never enough.

Perhaps the most important argument I made throughout this book, however, is that the policing of women athletes' identities around gender and sexuality is racialized. Anti-Blackness works in tandem with heteropatriarchy to differentially shape the experiences of White and Black athletes, in particular, in the sporting context. This is because ideals of femininity and womanhood, which are central to the lesbian stereotyping of women athletes and to the woman/athlete paradox, are centered on Whiteness and, as a result, have always excluded Black women. The policing of women athletes' identities is also especially acute for Black, queer, and/or masculine-presenting players where ideologies about race, gender, and sexuality collide to frame their bodies as illegible and dangerous. Explicitly and implicitly, these athletes are told to "tone it down," to modify their dress and behavior, and to choose activities to be more palatable for prospective players and their parents and, therefore, more profitable for the program. Straight, Black athletes like Rowan and Kameron who otherwise embody masculinity through their muscle mass are sent messages from others that they are too bulky or manly to be thought of as heterosexually attractive, feminine women. Such unforgiving and unrelenting social commentary leads some of them, like Rowan, to drastically alter their workout regimens or stop them completely to try to move closer to an idealized standard of beauty that is both wholly unattainable and detrimental to their performance in sport.

What Does Change Look Like?

As I have outlined throughout *Denied*, the institution of sport is a context that perpetuates structural inequities around race, gender, and sexuality at the micro-level.[3] And, yet, it remains an institution full of possibility and hope. There is "a long, albeit small, tradition of individuals who have used the playing field to advocate for political and social justice."[4] The last several years in particular have demonstrated the tremendous power of athlete activism in leading social change efforts. Women's National Basketball Association (WNBA) players have been especially instrumental in shining a spotlight on social justice issues even before Colin Kaepernick famously took a knee during the national anthem in 2016.[5]

> The breadth of action among W.N.B.A. players is unparalleled among professional sports leagues. They include singular efforts like Seim-

one Augustus's opposition to a ballot measure in Minnesota aimed at amending the state constitution to ban same-sex marriage, Maya Moore's basketball sabbatical to focus on criminal justice reform and Natasha Cloud's fight against gun violence. Often they include unified undertakings, such as the league's dedicating the 2020 season to Breonna Taylor, a Black woman who was killed by the police, and the players' collective stand against the co-owner of the Atlanta Dream, Senator Kelly Loeffler, Republican of Georgia, who had criticized their support for the Black Lives Matter movement. This off-season, many players have quickly transitioned from playing basketball to focusing on encouraging people to vote.[6]

Many Black and queer WNBA players have pointed out how their identities and their own experiences with marginalization have been central to their activism. "We are a walking protest at all times as a W.N.B.A. athlete," said Mistie Bass, who in 2016 took a knee during the national anthem while playing with the Phoenix Mercury. "If you think about it, we have so many different stigmas. We're just constantly in the fight. I don't think we have ever not been in a fight for equality, for justice."[7] Amira Rose Davis similarly argues that

> the WNBA is a league that is gritty by necessity. It catches so much hate because it's "too Black, too queer." It's full of women. And I think that it draws the ire of a lot of people. And so they as a league have always been fairly outspoken, because it's the only way to be. Their very presence on a court, their very insistence that they have the right to play and make a living by playing is a political act in and of itself. So I think they were already kind of primed towards action.[8]

Women's National Collegiate Athletic Association (NCAA) teams have been similarly engaged in advancing issues of racial justice and gender equity. In the 2021 NCAA tournament, the Notre Dame women's basketball team wore custom shoes and pregame shirts to promote racial justice featuring designs by a local Jamaican artist. The University of Michigan women's basketball team wore the slogan "Wolverine Against Racism" on their uniforms and warm-up jerseys. And the Texas El

Paso women's basketball team created a Black Lives Matter video featuring every one of its players. During the 2021 NCAA tournament, University of Oregon player Sedona Prince took to social media to expose the abysmal disparities between the men's and women's workout facilities, COVID-19 testing services, and meals offered to players. "I got something to show y'all," Prince opens with in the video. "So, for the NCAA March Madness, the biggest tournament in college basketball for women, *this* is our weight room," she says, pointing to a single rack of dumbbells. "Lemme show y'all the men's weight room," she continues, panning to a massive room filled with high-end weight-training equipment. She ends the video saying, "If you aren't upset about this problem, then you're a part of it."[9]

NCAA athletes are also speaking out against abusive coaching tactics. Texas Tech women's basketball coach Marlene Stollings was fired after twelve players left the program, alleging a toxic culture of "fear, anxiety, and depression" as well as sexual harassment by its strength and conditioning coach, Ralph Petrella.[10] Niecee Nelson, the women's basketball coach at Purdue Fort Wayne, was fired after twenty-two people, including players, parents, and team staff, alleged physical, emotional, and mental abuse.[11] Head women's basketball coaches at Syracuse, the University of Detroit Mercy, and the University of Florida have all been fired after similar allegations of bullying, harassment, physical and emotional abuse, and toxic environments. Athletes' willingness to speak out against abuse—perhaps buoyed by the increased awareness of sexual assault through the impact of #MeToo—is an important step in shifting the status quo in women's sports. Behavior that has been normalized for years will be less likely to flourish as more and more athletes share their experiences and demand accountability. Eliminating the "bad apples" within individual programs will not on its own change the culture of sports for women athletes. As Cynthia Enloe argues,

> The "bad apple" explanation always goes like this: the institution is working fine, its values are appropriate, its internal dynamics are of a sort that sustain positive values and respectful, productive behavior. Thus, according to the "bad apple" explanation, nothing needs to be reassessed or reformed in the way the organization works; all that needs to happen

to stop the abuse is to prosecute and remove those few individuals who refused to play by the established rules.[12]

Focusing on "bad apples" allows such scandals to shock us and "to be contained as aberrant, certainly, but isolated" as opposed to a natural outgrowth of the nature of sport itself, an institution steeped in many of the characteristics of toxic masculinity.[13]

Moreover, there is a significant difference between the absence of an abusive culture and an empowering and supportive culture. It is possible for coaches to not abuse their players physically, emotionally, or sexually while still not constructing a climate in which their players are flourishing; a lack of abuse does not equal well-being. Embracing athletes' identities, especially if they are marginalized, rather than seeing them as potentially detrimental, would go a long way toward cultivating a sporting context where athletes can thrive, personally and athletically. What would it look like, for example, if the presence of queer players on a team was framed as a positive for recruits (and their families) rather than something to be hidden? Or what if athletic departments invested in campaigns to educate their communities about the harmful effects of lesbian stereotyping of women athletes (or of athletes in general)? These are very real, practical things that programs can do to make meaningful change within an otherwise stubborn institution.

Changes in the institution of sport or within individual programs must, of course, coincide with broader societal shifts. As Maggie Hagerman argues, "This is not easy work, and it also may never be possible to solve structural problems entirely through individual acts."[14] Changing negative recruiting practices at MWSU, for instance, can only go so far if there are not corresponding shifts in the perceptions of and acceptance for LGBTQ people broadly and corresponding actions taken to eliminate gender- and sexuality-based discrimination. Upsettingly, as of August 2022, state legislatures across the country have introduced nearly 240 anti-LGBTQ bills, with the majority taking particular aim at transgender people, including trans athletes. The Mississippi Fairness Act, for example, "will bar trans students attending public schools in the state from participating in sports according to their gender identity and mandate that they do so according only to their gender assigned at birth."[15]

A Minnesota bill would allow any trans girl or woman who tried out for or participated in girls' or women's sports to be charged with a misdemeanor. Another, in Florida, titled the "Fairness in Women's Sports Act," initially contained provisions that would force some children to undergo a "routine sports physical examination" to inspect their genitals, genetic makeup, and testosterone levels. Lawmakers have since removed the genital inspections; the bill passed in both chambers [in 2021] and awaits the governor's signature.[16]

Such bills are a clear indication that change "does not inevitably mean movement toward equality. . . . [C]hange can mean the creation of sophisticated adaptations in defense of the status quo."[17]

Efforts at all levels—individual, institutional, and societal—can indeed create meaningful change at places like MSWU and within the institution of sport as a whole. It will require, among other things, a fundamental shift in how we think about what it means to be an elite-level athlete, and a commitment to valuing athletes as people first—with all of their complex identities—and as athletes second. It will mean supporting athlete activists and encouraging efforts to cultivate sport as a site for social change, rather than an institution that merely reproduces societal inequities. With this paradigm shift, a genuine and fundamental change in the institution of sport, athletics can become a context that embraces and encourages authenticity in all of its forms, and it might serve as a model of radical acceptance for other institutions to learn from.

* * *

The MWSU women's basketball season ended in late March, with them losing to their opponent by a handful of points in the second round of the NCAA tournament. Shortly after, Rowan Dawson was selected in the first round of the WNBA draft. Her teammates, Sara Parker and Kyle Kingsley, would go on to also have careers in the WNBA in subsequent years. Eve Callaway went on to work in the corporate sector, Kameron James works in public policy, and Tiffany Davidson is a lawyer. Naomi Pierce and Karolina Markovich followed their MWSU careers with professional ones internationally. Prince Davis became a police officer and Jizeal Lane became a teacher.

I think often of my time at MWSU and the players who shared so much of their lives with me. Wherever they are now, my hope is that they spend more time thinking of themselves as the talented, capable people that they are and less time wondering what they lack. I hope they are embracing their muscles, reveling in their queerness, and celebrating their Blackness—never too much and always enough.

ACKNOWLEDGMENTS

This book was made possible by the support, guidance, and love of so many people, including those named here and the countless others whom I have learned from and been inspired by but who are not formally named.

First and foremost, I owe tremendous gratitude to the Midwest State University athletes, coaches, and staff who invited me into their community and made me feel like a part of the team. Their willingness to share their lives, experiences, stories, and countless other moments with me—good, bad, and ugly as they say—for almost an entire year is the foundation upon which this book has been written. If I have one hope for this book, it is that I have represented them in ways they would believe to be true. I also owe sincere thanks to the many former athletes who agreed to be a part of this project, sharing with me their experiences of such an important, and often difficult, time in their lives. This book was made better by each and every one of their stories.

I am so fortunate to have brilliant friends and colleagues who have contributed to this book in various ways throughout the years. They have sent me citations, talked through ideas with me (often repeatedly), and listened to me complain or pontificate (often both). Thank you to Maggie Hagerman, Liz Alexander, and Donna Troka for helping me make this work so much better than it otherwise would have been. I am also grateful for my family and friends who have cheered me on as I have worked on this book, even if they didn't exactly know it. Thank you to my parents, my siblings, the Goodman family, and to Georgiann Davis, Emily Kropp, Lydia Prusinowski, Jes Hand, Sara Abelson, Linda Galib, Morgan Madison, Jody Ahlm, Shay Phillips, Jeni Meresman, Jordan Turner, Angela Walden, and Lisa Berube.

I have benefited from the insight of many intellectual mentors who have challenged my thinking and writing in incredibly important ways. Thank you to Tyrone Forman, Beth Richie, and Cathy Johnson for helping shape the early stages of this book; to Michelle Boyd for graciously providing me coaching during the middle; and to Maggie Andersen for offering critical and encouraging feedback and editing during the latter stages. Thank you to Maria Krysan, a longtime mentor and friend, for always encouraging me to push forward and showing me the value of the weekend writing retreat. Your unwavering support throughout the years, but especially during the final stages of this process, has been invaluable to me. I am also deeply appreciative for the several anonymous reviewers who provided thoughtful feedback, the editorial team at New York University Press, and my editor, Ilene Kalish, who believed in this book from the first time we had a conversation about it.

This book was barely an idea when I first met Amanda Lewis and it would still be just that if it were not for her. Amanda has been my mentor, friend, and biggest fan from the beginning. The ways I have benefited from her wisdom, generosity, and encouragement are too many to count. Thank you for reading countless drafts, talking through ideas, holding me accountable, and guiding me through this entire process. I would have given up on writing this book a long time ago if it weren't for your belief in me. Thank you so much.

While not often listed in book acknowledgments (for possibly obvious reasons), I owe special thanks to my animal companions, Dooley, Dillinger, Leonard, and Goose. They have been by my side, literally, every moment I have spent writing this book. They may never know what it has meant to me, but I do.

Finally, this book is dedicated to my partner and in-house editor, Leah Goodman. While I wrote most of this book before I knew her, I wrote the best of it after I did. Thank you for being such a constant, unconditional source of hype and for getting "hardcore" when I needed it. Your brilliance made this book better, and your humor and love made getting through it easier. I am forever grateful.

Admittedly, I found myself at Midwest State University (MWSU) out of luck. It's not that I didn't work hard to gain access to the program; I did. I made phone calls, sent emails, and hand-delivered letters, all in the hopes that I could get someone to invite me in. But my hard work isn't what got me into the team manager role at MWSU. When everything I tried had come up short, I called my former collegiate coach asking for help. Coincidentally, he knew assistant coach Grant Williams at MWSU and called him on my behalf. A few weeks later, I had a meeting with Coach Williams and about a month after that, I received a call from assistant coach Johnny Jacobs telling me that the project had been approved. Johnny then called back a couple of weeks later with bad news; one of MWSU's top athletic directors (ADs) did not approve of the project. He didn't tell me much as to why, but he felt certain that the project wouldn't be moving forward and that it wouldn't help to contact the AD directly. I did it anyway. I requested a meeting with the AD and brought my advisor with me. As the AD was a former collegiate athlete herself, we connected quickly and talked for an hour about various aspects of the project—why I wanted to conduct a study like this, issues of confidentiality, players' time commitments, and how much would be revealed about MWSU. Three weeks later, Johnny calls me back: the project has been re-approved. All of this is to say that access to MWSU was not easy. The approval process took almost five months and was ultimately a result of persistence, personal connections, and lived experience. As a former collegiate basketball player, I had connections to coaches that would not have existed otherwise, and I was able to talk about my own experiences as an athlete as a way to not only explain my project, but also ease concerns over having an "outsider" in the locker room. Connections to coaches gave me credibility and my status as a former athlete gave me leverage and insider status.

Importantly, the process of gaining access to MWSU was not a one-time event. Throughout the nine months I spent with the MWSU women's basketball team, I experienced numerous instances of gatekeeping. I was allowed to attend practices and games—indeed, that was part of my job as team manager—and, after much insistence, weightlifting sessions. I was not allowed, however, to attend classes with the players. The one time I tried attending classes with Rowan, Johnny Jacobs swiftly intervened, arguing that my presence could draw suspicion of providing extra help or cheating onto the players and the program. Sometimes I was blocked from watching film (tapes of previous MWSU games and/or games of upcoming opponents) while other times I was permitted. In some instances, I was told "no" then "yes" in a matter of a few minutes, always by Johnny, my direct supervisor. After the first few uncomfortable encounters with Johnny, I attempted to circumvent him by simply attending what I wanted to attend, without asking, since asking almost always brought with it an immense amount of anxiety for Johnny and awkward interactions between us. This strategy worked for a short while until he began arbitrarily calling me out of important team meetings and, on numerous occasions, literally intercepting me as I walked into team gatherings to have me do minor tasks such as inflate basketballs or fold towels.

After months of effort to gain access to MWSU, I learned quickly that access did not mean all-encompassing access. Rather, access at MWSU meant tightly controlled, circumscribed access that could change at any moment. This point is both methodologically important as well as substantively relevant, as these instances of gatekeeping illuminate the nature of hierarchy within MWSU as well as the institutional anxiety that exists within elite-level programs broadly. Top-tiered programs like MWSU and their athletes are under constant scrutiny by the National Collegiate Athletic Association (NCAA), the media, and the public. Protecting the images of the players, the program, and the university became almost as important as winning games. I became team manager of the MWSU team, but I was first and foremost a researcher, and these instances of gatekeeping were clear reminders that I was and would remain an insider/outsider.

THE TEAM

At the time of data collection, the MSWU women's basketball team comprised fifteen players and seventeen staff members. The staff consisted of seven coaches (including the head coach, several assistants, and the director of basketball operations), two full-time academic advisors, two team managers (myself and an MWSU undergraduate student), one film coordinator, one athletic trainer and one student-apprentice trainer, one team physician, one strength and conditioning coach, and one program administrator. The team also had at its disposal a number of other relevant volunteers and booster-club members who played both major and minor roles in the team's daily functions but were not officially considered staff. For example, one booster-club member volunteered her time to assist in tutoring players and often traveled with the team (sometimes at her own expense) to away games and tournaments to assist in various as-needed capacities (i.e., handing out pompoms to fans, setting up food for the team's pregame meal, etc.).

MY ROLE

For nine months I spent almost every day with the MWSU team, from the first day of preseason workouts in early August until their end-of-season banquet in May. While I was introduced to the team as a researcher, my official job title was volunteer team manager. In this role, my primary responsibilities were to set up the gym for practices and other practice-related duties: turning on lights; bringing out equipment from the locker room; running the clock and taking statistics during practice; cleaning up the gym and the locker room afterward; and picking up practice clothes and doing the laundry for that day. My responsibilities on game days were more involved and included setting up and cleaning up the MWSU pregame meal and hanging each player's uniform at their locker; setting up the opposing team's and the referee's locker room with towels, water and ice buckets, coolers full of Gatorade, bottled water, and soda; setting up the MWSU bench (towels on each player's assigned chair); managing equipment for the game (e.g., basketballs, clipboards, dry-erase markers); and preparing the MWSU uniforms for the professional laundry service after the game. I also assisted in various other functions that did not necessarily occur on a daily basis. For instance, before each road trip to an away game, every person traveling (players, coaches, other staff) was provided with a bag full of drinks and snacks to supplement their daily meals. These bags had to be prepared the night before each trip and be on the bus or charter plane on the day of travel. I also occasionally drove players to and from their classes, practice, or dorms.

Working as team manager was at times mundane, particularly during late nights in the locker room washing players' dirty socks and sports bras. But, more importantly, my role as team manager provided me with a level of access to these players' lives that I would have never been able to witness otherwise. The level of intimacy I was afforded as a result of being a member of the team, rather than just an outside observer, was not available to the average fan, reporter, friend, or parent. Being in this role also built trust between me and the players and coaches at MWSU. I was in it, just as they were—committed to supporting the daily operations and ultimate success of the program.

INSIDER/OUTSIDER STATUS

My insider status as a former collegiate basketball player was beneficial beyond the access process. Being able to draw on my own experiences as an athlete allowed me to form connections with the players that I would not have been able to do otherwise. As a former player, I was able to commiserate with the players about the cruelty of "suicides"—an unfortunately named running drill in which you sprint from the baseline to the near free-throw line, half court, and the far free-throw line and back before ending up at the other baseline, usually in under thirty seconds—as they sat in their ice baths after a long, grueling conditioning workout. I was able to connect with the players as I shared my own stories about how my coach used to set up garbage cans on the baseline and make us run until we puked. Swapping "war stories" about the everyday experiences and challenges of being an athlete became an exercise in bonding and trust-building. One of the players I became closest to, senior captain Eve, spent the entire season rehabilitating from an anterior cruciate ligament (ACL) tear she experienced during the previous year. Sitting with her in the training room before and after practices while she received treatments, I could empathize with her struggle because, as I showed her the scars on my own knee, I went through the exact same thing many years before. While possessing the literal battle scars of college athletics was perhaps not necessary, I do believe that our shared experience allowed us to gain a sense of rapport that would have been difficult to create otherwise.

While having insider knowledge and experience was crucial, I always also remained an outsider, and my age, race, and sexuality highlighted that outsider status. I was several years older than the players, making it difficult to connect to their contemporary cultural reference points in the same way I could connect to their experiences with basketball. Moreover, as a White person in a context in which all but one of the players were Black, my racial identity was a point of difference. There were times, for instance, where the players would be telling stories and make mention of "all White people" or "that White girl from Northeast State" and turn to me and say, "Sorry, Michelle. No offense." While I took no offense to these comments, the moments when the players explicitly acknowledged our racial difference highlighted my outsider-within status. While the players felt free to tell stories in front of me, their after-the-fact apologies for potentially offending me was a reminder that, despite having been an athlete, I would never truly share their experiences. Lastly, being out and visibly queer (a result of my gender expression) was something that made me both an insider and outsider, depending on the situation. For instance, talking with other queer players about bars, clubs, and girlfriends may have deepened my connection with them while simultaneously putting distance between some straight players and myself. Ultimately, my insider/outsider status more than likely opened up some doors while keeping others partially closed.

ETHNOGRAPHY

While there exists a spectrum of ways to conduct ethnographic fieldwork, I chose to employ participant observation by immersing myself into the daily lives of the MWSU women's basketball team. It was important to me to be a part of the athletes' everyday lived experiences so that I could see how their identities shaped those experiences in real time, from moment to moment, in big ways and small.

There are a number of practical limitations attached to this type of ethnographic research and they are worth outlining briefly. Observation and description are complex, and the representation of the "reality" of the social world under study is always reflexive. Participant observers must acknowledge that any and all descriptions of observations are always partial and selective.[1] During the course of an ethnography, you can observe countless events, interactions, and other commonplace activities. Deciding to focus specifically on a certain subset of those events and interactions is both theoretically and culturally driven and means that a number of other important observations will be ignored. Moreover, the representation of what is observed is not merely an objective description of reality. Ethnographic representation, rather, is a process of constructing reality through observation. As Robert Emerson notes, "An ethnographic description can never be an exact, literal picture of some 'thing' such as an event or social action. It is always a theory informed *re-presentation* of that 'thing,' a rendering of the event that transforms it in particular ways (e.g., by presenting 'what happened' in purposive, partial, and selective ways)."[2]

By transforming the event through the process of deciding what and how to observe and describe it, the ethnographer is an active participant in the construction of its reality. Events and experiences are constantly being shaped by the individuals involved within them and then reshaped in the process of their retelling. As a participant observer as MWSU, I brought with me into the field a series of theoretically driven research questions that I was interested in pursuing. As a result, my interactions with and observations of the team were always filtered through the lens of those questions. The things I focused on observing carefully compared to those that I, however unintentionally, overlooked were informed by those same questions. Ultimately, my representations of MWSU—its players, coaches, and events—are a compilation of many people's experiences, interactions, perspectives, and decisions, including my own.

Conducting ethnographic research also brings about important ethical issues—informed consent, deception, and confidentiality—that are sometimes challenging to negotiate during the course of data collection.[3] When I first joined the MWSU women's basketball program, I was introduced as a volunteer team manager interested in observing and recording the day-to-day activities of the team for a research project. I explained the purpose of my project to the team and gained their verbal consent to make observations. Because I was involved with the program for an extended period of time, I occasionally reminded the players and coaches of my dual roles so that they could opt out of participation if they wanted to. Gaining continuous consent was also important to avoid issues of deception. While at no time did I consider concealing my purpose for being involved with the team, it was important for me to be clear about the focus of my project. Often, players would come up to me and ask what I was observing, what I had written down, and other questions related to my research. It was not uncommon for me to get a question like "So what are you looking for again?" or "Observe anything good today?" These moments, while sometimes awkward, represented opportunities for continued informed consent, avoiding deception, and initiating some informal interviewing.

Being immersed in the daily operations of the MWSU program as team manager made data collection challenging. Taking field notes, one of the most important aspects of ethnographic data collection, was particularly difficult because my responsibilities required me to be both physically and mentally present every second. For example, while the logistics of running the clock during practice became routine very quickly, I had to remain alert at all times so as to never let the buzzer sound at the wrong moments, one of Coach King's pet peeves. Attempting to take notes on an interaction during practice meant risking losing focus on the task at hand and navigating the consequences. During one practice, I accidentally let the buzzer go off while King was lecturing the team. As the loud blare of the buzzer echoed through the stadium's rafters, King turned to Johnny, pointed at me, and screamed, "If she doesn't know how to work that damn thing, get me someone who can!" Needless to say, I didn't let the buzzer go off inadvertently again. At no time during the course of my data collection was I able to sit back and write notes while observing the team. I depended heavily on other strategies such as jottings—quick notes taken whenever possible (often in the bathroom during a water break) that I could expand on later. Ultimately, it was important to me to prioritize my role as team manager in order to gain the trust of the players and the coaching staff and become accepted as a true member of the team.

INTERVIEWS

Throughout the ethnography, I conducted brief, informal interviews with the MWSU players and coaches—an occasional follow-up question or two in the course of our regular day-to-day interactions. Following the ethnography, I conducted thirty-two semistructured, in-depth interviews; eighteen of those interviews were with MWSU players, coaches, or staff and fourteen were with former NCAA Division I women athletes, whom I included as a comparison group to the MWSU players. Twelve of the fourteen MWSU players and six of the thirteen staff members agreed to be formally interviewed. Perhaps the most significant omission from this group of staff is Coach King herself. I attempted several times to set up an interview with King through her assistant but was given various reasons each time as to why she was unavailable (e.g., traveling, too busy). I also set up interviews with assistant coaches Grant Williams and Johnny Jacobs but both interviews were canceled and never rescheduled.

The in-depth interviews provided firsthand accounts of the athletes' own experiences and allowed me to explore points of contradiction between what I observed during my time as team manager and what was being shared. For example, if I asked a particular athlete whether she felt like she ever did anything explicitly to avoid weight training and she said she did not, I could then compare that to what I observed her doing during my time as team manager. Contradictions shine a light on how the larger structures of race, gender, and sexuality operate—often without our knowing—in our everyday lives. These structures become so deeply ingrained within our collective imaginations that we think of them and talk about them as essential parts of who we are and what we do. It is also worth mentioning for methodological and substantive purposes that most of the MWSU players I interviewed admitted that had I not spent the season with them and formed relationships with them, they would have been unlikely to volunteer to be interviewed. Because they knew me, they agreed to be a part of an interview and felt comfortable talking with me about various aspects of their lives. Having established rapport with the players through my role as team manager acted as a gateway for accessing later interviews with them.

CONTENT ANALYSIS

In addition to the ethnographic and interview portions of this project, I also include data gathered from content analysis of popular culture materials in order to provide a broader historical and cultural context to my data. Various forms of difference such as gender, race, and sexuality are structural in nature, and our commonsense understandings of them are continually constructed within popular culture. Therefore, I examined and analyzed a vast amount of newspaper and magazine articles, blogs, videos, and images to situate my findings within the appropriate cultural context. For instance, while understanding that women athletes at MWSU engage in gender strategies may be interesting in and of itself, placing such behavior within a broader historical and cultural context that perpetuates the notion of the modern woman athlete as strong *and* sexy allows us to more fully understand how such behavior persists and also how we might approach efforts toward change. The data from this content analysis are interspersed throughout the chapters to add even more breadth and depth to the experiences of the women athletes in this study.

DATA ANALYSIS

The data analysis for this project was fundamentally inductive in nature. Throughout the course of my participant observation, I examined field notes and wrote memos about major themes and patterns that emerged. Doing this not only allowed me to organize and make sense of what I was experiencing on a daily basis but also served to inform how I would proceed with future data collection. I utilized the important issues I was witnessing as a stepping-stone off of which I wrote my interview guide. I was also able to bring in specific examples from my memos about incidents I observed and wanted the players' perspectives on. For example, one of the patterns that emerged early on from my memos of observing practice was how much the policing of gender through physical appearance came from the coaching staff, particularly Coach King. Drawing from this theme, I was able to construct a series of questions about appearance and whether the players felt pressured to look or act a certain way. Rather than merely asking about this in my interviews, however, I was able to recall specific instances in which I personally observed this type of policing happening and then ask my interviewees to respond to those observations.

HINDSIGHT

My time with the MWSU women's basketball team was methodologically challenging and at times personally difficult. But it was, above all else, a tremendous privilege. The entire team—even Johnny, however warily—accepted me and shared their lives with me every day I walked into the gym. I felt like part of the team. Their successes felt like mine, and I shared their heartbreak after their season-ending loss in the NCAA tournament. While I did not maintain relationships with any of the MWSU players or staff, I still occasionally check up on them through social media, curious about what and how they are doing. I probably always will.

NOTES

AUTHOR'S NOTE
1 Weisman and Bensinger (2022).

A NOTE ON LANGUAGE
1 Categories that were once included in the 1850 census for race, such as "mulatto," are no longer used today.
2 A. Lewis (2004), 624.
3 Ibid., 626.
4 Ewing (2020).
5 Ibid.

INTRODUCTION
1 Williams (2015).
2 Robson (2012).
3 ESPN (2014).
4 Bieler (2017).
5 Johnston (2016).
6 For additional analyses on the racial and gendered dimensions of the Williams sisters' experiences, see Douglas (2005, 2012); J. Hobson (2003); Leonard (2017); McKay and Johnson (2008); Messner (2002); and Schultz (2005).
7 Kilgannon (2001).
8 *Fairness and Accuracy in Reporting* (2007). Rosenberg was fired by Don Imus for his remarks but was reinstated after he issued an apology. Ironically, six years later, Don Imus would himself be fired from his show by referring to the mostly Black Rutgers women's basketball team as "nappy headed hoes" (ibid.).
9 Rodrick (2013).
10 Rankin (2014), 25.
11 M. Bailey (2021), 1.
12 Moyazb (2014).
13 For more detail on such commentary see Leonard (2012a).
14 Floyd (2012).
15 Leonard (2017), 177.
16 Ibid.

17 The Combahee River Collective statement is as follows: "The most general statement of our politics at the present time would be that we are actively committed to struggling against racial, sexual, heterosexual, and class oppression, and see as our particular task the development of integrated analysis and practice based upon the fact that the major system of oppression are interlocking. The synthesis of these oppressions creates the conditions of our lives" (Taylor (2017: 15).

18 Cooper (2017), 152.

19 Richie (2012), 128.

20 Scraton (2001).

21 For notable exceptions, see Anderson and McCormack (2010); Cahn (2015); and Leonard (2017).

22 Richie (2005). In academic scholarship, to queer something means to look for places to challenge or question previously held assumptions about a given topic and bring in new insights from outside disciplines to better understand a situation. In this case, queering sport scholarship means centering the experiences of Black women athletes and, importantly, to acknowledge how race, gender, and sexuality are equally important in shaping their experiences.

  Feminist sport scholars have noted the dearth of intersectional sport scholarship, particularly when it comes to integrating race into analyses of gender and sexuality in sport. Most of these scholars have made mention of the need to do such research, but they have stopped short of carrying it through.

23 Midwest State University (MWSU) is a pseudonym, created to protect the identities of those involved.

24 All names used in this book are pseudonyms, usually chosen by those involved. Every person interviewed for this book was given the opportunity to choose their own pseudonym. If they did not want to choose a pseudonym or were involved in the ethnography but not interviewed, I chose a pseudonym for them.

25 See the appendix for a full explanation of the methodology used in this study.

26 For research on middle and high school girls, see Enke (2005) and Malcolm (2003). For exceptions that study collegiate women athletes, see Blinde and Taub (1992a, 1992b); Krane et al. (2004); and Ross and Shinew (2008).

27 National Collegiate Athletic Association (2021).

28 Blinde and Taub (1992a; 1992b).

29 For instance, Black men make up most of the athletes in men's professional sports like the National Football League and the National Basketball Association but are significantly underrepresented when it comes to coaching, management, and ownership positions.

30 Messner (1992).

31 T. Collins (2013), viii.

32 Hartmann (2000); Messner (1988).

33 Neal (2013).

34 Pascoe (2007).

CHAPTER 1. "WE SHOULD GET YOU SKIRTS"

1 All names included in the book are pseudonyms.

2 Some of the direct quotations in this narrative were drawn from other related events in which Coach King was addressing her players (e.g., watching film or practice). I chose to combine some of those select quotes with the ones from this particular event in order to create a more comprehensive account of common and recurring coach-player interactions at MWSU.

3 During the time of data collection, MWSU was ranked among the top twenty-five women's basketball programs in the United States.

    Coach King's general coaching style involved frequent, violent verbal attacks on her players. During practices, for instance, she could be heard telling players that she was going to "punch them in the face" or "shove that ball up your ass."

    A number of studies have documented how sports culture can be emotionally, physically, and sexually abusive to athletes. See, for example, Brackenridge (1997) and Stirling and Kerr (2008a, 2008b, 2013, 2014). Sexual abuse of elite women athletes has received more attention recently due to the revelation that Larry Nassar, former doctor for Michigan State University athletes and the US Women's Olympic Gymnastics team, sexually abused more than 150 girls and women over a twenty-year span under the guise of medical treatment; he was sentenced in 2018 to 175 years in prison. For a firsthand account of her experience of abuse by Nassar, see Denhollander (2019).

4 Holt (1995).

5 Lewis and Diamond (2015), 5.

6 See Amanda Lewis's (2003a, 2003b; Lewis and Diamond [2015]) work on schools as race-making institutions.

7 Wacquant (2002).

8 Machado (2019).

9 Dworkin and Messner (2002), 27.

10 Acker (1992), 567.

11 Messner (2002), 66.

12 This is both a perception (see Shakib and Dunbar [2002]) and a reality in that many women's sports have different rules and equipment than their male counterparts. Women's basketballs are smaller than men's, for example, and the distance from the three-point line to the basket is closer for women than for men.

13 Hartmann (2003), 452.

14 A. Lewis (2003a).

15 *The Cut* (2018).

16 Connell (1987, 2020).

17 According to Connell (1987), for a masculinity to be hegemonic, it has to be centered on a relationship of dominance. Hegemonic masculinity is centered on men's domination over women as well as certain men's domination of other men. Connell argued, therefore, that femininity cannot be hegemonic since women do

not wholly dominate men and "women have few opportunities for institutionalized power relations over other women" (Pyke and Johnson 2003, 35). However, Pyke and Johnson (2003) argue that such a claim ignores how gender intersects with other axes of difference such as race and class. When multiple axes of power are taken into consideration, it is possible to see how, for example, the femininities of White, upper-class women are privileged whereas the femininities of women of color are subordinated. Thought of as the norm to which other femininities are compared and considered deviant, White, upper-class, heterosexual femininity is thus considered hegemonic.

18 Whether such an approach works is questionable. Mazer and colleagues (2013) found that college athletes were significantly less motivated by verbally aggressive coaches than those with affirming communication styles. Also see Kavanagh et al. (2017) and Stirling and Kerr (2013).

19 Ridgeway's use of gender as a cultural framing device is similar to the work of West and Zimmerman, who argue that gender is constructed primarily through our interactions with others. It is in this interactional space that we come to simultaneously define not only our own but also others' gender. In this way, gender can be seen as a "routine, methodical, and recurring accomplishment" (West and Zimmerman 1987, 126).

20 Ridgeway (2011), 44.

21 Prentice and Carranza (2002); Ridgeway (2011).

22 Ridgeway (2011).

23 Rudman et al. (2012), 165.

24 Sullivan et al. (2018), 2.

25 Yavorsky (2016), 957.

26 Schilt (2011).

27 "Dominance penalty" is from Schilt (2011). According to Rudman and colleagues (2012), women and men engage in backlash at similar rates and for the same primary motive—maintaining the gender hierarchy.

28 Dicaro (2017).

29 Ibid.

30 Mosbergen (2015).

31 Payne (2015).

32 Schmitz (2015).

33 Faludi (1991), 11.

34 Rudman and Glick (1999), 1009.

35 Ingraham (1994), 204.

36 Cahn (2015), 165.

37 Blinde and Taub (1992a, 1992b); Griffin (1998).

38 Frankenberg (1993); Le Espiritu (2008).

39 P. Collins (1986).

40 Crenshaw (1990), 1244.

41 Ritchie (2017); M. Bailey (2021); P. Collins (2004).

42 Cahn (2015), 127.
43 Leonard (2012b).
44 Crenshaw (1991), 1271.
45 P. Collins (1986), S17.
46 P. Collins (2004), 6.
47 "Jezebel" is a predominant racial trope portraying Black women as sexually pro-miscuous. Ritchie (2017), 15.
48 M. Bailey (2021), 2.
49 Morris (2016).
50 Wun (2018), 424.
51 Ibid.; Wun (2016a).
52 Wun (2016b), 748.
53 Morris (2016), 10.
54 Ibid., 34. Scholars have also documented how Black girls may be subject to harsher punishment in schools due to perceptions of them as much older than they actually are—adultification bias or age compression—thereby holding them to adult standards of behavior and, in particular, assumptions about Black women's behavior. See Epstein, Blake, and González (2017).
55 Vertinsky and Captain (1998); Leonard (2014).
56 As Menning and Holtzman (2014) argue, "It has also been suggested that gendered norms promoting niceness and deference in women interact with sexual scripts that confound seduction and acquaintance rape, thereby making it difficult for women to resist the pressure for sex or difficult for them to recognize a sexual encounter that qualifies as rape once it has occurred" (1074). See also Armstrong, Hamilton, and Sweeney (2006).
  Numerous scholars have articulated the existence of the "angry Black woman" stereotype (Childs [2005], Jones and Norwood [2016]), the lack of evidence for it (Walley-Jean [2009]), and the impact it has on Black women (Lewis and Neville [2015]).
57 Even women who theoretically could meet these numerous, conflicting expectations have a difficult time doing so. Examples abound in popular culture and scholarly literature condemning, for example, the trope of the "cool girl" perpetuated in literature and movies and the myth of "having it all." As Abi Turner (2020) argues, "Defining qualities of the cool girl is that she is one of the guys, has a passion for cars or sports or other stereotypical male activities. She's fun-loving, raunchy and uninhibited. She likes junk food and beer while maintaining an effortlessly hot body. She's easy-going and never gets angry. And, most importantly, *she is not like the other girls.*"
58 P. Collins (2004), 123.
59 Traister (2018).
60 Obama (2021), x.
61 Douglas (2002); Withycombe (2011).
62 Hong (2020), 55.

63 Ibid., 57.

64 Traister (2018).

CHAPTER 2. "DON'T BE SO BLUNT WITH IT"

1 Griffin (1998); Banet-Weiser (1999); Cahn (2015); Rauscher and Cooky (2017).

2 Unfortunately, I was not allowed to attend this meeting. As outlined in the appendix, not being invited to attend this meeting is but one instance of gatekeeping among many that I experienced while at MWSU. While I was considered part of the team in many ways, moments like this served as a reminder that I would always remain an outsider within. My being kept from the meeting is also, I argue, an indication of the seriousness with which the coaching staff took the video—it was truly a crisis that had to be dealt with swiftly and, most importantly, quietly.

3 As Crawley, Foley, and Shehan (2007) argue, "Social ideas determine behaviors that affect the sizes, shapes, and uses of bodies" (xiii).

4 Roberts (1997); Carrington (2002); P. Collins (2004).

5 P. Collins (2004), 27.

6 Carrington (2002); Leonard and King (2011); Neal (2013).

7 Carrington (2002), 35.

8 ross (2020).

9 Carrington (2002), 4.

10 Roberts (1997); P. Collins (2004).

11 Neal (2013), 5.

12 The stereotypical association of Black men and criminality is what Katheryn Russell-Brown (2008) has termed the "criminalblackman."

13 Neal (2013), 4.

14 Elliot is just one of a number of Black athletes who have been featured in *ESPN*'s body issue over the years. Regarding incarceration, see Alexander (2010).

15 The "Jezebel" is one of several controlling images of Black women. Others include the "Mammy," "Matriarch," and "Welfare Queen" (Roberts [1997]; P. Collins [2002, 2004]).

16 Roberts (1997), 10.

17 Ibid.

18 There are conflicting paradigms within the literature as to whether representations of Black women in hip-hop are fundamentally misogynistic or a source of agency and empowerment. For a review of this literature, see Herd (2015).

19 Menakem (2017), 36.

20 As Roberts (1997) argues, "The systematic, institutionalized denial of reproductive freedom has uniquely marked Black women's history in America" and has been justified by derogatory images of Black women that portray them as unfit for motherhood (4).

21 Mark Anthony Neal (2013) describes hip-hop masculinities as "essential tropes—playa, pimp, hustler, thug, and nigga—that define contemporary mainstream hip-hop masculinities" (37).

22 Leonard (2010), 259.

23 "Trolls" is a word used to describe individuals who purposely seek to create conflict on the internet by posting negative or hurtful comments with the intent of provoking others into arguments.

24 Abraham (2013).

25 Leonard (2006), 160.

26 Lewis and Diamond (2015), 48.

27 Treme, Burrus, and Sherrick (2011), 795.

28 Data were taken from the *2014–15 High School Athletics Participation Survey* conducted by the National Federation of State High School Associations. See www.scholarshipstats.com/varsityodds.html for more detail.

29 The high cost of attending recruiting showcases has led some coaches to refer to such events as "packet rackets," as they are often forced by event organizers to buy packets of information on high school athletes for hundreds of dollars per packet. See Parrish (2016).

30 There is some empirical evidence to suggest that having the most talented athletes does result in more wins. Treme and Burrus (2016), for example, found that "based on recruiting quality alone, a starting lineup comprised solely of five- and four-star freshman and sophomores generates more than twice the number of wins compared to a team with an average level of talent" (752).

31 Tracy (2017).

32 O'Neil (2016).

33 W. Hobson (2017).

34 An example of impermissible communication occurred with the Southeast Missouri State women's basketball program in 2014. An example of academic infractions occurred with the University of Mississippi women's basketball program in 2016.

35 See Griffin (1992); Wellman and Blinde (1997); Wolf-Wendel, Toma, and Morphew (2001).

36 Griffin (1998), 82.

37 Wellman and Blinde (1997).

38 Cyphers and Fagan (2011).

39 Ibid.

40 Antilesbian recruiting tactics are often aimed at parents as much as, if not more, than at potential recruits, perhaps because of the significant role parents can play in the decisions of recruits and because of their own insecurities around nonnormative sexualities. Indeed, the MWSU players asserted that often it was a recruit's parent(s) who asked the coaching staff about whether there were lesbians on the team. The little research that exists on antilesbian recruiting supports this perception; it is usually parents, not recruits, who are questioning coaches about lesbians on teams (Wellman and Blinde [1997]; Wolf-Wendel, Toma, and Morphew [2001]).

41 Wellman and Blinde (1997); Krane and Barber (2005).

42 I use the terms "gay" and "bisexual" here because that is how the players self-identified.

43 Hochschild (2012).

44 Mathers (2017), 304. This is especially true within a bathroom context where perceived gender transgressions can lead to violence against queer and trans people.

45 Former Penn State University women's basketball coach Rene Portland was known for having explicit rules against the presence of lesbian players on her team, inspiring a 2009 documentary film titled *Training Rules: No Drinking, No Drugs, No Lesbians.*

46 Morris (2016).

CHAPTER 3. "EVERYBODY KNOWS THAT ONE"

1 Hamilton et al. (2019), 326.

2 Pascoe (2007). More recent research by Bridges and Pascoe (2014) on "hybrid masculinities"—"the selective incorporation of elements of identity typically associated with various marginalized and subordinated masculinities and—at times—femininities into privileged men's gender performances and identities" (246)—opens up the possibility that there is a decreasing cultural association between masculinity and heterosexuality, and that a hybrid heterosexual masculinity might even incorporate elements of gay male culture.

3 Blinde and Taub (1992a, 1992b); Griffin (1998).

4 Pascoe (2007), 166.

5 Mogul, Ritchie, and Whitlock (2011).

6 Blinde and Taub (1992a, 1992b); Krane (1997); Griffin (1998); Krane et al. (2004); Kauer and Krane (2006); Cahn (2015); Fynes and Fisher (2016).

7 Del Rey (1978).

8 Kauer and Krane (2006), 46.

9 The average height for a women's college basketball player is between 5'6" and 6'0" and above, depending on position.

10 Griffin (1998), 55.

11 Kauer and Krane (2006), 47.

12 Banks (2000), 90.

13 Kauer and Krane (2006) found similarly that "having short hair evoked stereotypes about athletes" (48).

14 P. Collins (2004), 194.

15 Cottom (2019), 45.

16 Ibid., 43–44.

17 While gymnasts are commonly known for their musculature, they are not as subject to lesbian stereotyping as basketball players in part because they are usually much shorter and the sport context of gymnastics is feminine-identified—men participate, too, but it's still largely thought of as a women's sport.

18 As of 2021, White women make up 32 percent of Division I basketball players and 63 percent of volleyball players. For more student-athlete demographic data, see the National Collegiate Athletic Association (2021).

19 Rooted in the ideology of the sex/gender binary are the beliefs that sex, gender, and sexuality are dichotomous (i.e., that someone is born male or female, identifies as a man or a woman, and is either heterosexual or not heterosexual) and essential biological traits of an individual and that those traits align in normative ways (i.e., if someone is assigned male at birth, they will identify as a man and will be attracted to women).

20 Mogul, Ritchie, and Whitlock (2011).

21 Hart (2005), vii–iii.

22 Freedman (1996), 399.

23 Ibid., 400.

24 See Mogul, Ritchie, and Whitlock (2011) for more detailed examples of media representations of Black lesbians.

25 Ibid., 104.

26 Ibid.

27 Previous work on lesbian stereotyping of women athletes has discussed the role of jokes or gossip in perpetuating lesbian stereotyping but has done so by highlighting how lesbian athletes are often the subjects of gossip or how straight athletes use joking about lesbians as a means to distance themselves from lesbian athletes and avoid lesbian labeling (Blinde and Taub [1992a]; Krane [1997]; Griffin [1998]).

28 See Weaver (2011) for a discussion on how racist jokes perpetuate "serious racism."

29 Ford and Ferguson (2004), 91.

30 Research on the pervasiveness of everyday forms of racial discrimination against Black people over the life course reveals similar findings. See, for example, Forman and colleagues (1997) and Feagin (1991), who argue that because racial discrimination occurs at every turn (e.g., at restaurants, on the street, at work or school, while shopping), most Black people don't have the time or energy to confront it at every turn, leading to a "resigned acceptance" of the situation.

31 Krane (1997).

32 Steele (1997).

33 None of the athletes I spoke to explicitly questioned why their sexuality was up for discussion, debate, or humor in the first place. This, I assert, is the result of the long-standing pervasiveness of lesbian stereotyping in women's sports.

34 Krane (1997).

35 Fredrickson and Roberts (1997).

CHAPTER 4. "NOT A LOT OF LEADING LADIES HAVE MUSCLES"

1 Felshin (1974).

2 Del Rey (1978), 9.

3 Krane et al. (2004).

4 Blinde and Taub (1992b); Krane (2001).
5 Messner (1988); Cahn (1993); Clasen (2001); Paloian (2012).
6 Steinfeldt et al. (2011). For research regarding basketball, see Bennett et al. (2017). For soccer, see George (2005) and Devonport et al. (2019). For softball, see Malcolm (2003) and Ross and Shinew (2008). For gymnastics, see Ross and Shinew (2008). For weightlifting, see Vargas and Winter (2021). For swimming, see Howells and Grogan (2012). For golf, see Gregg, Taylor, and Hardin (2021). For ice hockey, see DiCarlo (2016). For track and field, see Krane et al. (2004) and Mosewich et al. (2009). For rugby, see Russell (2004).
7 Ross and Shinew (2008).
8 Knapp (2015); Washington and Economides (2016).
9 Douglas (2005).
10 Dworkin (2001).
11 Ibid., 334.
12 Krane et al. (2004), 326.
13 Dworkin (2001).
14 Steele (1997), 614; Pennington et al. (2016), 2.
15 The assumption that being cisgender—experiencing alignment between one's sex assigned at birth and one's gender identity—is the norm.
16 Heffernan (1999); Taub (1999); Krakauer and Rose (2002).
17 Myers et al. (1999), 21.
18 Ibid.; Pitman (2000); Acosta (2013); Grogan (2016).
19 Pitman (2000), 51.
20 Widdows (2018), 37.
21 Haley (2016), 5.
22 Ibid. As Haley notes, "White women were rarely imprisoned in Georgia and almost never sent to convict lease camps or chain gangs. In the rare instances in which they were given such punishment they often received special treatment, better conditions, and earlier release. From 1908 until 1936 black women were virtually the only female prisoners on the chain gang" (4).
23 Haley (2013). Haley (2016) calls the space outside "boundaries of humanness" a space of "non-being" (5).
24 Ibid., 20–21.
25 Haley (2013), 189; I. Perry (2005), 2.
26 Other physical characteristics such as skin tone came to be racialized during this time period as well. As Imani Perry (2005) notes, "In justification of slavery, imperialism, and colonialism, the dark skins of African and Asian peoples were associated with danger, savagery, primitiveness, and child-like intellects. Moreover, the rise of white supremacy was tied to Enlightenment matrices which associated the white male body with rationality while the darker and/or female bodies were linked with the irrational and sensual aspects of humanity" (2).
27 Gentles-Peart (2018), 199.

28 Maddie Sofia, interview with Sabrina Strings, NPR Shortwave, podcast transcript, July 21, 2020, www.npr.org/transcripts/893006538.

29 Strings (2019).

30 Hamad (2020), 15.

31 Gentles-Peart (2016); Hughes (2021). See Deliovsky (2008) for a discussion of a "benchmark woman."

32 Hamilton et al. (2019), 328. In addition to being raced, feminine beauty ideals are also classed. As the authors note, "Blondeness is a potentially expensive and time-consuming achievement; it is not a natural state for most adult women (with a few geographic exceptions) and thus also flags class privilege" (328).

33 P. Collins (2004), 199.

34 Gentles-Peart (2018).

35 "Gender testing" is inherently sexist and transphobic as it is rooted in fears of men dressing up as women in order to gain a competitive advantage, with the assumption that any man competing against any woman would be athletically superior by default. This same idea is used today to push back against trans athletes competing in sports that align with their gender identities.

36 Huber (2019).

37 North (2019).

38 Callow (2010).

39 As Moya Bailey (2016) outlines, "Her genitals were photographed and examined, her internal organs X-rayed. Genetic and chromosomal analysis were conducted all to determine if she was in fact a *she*, according to a multipronged medical rubric designed to identify 'true' sex through a process misleadingly called 'gender testing'" (4). Higher testosterone in women can be a result of hyperandrogenism, a difference of sexual development (DSD). For more on this, see Karkazis et al. (2012).

40 As Kim McCauley (2019) argues, "In the IAAF's argument, they state that the normal range of testosterone in cisgender women is 0.06 to 1.68 nmol/L, while the normal range in cisgender men is 7.7 to 29.4 nmol/L. How they used this information to argue for a limit of 5 nmol/L in female competitors is difficult to understand."

Other track and field athletes impacted by the World Athletics testosterone limit include, but are not limited to, Burundian runner Francine Niyonsaba, Ugandan runner Annet Negesa, and Indian runner Dutee Chand.

According to a World Athletics Q&A (n.d.), the response to the question "What do such athletes [those with DSD] have to do to be eligible to compete in the female classification?" is as follows: "If they are competing at international level, in one of the affected events (track races between 400m and one mile in distance), they first have to lower the level of testosterone in their blood down to below 5 nmol/L (because that is the highest level that a healthy woman with ovaries would have) for a period of six months, and maintain it below that level while they continue to compete at international level in such events. If they want to compete at international level in other events, again they can compete without restriction, i.e., without lowering their testosterone levels. To lower their testosterone levels in this way, affected athletes can either (a) take a daily oral contraceptive pill; or (b) take a monthly injection of a GnrH agonist; or (c) have their testes surgically removed (a 'gonadectomy'). It is their choice whether or not to have any treatment, and (if so) which treatment to have. In particular, the IAAF does not insist on surgery. The effects of the other two treatments are reversible if and when the athlete decides to stop treatment."

Ugandan runner Annet Negesa underwent a gonadectomy after being told she would not be allowed to compete in the 2012 Olympic Games in London. According to Negesa, this invasive and unnecessary medical procedure was recommended by a doctor for World Athletics. Following the surgery, Negesa has suffered from depression and joint pain, and she has not returned to competition. See Abdul (2019).

41 Karkazis and Jordan-Young (2018). The authors also point out the connection between the overreliance on testosterone to ideologies about gender and race rooted in colonialist practices.

42 Ibid., 3.

43 World Athletics (2019).

44 North (2019).

45 Semenya has been labeled "intersex" in the media, despite (as far as the author knows) not claiming the identity herself.

46 American swimmer Katie Ledecky, who is White and feminine-presenting, is often cited as an example of this. Ledecky is a five-time Olympic gold medal winner and holds fifteen world championship gold medals, more than any other female swimmer. She regularly dominates her competition yet has never been accused of being a man.

47 M. Bailey (2016), 9.

48 Adetiba (2020).

49 Callow (2010).

50 Ibid.

51 Ajayi (2018).

52 Stewart-Bouley (2018).

53 As Karen Grigsby Bates (2020) explains, "These Karens . . . make the choice to police people of color, especially Black people—everything from their legitimate right for their bodies to be in public spaces to their bodies period. And before there was all this focus on Karen, there was Becky . . . a certain kind of culturally oblivious white girl. But before there was Karen or Becky, there was Miss Ann who might go back as far as the antebellum South and who for sure was around in the Jim Crow era."

Many recent incidents have been documented online and in the media. A White woman working at a Starbucks in Philadelphia called the police on two Black men who were sitting in the coffee shop waiting for a friend, accusing them of "trespassing." Another White woman called the police on a family in Oakland, California, for using a charcoal grill instead of a non-charcoal grill in a park. Another White woman, Amy Cooper, was caught on video telling police that she was being threatened by a Black man, Christian Cooper, who was birdwatching in Central Park and had asked her to leash her dog.

54 Ibid.
55 Hamad (2020).
56 Stewart-Bouley (2018).
57 Leonard (2014), 211.
58 Sailes (1991); Miller (1998); Smith (2007).
59 Leonard (2017).
60 Ibid., 213.
61 A. Johnson (2020).
62 Racial battle fatigue, according to Smith and colleagues (2007), "addresses the physiological and psychological strain exacted on racially marginalized groups and the amount of energy lost dedicated to coping with racial microaggressions and racism" (555).

CHAPTER 5. "WE DON'T WANT YOU LOOKING ALL BEAT UP"

1 Felshin (1974); Wughalter (1978).
2 Musto and McGann (2016).
3 Blinde and Taub (1992b).
4 Blinde and Taub (1992a), 157.
5 Crosset (1995). A number of studies document the various types of strategies that women athletes use to align themselves with expectations of heterofemininity, including Griffin (1992); Cox and Thompson (2000); Dworkin (2001); Krane et al. (2004); Adams, Schmitke, and Franklin (2005); George (2005); Fallon and Jome (2007); Davis-Delano, Pollock, and Vose (2009); Ezzell (2009); Engh (2011); and Richard, Joncheray, and Dugas (2017).
6 Ross and Shinew (2008); Macro, Viveiros, and Cipriano (2009); Hardy (2015); Beaver (2016); Malcolm (2003); Sisjord and Kristiansen (2009); Broad (2001).
7 Carli (2017), 35.
8 Ibid., 33.
9 Carli (2001); Ridgeway (2001).
10 Klatt, Eimler, and Krämer (2016).
11 Hochschild (2012), 14.
12 Ibid.
13 Atkinson (2002), 220.
14 Thompson (2015).
15 Samuels (2012).
16 Baade and McGee (2021), 341.

17 Martin (2016).
18 Heywood and Dworkin (2003); Krane et al. (2004).
19 Lyng (2005).
20 Worthen and Baker (2016), 472.
21 H. Johnson (2020), 20.
22 Hochschild (2012); Chen (1999).
23 Sue (2010); Wang, Leu, and Shoda (2011); Lindert et al. (2021).
24 Krane (1997).
25 For examples of the effects of how the media portrays women athletes, see Creedon (1994); Kane, LaVoi, and Fink (2013); and Knight and Giuliano (2001, 2003).
26 For more on this, see Ryan (2008).
27 de la Cretaz (2019).
28 Ridgeway (2001), 650.
29 Ibid.

CONCLUSION

1 Carrington (2021).
2 Importantly, Richardson violated antidoping regulations whereas Semenya, Mboma, Masilingi, and Telfer failed to meet proper hormone requirements for competition.
3 Rees and Miracle (2000); Henricks (2006).
4 Kaufman and Wolff (2010), 158.
5 Garel (2020).
6 Abrams and Weiner (2020).
7 Ibid.
8 A. Perry (2020).
9 Prince (2021). Interestingly, the phrase "March Madness" was used only in reference to the men's tournament until the NCAA committed to using it for the women's tournament starting in 2022 following one of the recommendations from the Kaplan Hecker and Fink LLP (2021) gender equity review.

In response to critiques of the clear gender disparities in the handling of the tournament, the NCAA commissioned Kaplan Hecker and Fink LLP to conduct a gender equity review. In its final report, the reviewers argue that "the NCAA's broadcast agreements, corporate sponsorship contracts, distribution of revenue, organizational structure, and culture all prioritize Division I men's basketball over everything else in ways that create, normalize, and perpetuate gender inequities" (2).
10 Epstein and Libit (2020).
11 Benbow (2021).
12 Enloe (2004), 92.
13 McClintock (2009), 60.
14 Hagerman (2018), 207.

15 Luther (2021).
16 Ibid.
17 A. Lewis (2003b), 190.

APPENDIX

1 Emerson (2001), 28.
2 Ibid., 28–29.
3 C. Bailey and C. Bailey (2017).

REFERENCES

Abdul, Geneva. 2019, December 16. "This Intersex Runner Had Surgery to Compete. It Has Not Gone Well." *New York Times*.

Abraham, Laura. 2013, November 4. "How Slam-Dunking Gender-Bending WNBA Rookie Brittney Griner Is Changing the World of Sports." *Elle*.

Abrams, Jonathan, and Natalie Weiner. 2020, October 16. "How the Most Socially Progressive Pro League Got That Way." *New York Times*.

Acker, Joan. 1992. "From Sex Roles to Gendered Institutions." *Contemporary Sociology* 21, no. 5: 565–569. doi.org/10.2307/2075528.

Acosta, Katie L. 2013. *Amigas y Amantes: Sexually Nonconforming Latinas Negotiate Family*. New Brunswick, NJ: Rutgers University Press.

Adams, Natalie, Alison Schmitke, and Amy Franklin. 2005. "Tomboys, Dykes, and Girly Girls: Interrogating the Subjectivities of Adolescent Female Athletes." *Women's Studies Quarterly* 33, no. 1/2: 17–34.

Adetiba, Elizabeth. 2020, April 20. "Caster Semenya and the Cruel History of Contested Black Femininity." *SBNation*.

Ajayi, Luvvie. 2018, April 17. "About the Weary Weaponizing of White Women's Tears." *Awesomely Luvvie*, www.awesomelyluvvie.com.

Alexander, Michelle. 2010. *The New Jim Crow: Mass Incarceration in the Age of Colorblindness*. New York: New Press.

Anderson, Eric, and Mark McCormack. 2010. "Intersectionality, Critical Race Theory and American Sporting Oppression: Examining Black and Gay Male Athletes." *Journal of Homosexuality* 57, no. 8: 949–967. doi.org/10.1080/00918369.2010.503502.

Armstrong, Elizabeth A., Laura Hamilton, and Brian Sweeney. 2006. "Sexual Assault on Campus: A Multilevel, Integrative Approach to Party Rape." *Social Problems* 53, no. 4: 483–499. doi.org/10.1525/sp.2006.53.4.483.

Atkinson, Michael. 2002. "Pretty in Ink: Conformity, Resistance, and Negotiation in Women's Tattooing." *Sex Roles* 47, no. 5: 219–235. doi.org/10.1023/A:1021330609522.

Baade, Christina, and Kristin A. McGee, eds. 2021. *Beyoncé in the World: Making Meaning with Queen Bey in Troubled Times*. Middletown, CT: Wesleyan University Press.

Bailey, Carol R., and Carol A. Bailey. 2017. *A Guide to Qualitative Field Research*. Thousand Oaks, CA: Sage Publications.

Bailey, Moya. 2016. "Misogynoir in Medical Media: On Caster Semenya and R. Kelly." *Catalyst: Feminism, Theory, Technoscience* 2, no. 2: 1–31. doi.org/10.28968/cftt.v2i2.28800.

———. 2021. *Misogynoir Transformed: Black Women's Digital Resistance*. New York: New York University Press.

Bailey, Moya, and Trudy. 2018. "On Misogynoir: Citation, Erasure, and Plagiarism." *Feminist Media Studies* 18, no. 4: 762-768. doi.org/10.1080/14680777.2018.1447395.

Banet-Weiser, Sarah. 1999. "Hoop Dreams: Professional Basketball and the Politics of Race and Gender." *Journal of Sport and Social Issues* 23, no. 4: 403–420.

Banks, Ingrid. 2000. *Hair Matters: Beauty, Power, and Black Women's Consciousness*. New York: New York University Press.

Bates, Karen Grigsby. 2020, August 5. "What's in a Name: The History of Karens, Beckys, and Miss Anns." *NPR*.

Beaver, Travis D. 2016. "Roller Derby Uniforms: The Pleasures and Dilemmas of Sexualized Attire." *International Review for the Sociology of Sport* 51, no. 6: 639–657. doi.org/10.1177/1012690214549060.

Benbow, Dana Hunsinger. 2021, January 20. "Toxic Abuse Alleged Inside Purdue-Fort Wayne Women's Basketball: 'It Was Brutal.'" *Indianapolis Star*.

Bennett, Erica V., Louisa Scarlett, Laura Hurd Clarke, and Peter R. E. Crocker. 2017. "Negotiating (Athletic) Femininity: The Body and Identity in Elite Female Basketball Players." *Qualitative Research in Sport, Exercise and Health* 9, no. 2: 233–246. doi.org/10.1080/2159676X.2016.1246470.

Bieler, Des. 2017, January 19. "ESPN Analyst Says He Did Not Liken Venus Williams to a 'Gorilla' but a 'Guerrilla.'" *Washington Post*.

Blinde, Elaine M., and Diane E. Taub. 1992a. "Homophobia and Women's Sport: The Disempowerment of Athletes." *Sociological Focus* 25, no. 2: 151–166. doi.org/10.1080/00380237.1992.10570613.

———. 1992b. "Women Athletes as Falsely Accused Deviants: Managing the Lesbian Stigma." *Sociological Quarterly* 33, no. 4: 521–533. doi.org/10.1111/j.1533-8525.1992.tb00141.x.

Brackenridge, Celia. 1997. " 'He Owned Me Basically . . .': Women's Experience of Sexual Abuse in Sport." *International Review for the Sociology of Sport* 32, no. 2: 115–130. doi.org/10.1177/101269097032002001.

Bridges, Tristan, and Cheri J. Pascoe. 2014. "Hybrid Masculinities: New Directions in the Sociology of Men and Masculinities." *Sociology Compass*, 8, no. 3: 246–258. doi.org/10.1111/soc4.12134.

Broad, Kendal L. 2001. "The Gendered Unapologetic: Queer Resistance in Women's Sport." *Sociology of Sport Journal* 18, no. 2: 181–204. doi.org/10.1123/ssj.18.2.181.

Cahn, Susan K. 1993. "From the 'Muscle Moll' to the 'Butch' Ballplayer: Mannishness, Lesbianism, and Homophobia in US Women's Sport." *Feminist Studies* 19, no. 2: 343–368. doi.org/10.2307/3178373.

———. 2015. *Coming on Strong: Gender and Sexuality in Women's Sport*. 2nd edition. Champaign: University of Illinois Press.

Callow, James. 2010, August 23. "Caster Semenya Faces Growing Backlash after Competitors Have Their Say." *Guardian*.

Carli, Linda L. 2017. "Social Influence and Gender." In *The Oxford Handbook of Social Influence*, edited by S. G. Harkins, K. D. Williams, and J. M. Burger, 33–51. New York: Oxford University Press.

Carrington, Ben. 2002. " 'Race,' Representation, and the Sporting Body." *Centre for Urban and Community Research*. Goldsmiths University of London: 1–38.

———. 2021, July 2, 11:14 a.m. Twitter post. twitter.com/benhcarrington.

Chen, Anthony S. 1999. "Lives at the Center of the Periphery, Lives at the Periphery of the Center: Chinese American Masculinities and Bargaining with Hegemony." *Gender and Society* 13, no. 5: 584–607. doi.org/10.1177/089124399013005002.

Childs, Erica Chito. 2005. "Looking behind the Stereotypes of the 'Angry Black Woman': An Exploration of Black Women's Responses to Interracial Relationships." *Gender and Society* 19, no. 4: 544–561. doi.org/10.1177/0891243205276755.

Clasen, Patricia R. W. 2001. "The Female Athlete: Dualisms and Paradox in Practice." *Women and Language* 24, no. 2: 36–42.

Collins, Patricia Hill. 1986. "Learning from the Outsider Within: The Sociological Significance of Black Feminist Thought." *Social Problems* 33, no. 6: s14–s32. doi.org/10.2307/800672.

———. 2002. *Black Feminist Thought: Knowledge, Consciousness, and the Politics of Empowerment*. New York: Routledge.

———. 2004. *Black Sexual Politics: African Americans, Gender, and the New Racism*. New York: Routledge.

Collins, Tony. 2013. *Sport in Capitalist Society: A Short History*. New York: Routledge.

Connell, Raewyn. 1987. *Gender and Power*. London: Allen and Unwin.

———. 2020. *Masculinities*. New York: Routledge.

Cooper, Brittney C. 2017. "My Brother's Keeper and the Co-optation of Intersectionality." In *The Crunk Feminist Collection*, edited by Brittney C. Cooper, Robin M. Boylorn, and Susana M. Morris, 149–154. New York: Feminist Press at CUNY.

Cottom, Tressie McMillan. 2019. *Thick: And Other Essays*. New York: New Press.

Cox, Barbara, and Shona Thompson. 2000. "Multiple Bodies: Sportswomen, Soccer and Sexuality." *International Review for the Sociology of Sport* 35, no. 1: 5–20. doi.org/10.1177/101269000035001001.

Crawley, Sara L., Lara J. Foley, and Constance L. Shehan. 2007. *Gendering Bodies*. Lanham, MD: Rowman and Littlefield.

Creedon, Pamela J., ed. 1994. *Women, Media and Sport*. Thousand Oaks, CA: Sage.

Crenshaw, Kimberlé. 1990. "Mapping the Margins: Intersectionality, Identity Politics, and Violence against Women of Color." *Stanford Law Review* 43: 1241–1299.

———. 1991. "Race, Gender, and Sexual Harassment." *Southern California Law Review* 65: 1467–1476.

Crosset, Todd W. 1995. *Outsiders in the Clubhouse: The World of Women's Professional Golf*. Albany: SUNY Press.

Cyphers, Luke, and Kate Fagan. 2011, January 26. "Unhealthy Climate." *ESPN*.

Davis-Delano, Laurel R., April Pollock, and Jennifer Ellsworth Vose. 2009. "Apologetic Behavior among Female Athletes: A New Questionnaire and Initial Results." *International Review for the Sociology of Sport* 44, no. 2–3: 131–150. doi.org/10.1177/1012690209335524.

de la Cretaz, Britni. 2019, June 18. "Androgyny Is Now Fashionable in the W.N.B.A." *New York Times*.

Deliovsky, Kathy. 2008. "Normative White Femininity: Race, Gender and the Politics of Beauty." *Atlantis: Critical Studies in Gender, Culture and Social Justice* 33, no. 1: 49–59.

Del Rey, Patricia. 1978. "Apologetics and Androgyny: The Past and the Future." *Frontiers: A Journal of Women Studies*: 8–10. doi.org/10.2307/3345982.

Denhollander, Rachael. 2019. *What Is a Girl Worth? My Story of Breaking the Silence and Exposing the Truth about Larry Nassar and USA Gymnastics*. Carol Stream, IL: Tyndale House.

Devonport, Tracey J., Kate Russell, Kath Leflay, and Jennifer Conway. 2019. "Gendered Performances and Identity Construction among UK Female Soccer Players and Netballers: A Comparative Study." *Sport in Society* 22, no. 7: 1131–1147. doi.org/10.1080/17430437.2018.1545760.

DiCarlo, Danielle. 2016. "Playing Like a Girl? The Negotiation of Gender and Sexual Identity among Female Ice Hockey Athletes on Male Teams." *Sport in Society* 19, no. 8–9: 1363–1373. doi.org/10.1080/17430437.2015.1096260.

Dicaro, Julie. 2017, September 18. "Safest Bet in Sports: Men Complaining about a Female Announcer's Voice." *New York Times*.

Douglas, Delia D. 2002. "To Be Young, Gifted, Black and Female: A Meditation on the Cultural Politics at Play in Representations of Venus and Serena Williams." *Sociology of Sport Online* 5, no. 2: 1–16.

———. 2005. "Venus, Serena, and the Women's Tennis Association: When and Where 'Race' Enters." *Sociology of Sport Journal* 22, no. 3: 255–281. doi.org/10.1123/ssj.22.3.255.

———. 2012. "Venus, Serena, and the Inconspicuous Consumption of Blackness: A Commentary on Surveillance, Race Talk, and New Racism(s)." *Journal of Black Studies* 43, no. 2: 127–145. doi.org/10.1177/0021934711410880.

Dworkin, Shari L. 2001. " 'Holding Back': Negotiating a Glass Ceiling on Women's Muscular Strength." *Sociological Perspectives* 44, no. 3: 333–350. doi.org/10.1525/sop.2001.44.3.333.

Dworkin, Shari L., and Michael A. Messner. 2002. "Just Do . . . What? Sport, Bodies, Gender." In *Gender and Sport: A Reader*, edited by Sheila Scraton and Anne Fintoff, 17–29. New York: Routledge.

Emerson, Robert. 2001. "Introduction: The Development of Ethnographic Field Research." In *Contemporary Field Research: Perspectives and Formulations*, 1–54. Long Grove, IL: Waveland Press.

Engh, Mari Haugaa. 2011. "Tackling Femininity: The Heterosexual Paradigm and Women's Soccer in South Africa." *International Journal of the History of Sport* 28, no. 1: 137–152. doi.org/10.1080/09523367.2011.525311.

Enke, Janet. 2005. "Athleticism and Femininity on a High School Basketball Team: An Interpretative Approach." *Sociological Studies of Children and Youth* 11: 115–152. doi. org/10.1016/S1537-4661(05)11005-8.

Enloe, Cynthia. 2004. "Wielding Masculinity Inside Abu Ghraib: Making Feminist Sense of an American Military Scandal." *Asian Journal of Women's Studies* 10, no. 3: 89–102. doi.org/10.1080/12259276.2004.11665976.

Epstein, Jori, and Daniel Libit. 2020, August 5. "Texas Tech Women's Basketball Players Describe Toxic Culture: 'Fear, Anxiety, and Depression.'" *USA Today*.

Epstein, Rebecca, Jamilia Blake, and Thalia González. 2017. "Girlhood Interrupted: The Erasure of Black Girls' Childhood." Washington, DC: Georgetown University Law Center on Poverty and Inequality.

ESPN. 2014, October 17. "Shamil Tarpischev Fined, Banned Year."

Ewing, Eve L. 2020, July 2. "I'm a Black Scholar Who Studies Race. Here's Why I Capitalize 'White.'" *Zora*. www.zora.medium.com/.

Ezzell, Matthew B. 2009. " 'Barbie Dolls' on the Pitch: Identity Work, Defensive Othering, and Inequality in Women's Rugby." *Social Problems* 56, no. 1: 111–131. doi. org/10.1525/sp.2009.56.1.111.

Fairness and Accuracy in Reporting. 2007, April 9. "Racism Is to Be Expected from Don Imus." fair.org.

Fallon, Melissa A., and LaRae M. Jome. 2007. "An Exploration of Gender-Role Expectations and Conflict among Women Rugby Players." *Psychology of Women Quarterly* 31, no. 3: 311–321. doi.org/10.1111/j.1471-6402.2007.00374.x.

Faludi, Susan. 1991. *Backlash: The Undeclared War against American Women*. New York: Crown.

Feagin, Joe R. 1991. "The Continuing Significance of Race: Antiblack Discrimination in Public Places." *American Sociological Review*: 101–116. doi.org/10.2307/2095676.

Felshin, Jan. 1974. "The Triple Option . . . for Women in Sport." *Quest* 21, no. 1: 36–40. doi.org/10.1080/00336297.1974.10519789.

Floyd, Brian. 2012, July 11. "Every Time Brittney Griner Is on TV, This Happens." *SBNation*.

Ford, Thomas E., and Mark A. Ferguson. 2004. "Social Consequences of Disparagement Humor: A Prejudiced Norm Theory." *Personality and Social Psychology Review* 8, no. 1: 79–94. doi.org/10.1207/S15327957PSPR0801_4.

Forman, Tyrone A., David R. Williams, James S. Jackson, and Carol Gardner. 1997. "Race, Place, and Discrimination." *Perspectives on Social Problems* 9: 231–261.

Frankenberg, Ruth. 1993. *The Social Construction of Whiteness: White Women, Race Matters*. New York: Routledge.

Fredrickson, Barbara L., and Tomi-Ann Roberts. 1997. "Objectification Theory: Toward Understanding Women's Lived Experiences and Mental Health Risks." *Psychology of Women Quarterly* 21, no. 2: 173–206. doi.org/10.1111/j.1471-6402.1997.tb00108.x.

Freedman, Estelle B. 1996. "The Prison Lesbian: Race, Class, and the Construction of the Aggressive Female Homosexual, 1915–1965." *Feminist Studies* 22, no. 2: 397–423. doi.org/10.2307/3178421.

Fynes, Jamie M., and Leslee A. Fisher. 2016. "Is Authenticity and Integrity Possible for Sexual Minority Athletes? Lesbian Student-Athlete Experiences of US NCAA Division I Sport." *Women in Sport and Physical Activity Journal* 24, no. 1: 60–69. doi.org/10.1123/wspaj.2014–0055.

Garel, Connor. 2020, August 28. "WNBA Players Protested Police Brutality Even Before Colin Kaepernick. Remember That?" *Huffington Post.*

Gentles-Peart, Kamille. 2016. *Romance with Voluptuousness: Caribbean Women and Thick Bodies in the United States.* Lincoln: University of Nebraska Press.

———. 2018. "Controlling Beauty Ideals: Caribbean Women, Thick Bodies, and White Supremacist Discourse." *Women's Studies Quarterly* 46, no. 1/2: 199–214.

George, Molly. 2005. "Making Sense of Muscle: The Body Experiences of Collegiate Women Athletes." *Sociological Inquiry* 75, no. 3: 317–345. doi.org/10.1111/j.1475–682X.2005.00125.x.

Gregg, Elizabeth A., Elizabeth A. Taylor, and Robin Hardin. 2021. " 'I'm Too Sexy for My Shirt': The LPGA Dress Code." In *Sportswomen's Apparel in the United States: Uniformly Discussed,* edited by Linda K. Fuller, 217–229. London: Palgrave Macmillan.

Griffin, Pat. 1992. "Changing the Game: Homophobia, Sexism, and Lesbians in Sport." *Quest* 44, no. 2: 251–265. doi.org/10.1080/00336297.1992.10484053.

———. 1998. *Strong Women, Deep Closets: Lesbians and Homophobia in Sport.* Champaign, IL: Human Kinetics.

Grogan, Sarah. 2016. *Body Image: Understanding Body Dissatisfaction in Men, Women and Children.* New York: Routledge.

Hagerman, Margaret A. 2018. *White Kids: Growing Up with Privilege in a Racially Divided America.* New York: New York University Press.

Haley, Sarah. 2013. " 'Like I Was a Man': Chain Gangs, Gender, and the Domestic Carceral Sphere in Jim Crow Georgia." *Signs: Journal of Women in Culture and Society* 39, no. 1: 53–77. doi.org/10.1086/670769.

———. 2016. *No Mercy Here: Gender, Punishment, and the Making of Jim Crow Modernity.* Chapel Hill: University of North Carolina Press.

Hamad, Ruby. 2020. *White Tears Brown Scars: How White Feminism Betrays Women of Colour.* London: Hachette.

Hamilton, Laura T., Elizabeth A. Armstrong, J. Lotus Seeley, and Elizabeth M. Armstrong. 2019. "Hegemonic Femininities and Intersectional Domination." *Sociological Theory* 37, no. 4: 315–341. doi.org/10.1177/0735275119888248.

Hardy, Elizabeth. 2015. "The Female 'Apologetic' Behaviour within Canadian Women's Rugby: Athlete Perceptions and Media Influences." *Sport in Society* 18, no. 2: 155–167. doi.org/10.1080/17430437.2013.854515.

Hart, Lynda. 2005. *Fatal Women: Lesbian Sexuality and the Mark of Aggression.* New York: Routledge.

Hartmann, Douglas. 2000. "Rethinking the Relationship between Sport and Race in American Culture: Golden Ghettos and Contested Terrain." *Sociology of Sport Journal* 17, no. 3: 229–253. doi.org/10.1123/ssj.17.3.229.

——. 2003. "What Can We Learn from Sport If We Take Sport Seriously as a Racial Force? Lessons from C. L. R. James's *Beyond a Boundary.*" *Ethnic and Racial Studies* 26, no. 3: 451–483. doi.org/10.1080/0141987032000067282.

Heffernan, Karen. 1999. "Lesbians and the Internalization of Societal Standards of Weight and Appearance." *Journal of Lesbian Studies* 3, no. 4: 121–127. doi. org/10.1300/J155v03n04_16.

Henricks, Thomas S. 2006. *Play Reconsidered: Sociological Perspectives on Human Expression.* Champaign: University of Illinois Press.

Herd, Denise. 2015. "Conflicting Paradigms on Gender and Sexuality in Rap Music: A Systematic Review." *Sexuality and Culture* 19, no. 3: 577–589. doi.org/10.1007/s12119-014-9259-9.

Heywood, Leslie, and Shari L. Dworkin. 2003. *Built to Win: The Female Athlete as Cultural Icon.* Minneapolis: University of Minnesota Press.

Hobson, Janell. 2003. "The 'Batty' Politic: Toward an Aesthetic of the Black Female Body." *Hypatia* 18, no. 4: 87–105. doi:10.1111/j.1527-2001.2003.tb01414.x.

Hobson, Will. 2017, February 2. "Baylor Rape Scandal Involves Recruiting 'Hostess' Program. These Things Still Exist?" *Washington Post.*

Hochschild, Arlie, with Anne Machung. 2012. *The Second Shift: Working Families and the Revolution at Home.* New York: Penguin.

Holt, Thomas C. 1995. "Marking: Race, Race-making, and the Writing of History." *American Historical Review* 100, no. 1: 1–20. doi:10.2307/2167981.

Hong, Cathy Park. 2020. *Minor Feelings: An Asian American Reckoning.* New York: One World.

Howells, Karen, and Sarah Grogan. 2012. "Body Image and the Female Swimmer: Muscularity but in Moderation." *Qualitative Research in Sport, Exercise and Health* 4, no. 1: 98–116. doi.org/10.1080/2159676X.2011.653502.

Huber, Martin Fritz. 2019, May 3. "Did We Just See Caster Semenya's Last Race?" *Outside.*

Hughes, Elizabeth. 2021. " 'I'm Supposed to Be Thick': Managing Body Image Anxieties among Black American Women." *Journal of Black Studies* 52, no. 3: 310–330. doi.org/10.1177/0021934720972440.

Ingraham, Chrys. 1994. "The Heterosexual Imaginary: Feminist Sociology and Theories of Gender." *Sociological Theory*: 203–219. doi.org/10.2307/201865.

Johnson, Ayana Elizabeth. 2020, June 3. "I'm a Black Climate Expert: Racism Derails Our Efforts to Save the Planet." *Washington Post.*

Johnson, Harriet McBryde. 2020. "Unspeakable Conversations." In *Disability Visibility: First-Person Stories from the Twenty-First Century*, edited by Alice Wong, 3–27. New York: Knopf Doubleday.

Johnston, Chris. 2016, April 24. "Serena Williams Accuses Ilie Nastase of Racially Abusing Her and Unborn Child." *Guardian.*

Jones, Trina, and Kimberly Jade Norwood. 2016. "Aggressive Encounters and White Fragility: Deconstructing the Trope of the Angry Black Woman." *Iowa Law Review* 102: 2017–2069.

Kane, Mary Jo, Nicole M. LaVoi, and Janet S. Fink. 2013. "Exploring Elite Female Athletes' Interpretations of Sport Media Images: A Window into the Construction of Social Identity and 'Selling Sex' in Women's Sports." *Communication and Sport* 1, no. 3: 269–298. doi.org/10.1177/2167479512473585.

Kaplan Hecker and Fink LLP. 2021. *NCAA External Gender Equity Review.* Accessed September 2, 2021. kaplanhecker.app.box.com/s/6fpd51gxk9ki78f8vbhqcqhoboo95oxq.

Karkazis, Katrina, and Rebecca M. Jordan-Young. 2018. "The Powers of Testosterone: Obscuring Race and Regional Bias in the Regulation of Women Athletes." *Feminist Formations* 30, no. 2: 1–39. doi.org/10.1353/ff.2018.0017.

Karkazis, Katrina, Rebecca Jordan-Young, Georgiann Davis, and Silvia Camporesi. 2012. "Out of Bounds? A Critique of the New Policies on Hyperandrogenism in Elite Female Athletes." *American Journal of Bioethics* 12, no. 7: 3–16. doi.org/10.1080/15265161.2012.680533.

Kauer, Kerrie J., and Vikki Krane. 2006. " 'Scary Dykes' and 'Feminine Queens': Stereotypes and Female Collegiate Athletes." *Women in Sport and Physical Activity Journal* 15, no. 1: 42–55.

Kaufman, Peter, and Eli A. Wolff. 2010. "Playing and Protesting: Sport as a Vehicle for Social Change." *Journal of Sport and Social Issues* 34, no. 2: 154–175. doi.org/10.1177/0193723509360218.

Kavanagh, Emma, Lorraine Brown, and Ian Jones. 2017. "Elite Athletes' Experience of Coping with Emotional Abuse in the Coach–Athlete Relationship." *Journal of Applied Sport Psychology* 29, no. 4: 402–417. doi.org/10.1080/10413200.2017.1298165.

Kilgannon, Corey. 2001, June 8. "MediaTalk; Even Host is Offended By Talk on Imus Show." *New York Times.*

Klatt, Jennifer, Sabrina C. Eimler, and Nicole C. Krämer. 2016. "Makeup Your Mind: The Impact of Styling on Perceived Competence and Warmth of Female Leaders." *Journal of Social Psychology* 156, no. 5: 483–497. doi.org/10.1080/00224545.2015.1129303.

Knapp, Bobbi A. 2015. "Rx'd and Shirtless: An Examination of Gender in a CrossFit Box." *Women in Sport and Physical Activity Journal* 23, no. 1: 42–53. doi.org/10.1123/wspaj.2014–0021.

Knight, Jennifer L., and Traci A. Giuliano. 2001. "He's a Laker; She's a 'Looker': The Consequences of Gender-Stereotypical Portrayals of Male and Female Athletes by the Print Media." *Sex Roles* 45, no. 3: 217–229. doi.org/10.1023/A:1013553811620.

———. 2003. "Blood, Sweat, and Jeers: The Impact of the Media's Heterosexist Portrayals on Perceptions of Male and Female Athletes." *Journal of Sport Behavior* 26, no. 3: 272–284.

Krakauer, Ilana D., and Suzanna M. Rose. 2002. "The Impact of Group Membership on Lesbians' Physical Appearance." *Journal of Lesbian Studies* 6, no. 1: 31–43. doi.org/10.1300/J155v06n01_04.

Krane, Vikki. 1997. "Homonegativism Experienced by Lesbian Collegiate Athletes." *Women in Sport and Physical Activity Journal* 6, no. 2: 141–163. doi.org/10.1123/wspaj.6.2.141.

———. 2001. "We Can Be Athletic and Feminine, But Do We Want To? Challenging Hegemonic Femininity in Women's Sport." *Quest* 53, no. 1: 115–133. doi.org/10.1080/00336297.2001.10491733.

Krane, Vikki, and Heather Barber. 2005. "Identity Tensions in Lesbian Intercollegiate Coaches." *Research Quarterly for Exercise and Sport* 76, no. 1: 67–81.

Krane, Vikki, Precilla Y. L. Choi, Shannon M. Baird, Christine M. Aimar, and Kerrie J. Kauer. 2004. "Living the Paradox: Female Athletes Negotiate Femininity and Muscularity." *Sex Roles* 50, no. 5: 315–329. doi.org/10.1023/B:SERS.0000018888.48437.4f.

Le Espiritu, Yen. 2008. *Asian American Women and Men: Labor, Laws, and Love.* Lanham, MD: Rowman and Littlefield.

Leonard, David J. 2006. "The Real Color of Money: Controlling Black Bodies in the NBA." *Journal of Sport and Social Issues* 30, no. 2: 158–179. doi.org/10.1177/0193723506286725.

———. 2010. "Jumping the Gun: Sporting Cultures and the Criminalization of Black Masculinity." *Journal of Sport and Social Issues* 34, no. 2: 252–262. doi.org/10.1177/0193723510367781.

———. 2012a, July 12. "Brittney Griner, Women Athletes and the Erotic Gaze." *NewBlackMan in Exile.* www.newblackmaninexile.net.

———. 2012b, February 29. "Not Entertained?" *SLAM.* www.slamonline.com.

———. 2014. "Dilemmas and Contradictions: Black Female Athletes." In *Out of Bounds: Racism and the Black Athlete,* edited by Lori Latrice Martin, 209–230. Santa Barbara, CA: ABC-CLIO.

———. 2017. *Playing while White: Privilege and Power On and Off the Field.* Seattle: University of Washington Press.

Leonard, David J., and C. Richard King. 2011. "Lack of Black Opps: Kobe Bryant and the Difficult Path of Redemption." *Journal of Sport and Social Issues* 35, no. 2: 209–223. doi.org/10.1177/0193723511405482.

Lewis, Amanda E. 2003a. "Everyday Race-Making: Navigating Racial Boundaries in Schools." *American Behavioral Scientist* 47, no. 3: 283–305.

———. 2003b. *Race in the Schoolyard: Negotiating the Color Line in Classrooms and Communities.* New Brunswick, NJ: Rutgers University Press.

———. 2004. " 'What Group?' Studying Whites and Whiteness in the Era of 'Color-Blindness.'" *Sociological Theory* 22, no. 4: 623–646.

Lewis, Amanda E., and John B. Diamond. 2015. *Despite the Best Intentions: How Racial Inequality Thrives in Good Schools.* New York: Oxford University Press.

Lewis, Jioni A., and Helen A. Neville. 2015. "Construction and Initial Validation of the Gendered Racial Microaggressions Scale for Black Women." *Journal of Counseling Psychology* 62, no. 2: 289–302. doi.org/10.1037/cou0000062.

Lindert, Jutta, Kimberley C. Paul, E. Lachman Margie, Beate Ritz, and Teresa Seeman. 2021. "Social Stress and Risk of Declining Cognition: A Longitudinal Study of Men and Women in the United States." *Social Psychiatry and Psychiatric Epidemiology*: 1–10. doi.org/10.1007/s00127-021-02089-7.

Luther, Jessica W. 2021, May 17. "The Playing Field." *Vox.*

Lyng, Stephen. 2005. *Edgework: The Sociology of Risk-Taking*. London: Taylor and Francis.

Machado, Carmen Maria. 2019. *In the Dream House: A Memoir*. Minneapolis: Graywolf Press.

Macro, Ellen, Jennifer Viveiros, and Nick Cipriano. 2009. "Wrestling with Identity: An Exploration of Female Wrestlers' Perceptions." *Women in Sport and Physical Activity Journal* 18, no. 1: 42–53. doi.org/10.1123/wspaj.18.1.42.

Malcolm, Nancy L. 2003. "Constructing Female Athleticism: A Study of Girls' Recreational Softball." *American Behavioral Scientist* 46, no. 10: 1387–1404. doi.org/10.1177/0002764203046010007.

Martin, Renee. 2016, August 17. "The Real Reason People Keep Making Fun of Gabby Douglas' Hair." *Medium*.

Mathers, Lain AB. 2017. "Bathrooms, Boundaries, and Emotional Burdens: Cisgendering Interactions through the Interpretation of Transgender Experience." *Symbolic Interaction*, 40, no. 3: 295–316.

Mazer, Joseph P., Katie Barnes, Alexia Grevious, and Caroline Boger. 2013. "Coach Verbal Aggression: A Case Study Examining Effects on Athlete Motivation and Perceptions of Coach Credibility." *International Journal of Sport Communication* 6, no. 2: 203–213. doi.org/10.1123/ijsc.6.2.203.

McCauley, Kim. 2019, May 1. "9 Reasons the Caster Semenya Ruling Is Nonsense." *SBNation*.

McClintock, Anne. 2009. "Paranoid Empire: Specters from Guantánamo and Abu Ghraib." *Small Axe: A Caribbean Journal of Criticism* 13, no. 1: 50–74. doi.org/10.1215/07990537-2008-006.

McKay, James, and Helen Johnson. 2008. "Pornographic Eroticism and Sexual Grotesquerie in Representations of African American Sportswomen." *Social Identities* 14, no. 4: 491–504. doi.org/10.1080/13504630802211985.

Menakem, Resmaa. 2021. *My Grandmother's Hands: Racialized Trauma and the Pathway to Mending Our Hearts and Bodies*. London: Penguin.

Menning, Chadwick L., and Mellisa Holtzman. 2014. "Processes and Patterns in Gay, Lesbian, and Bisexual Sexual Assault: A Multimethodological Assessment." *Journal of Interpersonal Violence* 29, no. 6: 1071–1093. doi.org/10.1177/0886260513506056.

Messner, Michael A. 1988. "Sport and Male Domination: The Female Athlete as Contested Ideological Terrain." *Sociology of Sport Journal* 5, no. 3: 197–211. doi.org/10.1123/ssj.5.3.197.

———. 1992. *Power at Play: Sports and the Problem of Masculinity*. Boston: Beacon.

———. 2002. *Taking the Field: Women, Men, and Sports*. Minneapolis: University of Minnesota Press.

Miller, Patrick B. 1998. "The Anatomy of Scientific Racism: Racialist Responses to Black Athletic Achievement." *Journal of Sport History* 25, no. 1: 119–151.

Mogul, Joey L., Andrea J. Ritchie, and Kay Whitlock. 2011. *Queer (In)justice: The Criminalization of LGBT People in the United States*. Vol. 5. Boston: Beacon.

Morris, Monique. 2016. *Pushout: The Criminalization of Black Girls in Schools*. New York: New Press.

Mosbergen, Dominique. 2015, October 12. "Jessica Mendoza Makes Baseball History, Prompting Sexist Backlash." *Huffington Post.*

Mosewich, Amber D., Adrianne B. Vangool, Kent C. Kowalski, and Tara-Leigh F. McHugh. 2009. "Exploring Women Track and Field Athletes' Meanings of Muscularity." *Journal of Applied Sport Psychology* 21, no. 1: 99–115. doi.org/10.1080/10413200802575742.

Moyazb. 2010, March 14. "They Aren't Talking about Me . . ." Crunk Feminist Collective. crunkfeministcollective.com/2010/03/14/they-arent-talking-about-me/.

———. 2014, April 27. "More on the Origin of Misogynoir." Tumblr. moyazb.tumblr.com/post/84048113369/more-on-the-origin-of-misogynoir.

Musto, Michela, and P. J. McGann. 2016. "Strike a Pose! The Femininity Effect in Collegiate Women's Sport." *Sociology of Sport Journal* 33, no. 2: 101–112. doi.org/10.1123/ssj.2015–0034.

Myers, Anna, Jennifer Taub, Jessica F. Morris, and Esther D. Rothblum. 1999. "Beauty Mandates and the Appearance Obsession: Are Lesbian and Bisexual Women Better Off?" *Journal of Lesbian Studies* 3, no. 4: 15–26. doi.org/10.1300/J155v03n04_03.

National Collegiate Athletic Association. 2021, March. *NCAA Demographics Database* [Data visualization dashboard]. Distributed by the National Collegiate Athletic Association, ncaa.org.

Neal, Mark Anthony. 2013. *Looking for Leroy: Illegible Black Masculinities.* New York: New York University Press.

North, Anna. 2019, May 3. " 'I Am a Woman and I Am Fast': What Caster Semenya's Story Says about Gender and Race in Sports." *Vox.*

Obama, Michelle. 2021. *Becoming.* New York: Crown.

O'Neil, Dana. 2016, January 25. "Louisville, Pitino Fighting NCAA Allegations on Escort Scandal." *ESPN.*

Paloian, Andrea. 2012. "The Female/Athlete Paradox: Managing Traditional Views of Masculinity and Femininity." *Applied Psychology OPUS.* wp.nyu.edu/steinhardt-appsych_opus/the-femaleathlete-paradox-managing-traditional-views-of-masculinity-and-femininity/.

Parrish, Gary. 2016, July 22. "Inside College Hoops: The 'Packet Racket' Is Making Amateur Basketball Lucrative." *CBS Sports.*

Pascoe, C. J. 2007. *Dude, You're a Fag: Masculinity and Sexuality in High School.* Berkeley: University of California Press.

Payne, Marissa. 2015, February 7. "Clippers' Chris Paul Fined $25,000 for Critique of Female Referee." *Washington Post.*

Pennington, Charlotte R., Derek Heim, Andrew R. Levy, and Derek T. Larkin. 2016. "Twenty Years of Stereotype Threat Research: A Review of Psychological Mediators." *PloS One* 11, no. 1: e0146487. doi.org/10.1371/journal.pone.0146487.

Pereira Vargas, Maria Luisa Fernanda, and Stacy Winter. 2021. "Weight on the Bar vs. Weight on the Scale: A Qualitative Exploration of Disordered Eating in Competitive Female Powerlifters." *Psychology of Sport and Exercise* 52: 1–8. doi.org/10.1016/j.psychsport.2020.101822.

Perry, Alyssa Jeong. 2020, September 4. "How Black Women Athletes Paved the Way for the NBA Strike." *NPR*.

Perry, Imani. 2005. "Buying White Beauty." *Cardozo Journal of Law and Gender* 12: 579–607.

Pitman, Gayle E. 2000. "The Influence of Race, Ethnicity, Class, and Sexual Politics on Lesbians' Body Image." *Journal of Homosexuality* 40, no. 2: 49–64. doi.org/10.1300/J082v40n02_04.

Prentice, Deborah A., and Erica Carranza. 2002. "What Women and Men Should Be, Shouldn't Be, Are Allowed to Be, and Don't Have to Be: The Contents of Prescriptive Gender Stereotypes." *Psychology of Women Quarterly* 26, no. 4: 269–281. doi.org/10.1111/1471-6402.t01-1-00066.

Prince, Sedona. 2021, March 18, 9:26 p.m. Twitter post. twitter.com/sedonaprince.

Pyke, Karen D., and Denise L. Johnson. 2003. "Asian American Women and Racialized Femininities: 'Doing' Gender across Cultural Worlds." *Gender and Society* 17, no. 1: 33–53. doi.org/10.1177/0891243202238977.

Rankin, Claudia. 2014. *Citizen: An American Lyric*. Minneapolis: Graywolf Press.

Rauscher, Lauren, and Cheryl Cooky. 2016. "Girls and the Racialization of Female Bodies in Sport Contexts." In *Child's Play: Sport in Kids' Worlds*, edited by Michael Messner and Michela Musto, 61–81. New Brunswick, NJ: Rutgers University Press.

Rees, C. Roger, and Andrew W. Miracle. 2000. "Education and Sports." *Handbook of Sports Studies*: 277–290.

Richard, Rémi, Helene Joncheray, and Eric Dugas. 2017. "Disabled Sportswomen and Gender Construction in Powerchair Football." *International Review for the Sociology of Sport* 52, no. 1: 61–81. doi.org/10.1177/1012690215577398.

Richie, Beth E. 2005. "Queering Antiprison Work: African American Lesbians in the Juvenile Justice System." In *Global Lockdown: Race, Gender, and the Prison-Industrial Complex*, edited by Julia Sudbury, 73–85. New York: Routledge.

———. 2012. *Arrested Justice: Black Women, Violence, and America's Prison Nation*. New York: New York University Press.

Ridgeway, Cecelia L. 2001. "Gender, Status, and Leadership." *Journal of Social Issues* 57, no. 4: 637–655.

———. 2011. *Framed by Gender: How Gender Inequality Persists in the Modern World*. New York: Oxford University Press.

Ritchie, Andrea J. 2017. *Invisible No More: Police Violence against Black Women and Women of Color*. Boston: Beacon.

Roberts, Dorothy E. 1997. *Killing the Black Body: Race, Reproduction, and the Meaning of Liberty*. New York: Vintage.

Robson, Douglas. 2012, December 19. "Serena Untroubled by Wozniacki's Parody." *USA Today*.

Rodrick, Stephen. 2013, June 18. "Serena Williams: The Great One." *Rolling Stone*.

ross, kihana miraya. 2020, June 4. "Call It What It Is: Anti-Blackness." *New York Times*.

Ross, Sally R., and Kimberly J. Shinew. 2008. "Perspectives of Women College Athletes on Sport and Gender." *Sex Roles* 58, no. 1: 40–57. doi.org/10.1007/s11199-007-9275-4.

Rudman, Laurie A., and Peter Glick. 1999. "Feminized Management and Backlash toward Agentic Women: The Hidden Costs to Women of a Kinder, Gentler Image of Middle Managers." *Journal of Personality and Social Psychology* 77, no. 5: 1004–1010. doi.org/10.1037/0022-3514.77.5.1004.

Rudman, Laurie A., Corinne A. Moss-Racusin, Julie E. Phelan, and Sanne Nauts. 2012. "Status Incongruity and Backlash Effects: Defending the Gender Hierarchy Motivates Prejudice against Female Leaders." *Journal of Experimental Social Psychology* 48, no. 1: 165–179. doi.org/10.1016/j.jesp.2011.10.008.

Russell, Kate M. 2004. "On Versus Off the Pitch: The Transiency of Body Satisfaction among Female Rugby Players, Cricketers, and Netballers." *Sex Roles* 51, no. 9–10: 561–574. doi.org/10.1007/s11199-004-5466-4.

Russell-Brown, Katheryn. 2008. *The Color of Crime: Racial Hoaxes, White Fear, Black Protectionism, Police Harassment, and Other Macroaggressions.* New York: New York University Press.

Ryan, Shannon. 2008, May 4. "Banking on Beauty." *Chicago Tribune.*

Sailes, Gary A. 1991. "The Myth of Black Sports Supremacy." *Journal of Black Studies* 21, no. 4: 480–487.

Samuels, Allison. 2012, August 2. "Gabby Douglas Takes Two Olympic Golds—and Hair Criticism." *Daily Beast.*

Schilt, Kristen. 2011. *Just One of the Guys? Transgender Men and the Persistence of Gender Inequality.* Chicago: University of Chicago Press.

Schmitz, Melanie. 2015, February 9. "Chris Paul Isn't Sexist, but His Defenders Are." *Bustle.*

Schultz, Jaime. 2005. "Reading the Catsuit: Serena Williams and the Production of Blackness at the 2002 US Open." *Journal of Sport and Social Issues* 29, no. 3: 338–357. doi.org/10.1177/0193723505276230.

Scraton, Sheila. 2001. "Reconceptualizing Race, Gender and Sport." In *"Race," Sport and British Society*, edited by Ben Carrington and Ian McDonald, 170–187. New York: Routledge.

Shakib, Sohaila, and Michele D. Dunbar. 2002. "The Social Construction of Female and Male High School Basketball Participation: Reproducing the Gender Order through a Two-Tiered Sporting Institution." *Sociological Perspectives* 45, no. 4: 353–378. doi.org/10.1525/sop.2002.45.4.353.

Sisjord, Mari Kristin, and Elsa Kristiansen. 2009. "Elite Women Wrestlers' Muscles: Physical Strength and a Social Burden." *International Review for the Sociology of Sport* 44, no. 2–3: 231–246. doi.org/10.1177/1012690209335278.

Smith, Earl. 2007. *Race, Sport, and the American Dream.* Durham, NC: Carolina Academic Press.

Smith, William A., Walter R. Allen, and Lynette L. Danley. 2007. " 'Assume the Position . . . You Fit the Description': Psychosocial Experiences and Racial Battle Fatigue among African American Male College Students." *American Behavioral Scientist* 51, no. 4: 551–578. doi.org/10.1177/0002764207307742.

Sofia, Maddie. 2020, July 21. Interview with Sabrina Strings. *NPR Short Wave.* Podcast transcript, npr.org/transcripts/893006538.

Steele, Claude M. 1997. "A Threat in the Air: How Stereotypes Shape Intellectual Identity and Performance." *American Psychologist* 52, no. 6: 613–629. doi.org/10.1037/0003-066X.52.6.613.

Steinfeldt, Jesse A., Hailee Carter, Emily Benton, and Matthew Clint Steinfeldt. 2011. "Muscularity Beliefs of Female College Student-Athletes." *Sex Roles* 64, no. 7–8: 543–554. doi.org/10.1007/s11199-011-9935-2.

Stewart-Bouley, Shay. 2018, April 17. "Weapon of Lass Destruction: The Tears of a White Woman." *Black Girl in Maine*. www.blackgirlinmaine.com.

Stirling, Ashley E., and Gretchen A. Kerr. 2008a. "Defining and Categorizing Emotional Abuse in Sport." *European Journal of Sport Science* 8, no. 4: 173–181. doi.org/10.1080/17461390802086281.

———. 2008b. "Elite Female Swimmers' Experiences of Emotional Abuse across Time." *Journal of Emotional Abuse* 7, no. 4: 89–113. doi.org/10.1300/J135v07n04_05.

———. 2013. "The Perceived Effects of Elite Athletes' Experiences of Emotional Abuse in the Coach–Athlete Relationship." *International Journal of Sport and Exercise Psychology* 11, no. 1: 87–100. doi.org/10.1080/1612197X.2013.752173.

———. 2014. "Initiating and Sustaining Emotional Abuse in the Coach–Athlete Relationship: An Ecological Transactional Model of Vulnerability." *Journal of Aggression, Maltreatment and Trauma* 23, no. 2: 116–135. doi.org/10.1080/10926771.2014.872747.

Strings, Sabrina. 2019. *Fearing the Black Body: The Racial Origins of Fat Phobia*. New York: New York University Press.

Sue, Derald Wing. 2010. *Microaggressions in Everyday Life: Race, Gender, and Sexual Orientation*. Hoboken, NJ: John Wiley and Sons.

Sullivan, Jessica, Corinne Moss-Racusin, Michael Lopez, and Katherine Williams. 2018. "Backlash against Gender Stereotype–Violating Preschool Children." *PLoS One* 13, no. 4: 1–24. doi.org/10.1371/journal.pone.0195503.

Taub, Jennifer. 1999. "Bisexual Women and Beauty Norms: A Qualitative Examination." *Journal of Lesbian Studies* 3, no. 4: 27–36. doi.org/10.1300/J155v03n04_04.

Taylor, Keeanga-Yamahtta, ed., 2017. *How We Get Free: Black Feminism and the Combahee River Collective*. Chicago: Haymarket Books.

The Cut. 2019, March 11. "The Women of How I Get It Done Day."

Thompson, Beverly Yuen. 2015. *Covered in Ink: Tattoos, Women and the Politics of the Body*. New York: New York University Press.

Tracy, Marc. 2017, September 26. "N.C.A.A. Coaches, Adidas Executive Face Charges; Pitino's Program Implicated." *New York Times*.

Traister, Rebecca. 2018. September 9. "Serena Williams and the Game That Can't Be Won (Yet)." *The Cut*.

Treme, Julianne, and Robert T. Burrus. 2016. "NCAA Basketball: When Does Recruiting Talent Translate into Wins for Power Conferences?" *Journal of Economics and Finance* 40, no. 4: 735–753. doi.org/10.1007/s12197-015-9323-9.

Treme, Julianne, R. Burrus, and Bruce Sherrick. 2011. "The Impact of Recruiting on NCAA Basketball Success." *Applied Economics Letters* 18, no. 9: 795–798. doi.org/10.1080/13504851.2010.507171.

Turner, Abi. 2020, February 11. "I Am Like the Other Girls: Examining the Cool Girl Trope." *Keke*.

Vargas, Maria Luisa Fernanda Pereira, and Stacy Winter. 2021. "Weight on the Bar vs. Weight on the Scale: A Qualitative Exploration of Disordered Eating in Competitive Female Powerlifters." *Psychology of Sport and Exercise* 52 (2021): 101822. doi. org/10.1016/j.psychsport.2020.101822.

Vertinsky, Patricia, and Gwendolyn Captain. 1998. "More Myth Than History: American Culture and Representations of the Black Female's Athletic Ability." *Journal of Sport History* 25, no. 3: 532–561.

Wacquant, Loïc. 2002. "Slavery to Mass Incarceration." *New Left Review* 13: 41–60.

Walley-Jean, J. Celeste. 2009. "Debunking the Myth of the 'Angry Black Woman': An Exploration of Anger in Young African American Women." *Black Women, Gender and Families* 3, no. 2: 68–86.

Wang, Jennifer, Janxin Leu, and Yuichi Shoda. 2011. "When the Seemingly Innocuous 'Stings': Racial Microaggressions and Their Emotional Consequences." *Personality and Social Psychology Bulletin* 37, no. 12: 1666–1678. doi. org/10.1177/0146167211416130.

Washington, Myra S., and Megan Economides. 2016. "Strong Is the New Sexy: Women, CrossFit, and the Postfeminist Ideal." *Journal of Sport and Social Issues* 40, no. 2: 143–161. doi.org/10.1177/0193723515615181.

Weaver, Simon. 2011. "Jokes, Rhetoric and Embodied Racism: A Rhetorical Discourse Analysis of the Logics of Racist Jokes on the Internet." *Ethnicities* 11, no. 4: 413–435. doi.org/10.1177/1468796811407755.

Weisman, Jonathan, and Ken Bensinger. 2022, December 9. "Blowback over Griner's Release Exposes Depth of America's Divisions." New York Times.

Wellman, Susan, and Elaine Blinde. 1997. "Homophobia in Women's Intercollegiate Basketball: Views of Women Coaches Regarding Coaching Careers and Recruitment of Athletes." *Women in Sport and Physical Activity Journal* 6, no. 2: 63–82. doi. org/10.1123/wspaj.6.2.63.

West, Candace, and Don H. Zimmerman. 1987. "Doing Gender." *Gender and Society* 1, no. 2: 125–151. doi.org/10.1177/0891243287001002002.

Widdows, Heather. 2018. *Perfect Me*. Princeton, NJ: Princeton University Press.

Williams, Serena. 2015, February 4. "Serena Williams: I'm Going Back to Indian Wells." *Time*.

Withycombe, Jenny Lind. 2011. "Intersecting Selves: African American Female Athletes' Experiences of Sport." *Sociology of Sport Journal* 28, no. 4: 478–493. doi. org/10.1123/ssj.28.4.478.

Wolf-Wendel, Lisa E., J. Douglas Toma, and Christopher C. Morphew. 2001. "How Much Difference Is Too Much Difference? Perceptions of Gay Men and Lesbians in Intercollegiate Athletics." Journal of College Student Development 42, no. 5: 465–479.

World Athletics. 2019, May 1. "CAS Upholds IAAF's Female Eligibility Regulations." www.worldathletics.org/news/press-release/cas-female-eligibility-regulations.

World Athletics. N.d. "IAAF Publishes Briefing Notes and Q&A on Female Eligibility Requirements." www.worldathletics.org.

Worthen, Meredith G. F., and S. Abby Baker. 2016. "Pushing Up on the Glass Ceiling of Female Muscularity: Women's Bodybuilding as Edgework." *Deviant Behavior* 37, no. 5: 471–495. doi.org/10.1080/01639625.2015.1060741.

Wughalter, Emily. 1978. "Ruffles and Flounces: The Apologetic in Women's Sports." *Frontiers: A Journal of Women Studies*: 11–13. doi.org/10.2307/3345983.

Wun, Connie. 2016a. "Against Captivity: Black Girls and School Discipline Policies in the Afterlife of Slavery." *Educational Policy* 30, no. 1: 171–196. doi.org/10.1177/0895904815615439.

———. 2016b. "Unaccounted Foundations: Black Girls, Anti-Black Racism, and Punishment in Schools." *Critical Sociology* 42, no. 4–5: 737–750. doi.org/10.1177/0896920514560444.

———. 2018. "Angered: Black and Non-Black Girls of Color at the Intersections of Violence and School Discipline in the United States." *Race Ethnicity, and Education* 21, no. 4: 423–437. doi.org/10.1080/13613324.2016.1248829.

Yavorsky, Jill E. 2016. "Cisgendered Organizations: Trans Women and Inequality in the Workplace." *Sociological Forum* 31, no. 4: 948–969. doi.org/10.1111/socf.12291.

INDEX

abortion, ix
Abraham, Laura, 42
abuse/abusive, 15–18, 20–21, 163–64, 181n3
academics for collegiate athletes, 45, 185n34
Academy Awards, 1
access/accessibility, 11, 169–73
activism, 6, 161–62
Adidas, 44
Adler, Doug, 3
adultification bias, 183n54
age compression, 183n54
agency, 8, 23–24, 122, 155–57, 184n18;
    "dominance penalty" and, 24, 182n27
ambivalence, 37–38, 86–88, 129, 134, 136–38, 140
androgyny, 6, 105
"angry Black woman" stereotype, 31, 183n56
anti-Blackness, xv, 5, 10, 38, 62, 92, 112;
    heteropatriarchy and, 42, 131, 161
antilesbian recruitment, 45–53, 185n40, 186n45; unintended consequences in, 54–57
anxiety, 84, 163, 170
"apologetics," 62, 94, 121–23
"Apologetics and Androgyny" (Del Rey), 94
"appropriateness," 29, 52, 54, 94, 104–5, 111, 116, 139, 151–54
arms, musculature of, 93, 135, 137, 141–42, 148, 150
assumptions, 5, 22, 25, 69, 108; stereotypes and, 63–65, 82–85, 125

athletes. *See specific topics*
athletes of color, 5, 7, 10
athletic: careers, 1–3, 142, 147–49, 165;
    identities, 94–97, 100–107, 109–17, 122;
    performance, 18–19, 21, 99, 141–42,
    144–47, 160; scholarships, 11, 43, 147–48
Atlanta Dream (WNBA team), 162
attractiveness, heterosexual, 5, 69–72, 84,
    97–99, 104, 115, 136–41, 146, 156, 161
Australian Open (competition), 3

"backlash effect," gender proscriptions,
    23–25, 30, 182n27
"bad apples," collegiate athletic coaches as,
    163–64
Bailey, Moya, xv, 4, 111, 189n39
Baker, S. Abby, 140
Banks, Ingrid, 67
basketball. *See specific topics*
Bass, Mistie, 162
Bates, Karen Grigsby, 190n53
bathrooms, 50, 186n44
Baylor University, 44
beauty, 67–70, 98; ideals, 69, 106–9, 156–
    57, 189n32; standards, 26–27, 108, 125,
    131–33, 149–50
behaviors, xv, 22–23, 64, 73, 103–4, 129, 177;
    "apologetic," 62, 94, 121–23
Biles, Simone, 4, 30
binary, gender, xii, xv, 23, 104, 187n19
biracial people, 4, 10
bisexuality/bisexual people, xi, 49–50, 72–
    73, 106, 186n42
Black athletes, 68, 115, 161, 184n14

ABOUT THE AUTHOR

MICHELLE J. MANNO is Assistant Provost for Diversity and Inclusion in the Office of Institutional Diversity and Inclusion at Northwestern University.